# Anti-Genocide

# Anti-Genocide

## Building an American Movement to Prevent Genocide

**Herbert Hirsch**

Westport, Connecticut
London

Library of Congress Cataloging-in-Publication Data

Hirsch, Herbert, 1941–
    Anti-genocide : building an American movement to prevent genocide / Herbert Hirsch.
        p. cm.
    Includes bibliographical references and index.
    ISBN 0–275–97676–9 (alk. paper)
    1. Genocide—Prevention.   2. Genocide—Government policy—United States—Citizen participation.   3. Genocide—United States—Public opinion.   I. Title.
    HV6322.7 .H547 2002
    364.15′1—dc21                                                                    2002067298

British Library Cataloguing in Publication Data is available.

Copyright © 2002 by Herbert Hirsch

All rights reserved. No portion of this book may be reproduced, by any process or technique, without the express written consent of the publisher.

Library of Congress Catalog Card Number: 2002067298
ISBN: 0–275–97676–9

First published in 2002

Praeger Publishers, 88 Post Road West, Westport, CT 06881
An imprint of Greenwood Publishing Group, Inc.
www.praeger.com

Printed in the United States of America

The paper used in this book complies with the Permanent Paper Standard issued by the National Information Standards Organization (Z39.48–1984).

10  9  8  7  6  5  4  3  2  1

Copyright Acknowledgment

Grateful acknowledgment is given for permission to reprint derivations of chapters 13 and 14, *Genocide and the Politics of Memory: Studying Death to Preserve Life* by Herbert Hirsch. Copyright © 1995 by the University of North Carolina Press. Used by permission of the publisher.

To Susan
    For Everything

# Contents

| | |
|---|---|
| *Tables* | ix |
| *Preface* | xi |
| *Acknowledgments* | xv |
| *Introduction: Genocide, Politics and Human Behavior* | 1 |
| **Part 1: Genocide and Political Movements** | **19** |
| 1. Building a Movement to Stop Genocide | 21 |
| 2. Genocide and Public Opinion: A Comparison of the Policy-Making Elite and the General Public | 39 |
| 3. Putting Pressure on U.S. Political Institutions | 57 |
| **Part II: Guilty Secrets: Genocide and the Failure of U.S. Foreign Policy During the Clinton and Bush Administrations** | **69** |
| 4. The Failure of Prevention: Bosnia | 73 |
| 5. A Second Failure of Prevention: The Rwandan Genocide | 89 |
| 6. Lessons from the Late Twentieth and Early Twenty-First Centuries: Kosovo, Clinton and Bush | 95 |

**Part III: Genocide and the Politics of Prevention**     119

7. A Foreign Policy to Prevent Genocide: The Practicality of Morality     123

8. U.S. Foreign Policy in the New Century     143

9. Reflections on "Ethics," "Morality" and "Responsibility": Thinking about a New Political Consciousness for a New Century     151

10. Inculcating an Ethic to Prevent Genocide     163

*Conclusion: A Politics to Prevent Genocide*     175

*Notes*     187

*References*     193

*Index*     207

# Tables

| | |
|---|---|
| 2.1 Percentage of People Who Say They Follow the "Civil War in Bosnia" "Very Closely" | 41 |
| 2.2 Top News Stories of 2001 | 43 |
| 2.3 Perceptions of the Holocaust | 45 |
| 2.4 Perceptions of Bosnia | 47 |
| 2.5 Perceptions of Rwanda | 49 |
| 2.6 Support for U.S. Ground Troops in Kosovo | 50 |

# Preface

There is an old adage, attributed to Karl Marx, that goes something like: People make their own history. Since I believe that our lives are a mixture of work, luck and random occurrence, as opposed to the intervention of omnipotent forces, I also believe we have at least the potential to improve, to a certain extent, the conditions under which we live with our partners on the planet. Therefore, in understanding whether we are able to live together peacefully or kill each other repeatedly, we have to begin with ourselves. Which means, obviously, that I must look not only at the behavior of others, but my own and my perceptions of what I see as well. Honestly, then, I am writing a book to advocate something that I believe may be highly unlikely to take place. Given the sad reality of modern politics, I do not really think a movement to stop genocide will happen. Yet, I want it to happen and hope that my pessimism does not become a self-fulfilling prophecy.

Because of the serious nature of the topic, this is a critical and idiosyncratic book, hopefully, without scholarly pretensions. I plan to keep academic jargon to a minimum and use as few footnotes as possible. I am sure I will "borrow," a euphemism for "appropriate," the work of others, but at this point I have been studying genocide and human violence for such a long period of time that there are occasions when I am not able to ascertain honestly whether a statement is my own or taken from the work of another writer. I, therefore, apologize in advance for any slight or oversight on my part.

Generally, I hope this book will prove to be an enlightening and forthright confrontation with the problems facing humanity as we try to move toward a more peaceful world.

As noted, I am going to attempt to leave some of my pretensions to scholarly objectivity, whatever that might be, in order to try to make this work more accessible. In fact, I have a severe objection to the manner in which we pretend to talk and teach about genocide. If pushed, I argue that our pretense to objectivity contributes to the very problems we are unwilling to confront and this is a book about why we must be willing to confront problems.

For example, if one were writing such a work in Germany sometime between 1933 and 1945 and one noted that his was an objective presentation because he was simply describing how the system works, he would be an accomplice, if not a participant, in one of the greatest immoral actions in the history of the world—the extermination of European Jews. Of course, today, we find that stance unacceptable. Yet, we are perfectly content when we are told, for example, that teachers of U.S. politics are "objective" only when describing the system even when that system has internal problems such as inequality, homelessness, poor or nonexistent health care, or when the leaders of that system hesitate and often do not take action to save lives threatened by genocide. Writers have a responsibility, and this is where our notions of responsibility begin—with those who think, write, speak about genocide, to make very clear what their positions are and where those positions originate.

I mean, therefore, to be more candid about my biases, and we all have them. It matters little what the topic: If it is remotely related to politics any discussion proceeds from a point of view from a view of the world as seen by the author—or, perhaps, as he or she would like the world to be. Often these perspectives may appear contradictory. I might, for example, see a world in which large numbers of people kill each other, wish it were different, and at the same time believe that change is unlikely. Therefore, while I would like to see a world in which people made the choice to preserve rather than destroy life, a place where, whenever possible, the overall goal of human behavior would be to help create the conditions under which people's everyday lives are as enjoyable and free of pain and suffering as possible, I also find that my observations of politics indicate to me that there are profound impediments to reaching these goals.

In confronting the hard reality of human destructiveness I am trying to leave behind much of the naiveté that characterizes many other works advocating less violence. In spite of my attempted confrontation with reality, I realize that many will find these meditations to be foolishly idealistic and at odds with the reality of human interaction. Yet, most people most of the time are not harming others. Moreover, if, as I just noted, we possess at least the potential to create our own history, there is a strong element of the self-fulfilling prophecy in what we do. If we believe we can get along, then we act to make that a reality. On the other hand, if we allow ourselves to be driven by greed, hate or some other perceived reason to commit violence, we will do that as well.

Humans dredge, from the rivers of life, memories that condition their actions. This behavior is often a result of good fortune, luck and hard work. All of us face alternative realities, which means that for reasons beyond our control we could just as easily been born to a different context. Instead of sitting at this computer I could just as easily have been caught in the Nazi exterminations if my family had not fled Europe or been the victim of any number of untold tragedies that have plagued the world in the last century. In a fashion, then, this is an examination of how to overcome unlucky circumstances and create a world in which all people have the opportunity to at least survive without genocide threatening their lives.

As I ponder these issues, I find that I often think about how I came to these reflections. I have taught and studied politics as a full-time vocation and avocation since 1959, when I entered college and decided to major in political science. In my journey I flirted with many views, assorted and sometimes contradictory ideologies and political perspectives. This is not, I hope, unusual when one attempts to encounter the depressing and difficult problem of genocide in the modern world. In the search for solutions, scholars and other observers seek to solve the enigma of genocide by grasping at whatever straws they believe will help. Many have pointed out that traditional academic perspectives suffer from serious limitations about which we should, over the years, have become very conscious.

W.H. Auden wrote of many things, but of affirmation more than anything. On September 1, 1939, Auden wrote about a voice "to undo the folded lie" of "Authority" as a means to bring humanity "into the ethical life" (Mendelson, 1995, pp. 86–89). Have we, I wonder, wandered away from the "ethical life" to accept the lie of Authority? Do we understand, as Auden, the importance of raising our voices to question these lies in order to, as he stated, "show an affirming flame"? This book is my flame.

# Acknowledgments

I want to thank the Earhart Foundation for providing a grant that allowed me the time to work on this project and also Virginia Commonwealth University, which provided me with a research leave. There are so many individuals to thank that I cannot name them all. Many are participants in several organizations and conferences that I attend to find stimulation and renewal. One such group is the Pastora Goldner Holocaust Symposium convened on alternative even-numbered years at Wroxton College at Oxfordshire, England. The participants gather there to discuss issues such as those cited in this book and to talk and debate in a mutually supportive atmosphere, which makes this conference most unlike other academic conferences. As a result, friendships and mutual respect help to guide our related undertakings. Other individuals, in ways they have not realized, contributed to the thought that has gone into this project. Hubert Locke, the finest gentleman I know, and Franklin Littell, co-founders of the Annual Scholar's Conference on the Holocaust and the Churches, were pioneers in the field of preventing genocide. Leo Kuper wrote what remains the best single book *The Prevention of Genocide*, on the prevention of genocide. My own work here is derivative. Roger Smith has been a friend and constant source of ideas and criticism; he remains one of the most perceptive scholars in this field. Paul Bartrop continues to motivate me with his ideas and his own insatiable energy.

Others helped in ways they cannot know—unless they have had the experience of sitting at a computer, trying to make sense out of something that, when all is said and done, is hard to understand. In particular, I acknowledge my four children, my grandchildren and their parents, and, most important, Susan. Susan and I found each other in a time of loneliness and have created a life together that allows me to hope that all may have such a future. That is why, even when despair sets in and we feel as though any attempt to change the particularly discouraging display of human behavior that takes rather than saves human life may be futile, we must always continue to hope for improvement.

In that sense I am trying to affirm something I learned as a freshman in college. I was never more moved than when my English instructor had us read Robert Browning and explained to us Browning's idea of attempting to attain the unattainable. It is in the quest for that ideal that the essence of life is found. When the search is abandoned, so is hope, and when hope dies so do people.

# Anti-Genocide

# Introduction: Genocide, Politics and Human Behavior

Human interaction is a tenuous thing. Cultures, societies and political systems are fragile. They are bound by threads that may unravel with incredible ease. A single person with a gun, or even a knife, or many people with guns, or, in some cases, a misplaced word or words, may cut the thread. The fabric is so finely woven, with trust and responsibility intertwined. Trust that you may walk the street, drive the highway, pursue the activities of everyday life with a low probability of encountering someone who may, in an instant, shatter that trust and forever alter a life. In addition, one must assume the responsibility that they will not be the one to undertake that particular activity and will be accountable for their behavior.

If both trust and responsibility unravel, if they are not part of the cultural diffusion flowing into the heads and hearts of all of us, our neighbors, our children, we might easily regress to a state of uncontrolled violence and perpetual insecurity. For without trust and responsibility there can be no security, no, however ephemeral, minimal certitude that life goes on. It is not difficult to imagine how easy it is to unravel the tenuous threads.

Every minute of our lives we are at the mercy of other people. Every action potentially determines our life or death. When we open our front doors to pick up the morning paper, we trust our neighbors will not be waiting to pick us off like snipers in Sarajevo during the genocide in Bosnia. When we start our cars we trust they have not been rigged with explosive devices, and when we drive on the road we trust those in the opposite lane to stay there. When we eat our food, we trust it has not been poisoned, and on and on and on.

When these threads unravel, when trust, or perhaps faith, begin to fray, we begin to feel threatened. We react by attempting to preserve some semblance of peaceful civic life. Generally, we seek some form of immediate protection: purchase a weapon, move to a walled suburb protected by private police guards, withdraw emotionally and psychologically, look for scapegoats who, to protect ourselves, must be killed. Tenuously, we remain a social fabric held together by threads that appear to have unraveled with daunting frequency in the last century.

There has been no shortage of genocides in the twentieth century. In fact, some argue that there have been up to two dozen genocides or genocidal massacres since 1945 alone. If we listed only the better known genocides that would certainly allow one to label, as many have, the last century an age of genocide.[1] Of course, there is no consensus on whether these are all examples of genocide as defined by the UN or whether the most recent atrocities in East Timor and Kosovo fit that definition. The debate over the definition, while not irrelevant, is, in my opinion, less important than what causes and how to prevent atrocity—be it defined as genocide or some "near genocide-like" event. Yet, even though I believe that the arguments over definitions are less important then developing a politics of prevention, it is still necessary to define exactly what it is we are discussing.

## What is Genocide?

It is common knowledge among genocide scholars that the term "genocide" was coined by Raphael Lemkin when he introduced it into our vocabulary in his 1944 book, *Axis Rule in Europe*. According to Lemkin, genocide is derived from the Greek word "genus" (race, tribe) and the Latin word "cide" (killing), corresponding in its formulation to such words as tyrannicide, homicide, etc. Lemkin defined genocide as "a coordinated plan of different actions aiming at the destruction of the essential foundation of the life of national groups, with the aim of annihilating the groups themselves. . . . Genocide is directed against individuals not in their individual capacity, but as members of the national group." He identifies two phases in the process of genocide. The first is the "destruction of the national patterns of the oppressed group," and the second is the "imposition of the national pattern of the oppressor" (pp. 79–80). Lemkin elaborates his exposition at great length, pointing out that the Third Reich carried out genocide in seven areas: political, social, physical, cultural, economic, biological, religious and moral. He proposed that the way to prevent such terrible actions was for the UN to adopt an international, multilateral treaty prohibiting genocide and

## Introduction: Genocide, Politics and Human Behavior

that this treaty be incorporated into the constitutions and criminal codes of nation-states who were members of the UN.

The treaty or convention, as visualized by Lemkin, would protect the lives, liberty and property of minority groups and would impose criminal liability on any individual who committed genocide, ordered others to commit genocide or incited genocide. In addition, an international tribunal would be established to examine allegations of genocide brought against government leaders. Finally, in order to prevent the occurrence of genocide during periods of war, an international nongovernmental organization, such as the Red Cross, was to be charged with the responsibility of supervising the treatment of civilians.

Lemkin's proposals were far-reaching and dramatic. They would have created an international tribunal to judge crimes and to pinpoint responsibility. Unfortunately, his early language and intent were diluted by the political debates prior to the December 9, 1948, adoption by the UN of the International Convention on the Prevention and Punishment of the Crime of Genocide.

The general story of how Lemkin's original language was changed as the proposal traveled through international and national political institutions is common fare in all works dealing with genocide and international law. Generally, the debates that took place prior to the final adoption of the Convention make depressing reading and give an early indication of the overall lack of impact the Convention would have on international politics—it would not prevent or punish any crime of genocide.

There were major controversies over what types of groups would be protected, how to measure intention to commit genocide, how to implement punishment and how much destruction was necessary to constitute genocide. In sum, the result was that political groups were excluded from coverage, and there were no mechanisms for enforcement. The delegates could not even agree on what genocide was, and absent was any moral or legal commitment to the eventual eradication of mass murder.

The basic argument against including political groups stated that membership in a political group was voluntary and not permanent, while membership in racial or religious groups was involuntary and generally permanent. The states opposing the inclusion of political groups also argued that their inclusion would weaken the Convention and expose nations to external intervention in their domestic concerns. This would endanger the future of the Convention because many nations would be unwilling to ratify it, fearing the possibility of being called before an international tribunal to answer charges made against them. For example, opponents of the Convention in the United States, as Smith (1992b) notes, feared that the United States could be charged with genocide for its harsh treatment of African Americans and Native Americans. They reasoned that lynching could be construed as genocide since it involved the killing of a "part" of a group for racial reasons, and that discrimination could be equated with "mental harm" to a group, an act defined under the Convention as genocide. (Pp. 229–30)

Many of these basic arguments were verbalized in debates involving U.S. attempts to ratify the UN Convention on the Prevention and Punishment of the Crime of Genocide.

## U.S. Ratification of the Genocide Convention

On September 5, 1984, then president of the United States Ronald Reagan, asked the U.S. Senate to ratify the UN Convention on the Prevention and Punishment of the Crime of Genocide. This was thirty-six years after the Convention had been passed originally by the UN and thirty-nine years after the conclusion of World War II. When the Convention was finally ratified by the U.S. Senate in 1986, "it had been before that body longer than any other treaty in United States history" (Smith, 1992b, p. 227).

The twisting road to ratification offers an unobstructed view of the way sovereignty has restricted the power of the UN to force nations to comply with the eloquent human rights provisions to which it has given verbal approval.

The Convention was first sent to the Senate in 1949 by President Harry Truman. The 1950 hearings were, as Smith points out, "acrimonious in the extreme, characterized by charges that the Convention was a 'sell-out' to the Communists, an attack on fundamental civil liberties, a grab for power by the President, and a threat to the powers of the states within the federal system" (ibid.). These charges were repeated whenever the Convention was submitted or considered. No new hearings were held for twenty years, and the Convention received no support from President Eisenhower and little from presidents Kennedy and Johnson. President Nixon did offer support, and hearings were held in 1970. It was not until 1984 that it was again submitted by President Reagan. When the Senate finally ratified the Convention, the ratification was conditional since two reservations, five understandings and one declaration were attached as integral parts of the treaty. The most important condition was the rejection of the compulsory jurisdiction of the International Court of Justice, which clearly indicated that the United States had no intention of being bound by the Convention and did not take international judicial institutions seriously.

During the Senate debates over ratification this was abundantly clear.

Senator Jesse Helms (R–N.C.) argued: "I think we should pass a Genocide Convention, but only if we can make it work so that our domestic affairs are not subjected to the supervision of international bodies, and that our security interests and those of our allies are not jeopardized" (U.S. Senate Committee, 1985, p. 8). This provided a very clear indication of the power of the beliefs in national interest and sovereignty and produced a rather unusual conceptualization of making the Convention "work." What Senator Helms actually meant was not work, since all provisions of enforcement were to be gutted from the Convention and it would be operational only if the United States was not subject to its provisions. Clearly, if the same type of thinking were applied to domestic law, chaos and anarchy would reign supreme.

When asked by Senator Pell (D–R.I.) why, when the United States is a party to at least eighty different treaties under which they accept the jurisdiction of the International Court of Justice, was it necessary to have reservations about the Convention, Mr. Robinson, legal adviser to the State Department, responded by arguing that the Senate might not pass it without the reservation, but, more important, he cited the Nicaragua case[2] and went on to state:

> We believe that the question of genocide could be a highly charged issue. Of course, we believe it would be preposterous that ever anybody could make any valid accusation against the United States that it had engaged in any acts or offenses involving genocide....
>
> Nonetheless, with the experience that we have recently undergone, and when combined with the practicalities, we think that a World Court reservation would be not only wise, but desirable at this point. (Ibid., p. 12)

Consequently, while the Convention was eventually ratified, it was accomplished in such a fashion as to guarantee that it would have little or no impact on national policy. To ensure this, when the Senate finalized its ratification on February 19, 1986, it attached, as noted above, two reservations and five understandings.[3]

Finally, the Senate forbade the president to implement the treaty until implementing legislation was enacted. This occurred on January 25, 1988, when the Congress defined genocide as being within the criminal code of the United States (S. 1851). The legislation adopted the UN definition and then set penalties of a "fine of not more than $1 million and imprisonment for life" for killing members of a group; and "a fine of not more than $1 million or imprisonment for not more than twenty years, or both, in any other case." If a person "directly and publicly incites another to violate subsection (a)" the punishment is a fine of "not more than $500,000 or imprison[ment] for not more than five years, or both." For these to be implemented the offense must be committed in the

United States or the offender must be a U.S. citizen. In spite of its incorporation into U.S. law, these reservations and understandings may act to seriously undermine the credibility of the United States should it attempt to lead a coalition to prevent and punish genocide. It might be prudent for the United States, at some future time, in order to forestall the possibility that other states will invoke the record of U.S. indifference, to think seriously about repealing the understandings and reservations as a first step to demonstrate its sincerity and commitment to the prevention of genocide and political massacres.

Even though the Convention has not deterred, prevented or punished any genocide, it served symbolic notice on the world that genocide is not an acceptable activity for states to pursue. Without enforcement provisions and a clear and generally applicable definition of genocide, however, action to prevent its occurrence is unlikely.

## Issues of Definition

Lack of definitional clarity continues to plague the Convention. Some scholars have, in fact, argued that the definition of genocide found in the Convention does not cover all the possible manifestations of the crime because the destruction of a large number of people may take additional forms, such as deportations or mass displacement, internment and enslavement with forced labor, denationalization by systematic terrorism, torture, and so forth.

A second stumbling block is the language involving intent to commit genocide. If one adheres to a strict interpretation of the language of intent, then the Serbs were, for example, able to argue that their intent was not to commit genocide, but to acquire territory, or as perpetrators often argue, to protect themselves from the threat raised by the Bosnian Muslims or Croatians. The concept of "intent" is, ambiguous. If a group or nation intends to acquire another group or nation's territory but ends up killing a large number of the people, they should still be liable for prosecution for both war crimes and genocide. If the interpretation is so broadened, then the conditions stated in Article II of the Convention concerning intent to commit genocide are satisfied. Under this and Article VIII (Article VIII: "Any Contracting Party may call upon competent organs of the United Nations to take action under the Charter of the United Nations as they consider appropriate for the prevention and suppression of acts of genocide [35:68]), combined with the Nuremberg principles, there appears ample precedent for war crimes trials. In short, instead of emphasizing an obscure and impossible-to-define psychological state of intent, the Convention should focus on an easily identifiable action or behavior and infer intent from that behavior.

Not only is there a problem with "intent," but, as Freeman (1991) points out, the UN also stipulates that the genocidal intent has to be to

## Introduction: Genocide, Politics and Human Behavior

destroy a listed group "in whole or in part" (p. 187). This creates additional uncertainty as to the size of the "part" necessary to constitute genocide. Lacking definitional specificity and the narrowing of Lemkin's original proposal lead to the quest for new conceptualizations of genocide.

Freeman refers to this as the "definitional problematic," and it is not merely an academic exercise since definitions are tied to politics and political action. How an idea is defined has important consequences for how it is implemented. As a result, there have been a number of attempts to reconceptualize genocide.

Chalk and Jonassohn (1990), for example, defined genocide as "a form of one-sided mass killing in which a state or other authority intends to destroy a group, as that group and membership in it are defined by the perpetrator" (p. 23). In this case, the definition is hardly an improvement over the UN definition since the question of intent not only remains, but is raised to a preeminent level. Freeman's analysis is, it seems to me, an important step away from many of the problems of definitional ambiguity.

According to Freeman genocide is a "social process, initiated and implemented by various social agents in structured social situations. It consists of many different agents located in different positions in the social structure. The central genocidal relation is that of perpetrator domination and victim subordination" (p. 188). Genocide is a series of relationships involving both power and violence. Generally, in modern times, the state has control of the forces of violence and, therefore, states are "the most likely perpetrators of genocide, although genocide can also be committed by others with the connivance of states or by powerful social groups which states are too weak to control" (ibid.).

Since modern states are very powerful, often accumulating the necessary weaponry from other states, they are particularly well equipped to commit genocide. To move ahead with the planned destruction the "perpetrator must prevent or overcome resistance by the victim, isolate the latter from potential allies, cut off escape routes and ensure an appropriate combination of collaboration, acquiescence and ignorance among the rest of the population" (Freeman, 1991, p. 199). The modern state, or forces supported in one or another fashion by the state, is in a position to accomplish these ends. If genocide is most often committed by the nation-state or with its active support or collaboration, this implies that there must be conditions of pluralism within the state. But the state and pluralism are only sufficient conditions for genocide. What is necessary, as Freeman argues is a "genocidal ideology." The ideology is the motivating factor.

> Such ideologies construct genocide as natural, necessary, rational and/or obligatory. To understand genocide, we must understand what problems

the perpetrators were trying to solve, why they defined their problems as they did, and in particular, why they defined the victim as part of the problem, and why genocide seemed to them a rational solution. (P. 189)

Genocidal ideologies take many forms, including utopian fantasies and realistic projects for development or expansion. Often they dehumanize the potential victims, identifying them as animals, vermin, carriers of disease or as a threat and contrast the purity of the perpetrator with the corruption of the victim arguing that the extermination is necessary to protect the perpetrators from the threat posed by the victims. Genocidal ideologies may find their roots in the myths and cultures of a society or they may come into being to explain the action taken.

According to Freeman, one "common precipitant of genocide is societal crisis" (p. 190), because crisis calls for blame to be allocated to explain what is occurring. Since modern states experiencing crisis, such as the dissolution of the former Yugoslavia, become vulnerable to groups which hope to gain from the crisis, nation-state building may result in genocide.

Thus viewed, genocide becomes a relationship between victims and perpetrators and is seen as

> a complex set of social relations: different social agents in different social roles are motivated to perform different sorts of actions. Even the decision-making elites may not be unified: some may be true believers, others cynical careerists, and there may be factional power struggles within this group. Ideology may motivate the executives but theories of bureaucratic behavior and obedience to authority teach us that genocidal elites do not need to achieve high levels of ideological mobilization in order to implement genocidal policies. (Pp. 191–92)

It is important to note that genocide is not a pure, easily defined phenomenon and that events are not, as Freeman points out, "either genocidal or non-genocidal but more or less genocidal, and there is simply no cut-off point" (p. 193).

According to this conceptualization, genocide requires at least three ingredients: (1) murderous elites motivated by a genocidal ideology, (2) obedient perpetrators, and (3) acquiescent bystanders. Throughout the ages genocide has been justified by tribalism, nationalism, racism, religion and science, and no historic epoch has a monopoly on these conditions. There is even among scholars some agreement regarding which historical events might be classified as genocides as noted in the list above.

## Weaknesses of the Convention

Even the UN realized the genocide Convention was not effective and commissioned several reports to examine the weaknesses. In 1985 the UN commissioned another report on genocide that was prepared by Mr. B. Whitaker. The Whitaker Report also pointed out that genocide had occurred both before and after the adoption of the Convention and concluded that the Convention had not been effective. It also recommended a series of remedies.

> These are to explicitly include acts of "advertent omission" (within the Convention's meaning of "intent"); protection for "political groups"; the nonavailability of a "superior orders" defense; state responsibility and liability for damages and restitution; a tightened "non-extradition" clause; a Committee on Genocide (under Articles VIII) with powers to investigate and communicate to the Secretary General; an anti-genocide educational plan; an early warning system; an International Court of Human Rights, endowing the World Court with criminal jurisdiction; and further study of "cultural genocide," "ethnocide" and "ecocide." (Hawk, 1986, p. 3)

Upon inspection, it becomes quite clear that independent scholars as well as the UN itself are well aware of the weaknesses confronting the Convention as a means to prevent and punish genocide. In reality most of the proposals for reform harken back to Lemkin's original formulation and link the idea of genocide to the precedents set up under the laws of war.

As a result of the attention focused on genocide in the last half of the twentieth century a series of important steps toward possible deterrent mechanisms to prevent future genocides have been taken. So, in the beginning of the twenty-first century it is entirely appropriate to reflect back on the previous century and to attempt to ascertain what, if anything, might be done to lessen the magnitude of these tragedies in the future.

We begin with the fact that there is apparently nothing unique about humans killing other humans in relatively large numbers. Our methods of destruction have certainly become more sophisticated, enabling fewer people to kill many people in a short period of time, but contemporary genocides such as those in Rwanda and Cambodia were still carried out with cruder, simpler methods of killing. It is the phenomenon of genocide itself that appears to have been with us since we began to record our worst excesses.

Or is it that we are better informed since we are now able to witness the brutality firsthand, or at least on the small screen, where in times past we relied on the accounts of others. Whatever the case, the end of the twentieth century certainly brought genocide to the forefront of human consciousness.

Indeed, it often appears as though we are hell-bent on making ourselves extinct, on killing each other in such large numbers that the continuation of the species will be questionable. Yet, there remains an enigma at the heart of genocidal, if not all, human behavior: namely, that while there are numerous ongoing atrocities taking place around the globe, most people, most of the time are not determined to destroy each other and live in relative peace. We humans are capable of great violence and great love. This means that if we are ever to confront successfully and prevent, or at least control the most egregious aspects of genocidal violence, it will be necessary to create some mechanisms, some political institutions, to contain violence in the short run and to change, or try to change, human behavior in the long run. There are, consequently, complex realities to be examined. In addition, the politics of genocide must be confronted in the international realm where policies to control genocidal violence will be focused, and at the same time at the national level, in particular in the United States, where a political movement needs to be built to support the politics of prevention in the international realm.

These are the short-term politics of prevention. If we are, in the long run, to continue to control genocidal behavior it will be necessary to began to change the way humans view each other.

Therefore, while I am in the process of outlining how prevention might proceed, I remain, as I noted above, pessimistic concerning the actual implementation and accomplishment of that elusive goal. Even though I do not believe, deep down, that we will achieve the overall goal of prevention, I also hope that we will at least move toward control and that we have the knowledge to show us how to go in that direction. Whether we travel that road is up to us, and it depends on the decisions and choices we make. To begin the journey, therefore, I want to examine the connection between genocide and politics.

In pursuit of this examination there are several self-imposed limitations that will regulate this inquiry. First, I am assuming that, in the modern era, most genocide has been a political tool of the modern nation-state. Second, I am looking only at politics. In my last book, *Genocide and the Politics of Memory* (1995), I examined cultural and psychological dimensions of genocide. Here, however, I am looking at the process of politics. Third, and perhaps most important, while genocide is as old as history and occurs all over the world, I am limiting my inquiry to twentieth-century genocides and emphasizing that any politics of prevention must begin with the United States. While I am not arguing that the United States is able, by itself, to prevent genocide, I am convinced that the preeminence of U.S. power in the post–Cold War world means that it must be involved in any attempts to prevent genocide and

# Introduction: Genocide, Politics and Human Behavior

that to make that happen it is necessary to build an indigenous movement within the United States to support preventive action.

Then, on September 11, 2001, another aspect of human destructiveness shifted our attention from the many genocidal acts of the last century and focused the nations of the world on terrorism. In spite of the fact that the tragic loss of human life in the September 11 terrorism did not approach the millions exterminated in the genocides of the last millennium, terrorism became the main topic largely because the United States was the target. This illustrates very dramatically how important the United States is in forming international policy to combat or ignore the destruction of human life.

## Genocide and Politics

As reductionist as it may appear, at whatever level we are focusing our attention, the ultimate focus is on human choice and decision. An individual, when given an order to commit an act of violence, makes a choice whether it be in pursuit of his role as a foot soldier, a citizen, a person in a position of political or moral leadership within a national or international institution. No matter how we would like to slice it, the politics of genocide is related to the choices made by individual human persons.

Participants in genocidal massacres have always pointed in this direction. For example, one of the American soldiers who killed Vietnamese women and children at My Lai noted:

> Do you realize what it was like killing five hundred people in a matter of four or five hours? It's just like the gas chambers—what Hitler did. You line up fifty people, women, old men, children, and just mow 'em down. And that's the way it was—from twenty-five to fifty to one hundred. Just killed. We just rounded 'em up, me and a couple of guys, just put the M-16 on automatic, and just mowed 'em down. (Bilton and Sim, 1992, p. 131)

Varnado Simpson, quoted above, was personally responsible, by his own admission, for killing about twenty-five people. "Men, women. From shooting them, to cutting their throats, scalping them, to . . . cutting off their hands and cutting out their tongue. I did it" (ibid., p. 7). This is the hidden side of war, as violence is the submerged side of humanity. We only discuss it in terms of how horrible it is and how it can be controlled by getting rid of the really "bad" people who, we desperately want to believe, are the ultimate causes of the problem. And so we hide from the reality of violence and from the possibility that under certain conditions it might be possible for any person to commit the most horrible acts. This, of course, is the great enigma of human violence: how the very same person who might nurse a child fallen from his bicycle in the neighborhood could conceivably kill women and children in My Lai or how a person who is one of the most notorious serial killers in U.S. history could be handsome, charming and appealing or how the commandant of a concentration camp is able to return home after a "day's work," have dinner with wife and children, enjoy a glass of fine wine, listen to classical music and awaken the next morning to supervise that day's quota of exterminations.

Of course there is something in all of us that would like to be able to explain away the worst side of humanity—to be persuaded, once and for all, that only psychopaths commit violence and that, after all, we certainly would never do anything so horrible. Yet, as the evidence accumulates, there appears to be less reason for optimism. We both fear and love violence. It terrifies us and, in certain circumstances, propels us to undreamed-of heights of ecstasy and exhilaration. We run from it, and we revel in and are fascinated by it, and we are fed a daily diet of it.

In spite of our wishes and protestations to the contrary, people do commit unspeakable acts of violence, and we must remember that for people to die, other people have to pull the triggers, release the gas and drop the bombs. Their behavior occurs within a structural context, within an environment where they are faced with a set of conditions that propels them to commit violence. If, therefore, these conditions could be altered or, alternatively, we could understand what propels individuals to commit violence, there conceivably could be greater opportunities to stop genocidal violence.

These contextual factors appear to be related in a causal fashion to the level of violent behavior. In order to understand why we were so unsuccessful in the late twentieth century in preventing national and international violence in general, and genocidal violence in particular, we have to study not only these conditions but also the people acting within these structural boundaries. Trying to find out why people kill without remorse and how they might be able to convince themselves that hate, torture and murder are justifiable, even honorable and ethical activities is a depressing undertaking. This is where politics enters the equation.

If violence is precipitated by specific political conditions, and here I include economic and structural conditions such as the transmission of cultural identity, we have to examine these briefly. There are disturbing parallels between conditions within the United States, national factors, and those linked to genocidal violence internationally.

In both the United States and in international politics there is a dynamic and profitable trade in weapons. The urban arms race in the United States has resulted in over 200 million hand guns flooding the society. Likewise, arms are sold to any customer in the international arms bazaar, and most of the industrialized nations of the world have an active business in selling the most sophisticated weapons of destruction.

Terrorism is a common feature of both national and international politics. What, after all, are drive-by shootings but a form of terrorism hardly different in effect or cause from the methods used by terrorists in international politics. As I was writing this it became all too real when, on September 11, 2001, hijacked airliners were flown into the World Trade Center towers in New York City and into the Pentagon in Washington, D.C. Terrorist violence, like genocidal violence, is persistent and there appears to be a large and willing supply of individuals willing to kill others in the service of some ideology or cause. Yet, in spite of the immediacy of these events, I must return to my main theme.

The chief cause of death among young African American males in the United States is homicide. The chief cause of death among the Kurds in southeastern Turkey is also a form of homicide, as they are killed by the government.

Anarchy, not law, rules both the national and international systems. People in the urban areas of the United States feel as though they are living in a war zone. In a war zone, how do you survive? You become a killer rather than a victim. You adapt to the circumstances that will most readily assure your survival. As the social order breaks down, symbols of respect become important and people will kill if they are insulted. Individuals must depend on themselves, and they arm and use weapons to achieve what cannot be achieved through other means. The code of the street becomes the rules of the game and the socialization of the street guarantees a form of often brief survival. Similarly, in international politics there are few if any institutional controls on the behavior of states. Anarchy characterizes the international state system as sovereignty allows the nation-states of the world to treat their internal populations however they wish without fear of outside interference. And all of this is exacerbated by the realities of politics that await those who are forced to survive under the often abysmal conditions.

Reflect for a moment on some of the more somber realities. Within the United States individuals face poverty, homelessness, environmental destruction and disintegration, increasing gaps between rich and poor, unemployment, recession, drugs, violence, disintegrating cities and a disintegrating infrastructure, and increases in the incidents of racism, sexism and anti-Semitism. Internationally, individuals are confronted with and exposed to war, nationalism and ethnic hostility; these forces often foster increasing interethnic violence and genocide, widening inequality between rich and poor nations, growing occurrences of starvation and famine, expanding destruction of the rain forest and genocide against indigenous populations. The list is almost beyond comprehension and almost immediately depressing.

Politics, it seems, is an integral part of our daily diet of overwhelming information, and it intrudes into our everyday existence. We are unable to escape, and there are complex reasons that help turn these political factors into atrocity.

How, within these settings, would it be possible for a person to develop the essential qualities that allow him to see other people as fully human? Where in these settings is the person encouraged to develop the moral compacts and ethical rules that theoretically should govern human relationships?

If a culture becomes increasingly accustomed to violence, people lose their awareness of the sadness and tragedy of death. The commonness of violence erodes the understanding of the pricelessness of life along with a capacity for outrage at injustice and cruelty that appears, in the modern period, to be the "normal" state of human existence. People are desensitized or numbed and no longer react with horror and disgust at the destruction of life. If this is indeed a growing tendency in many cultures, and in modern American culture in particular, why do we continue to celebrate violence and elevate those who commit violence to the level of modern heroes?

Growing up in a small town in northeastern Pennsylvania, my heroes were baseball stars like Phil Rizzuto and Mickey Mantle. I wanted to play for the New York Yankees and be like I thought they were—all-American, Boy Scouts and honorable men, like George Washington and Abe Lincoln. One of my heroes, Mickey Mantle, admitted his flaws with alcohol abuse several years ago, and another American sports hero, football great O.J. Simpson, remains in the national headlines as his acquittal continues to stir controversy. Like many American children in the 1950s, my friends and I also celebrated violent destroyers. We romanticized the Western cowboys who murdered Native Americans, and we idolized notorious robbers and killers such as Jesse James, Billy the Kid, and Bonnie and Clyde. Surely these are not models of how we all should live, but we were mesmerized by the excitement that was conveyed in their stories. If a culture makes heroes out of sports figures and individuals who have gained notoriety through the use of violence, how can one expect a nonviolent society?

I often ask my classes to remember the Vietnam War and, in so doing, ask how many are able to recall the name of the helicopter pilot who landed his aircraft between a group of Vietnamese and American soldiers who were about to kill them and ordered his crew to turn their guns on the Americans if they began to fire? Or, who remembers the names of the soldiers who refused to obey orders at My Lai to execute civilian elderly men, women and children? Yet, how many of us know William Calley, or William Westmoreland or take your pick? If the latter, we must then inquire into the cultural context and scrutinize the structure of rewards in that particular culture. Doing so cannot but help lead to troubling conclusions. In a time of fear and uncertainty, frustration and anger, people look for strong leaders, for the man on the white horse, as they try, to use an old book title, "To Escape From Freedom." In their rapid pursuit of salvation through obedience they surrender the essence of humanity and give up control of their decision-making capability. Listen to Varnado Simpson as he tells why he killed all those people at My Lai. Simpson's first victim was a baby. After killing her he recounts his reaction:

> My mind just went. The training came to me and I just started killing. Old men, women, children, water buffalos, everything. We were told to leave nothing standing. We did what we were told, regardless of whether they were civilians. They was the enemy. Period. Kill. . . .
> I just started killing any kinda way I can kill. It just came. I didn't know I had it in me. After I killed the child my whole mind just went. I just went. And after you start it's very easy to keep on. The hardest is to kill the first time but once you kill, then it becomes easier to kill the next person and the next one and the next one. Because I had no feeling, no emotions . . . nothing. (Ibid., p. 130)

And William Calley noted:

> I was a run-of-the mill average guy: I still am, I always said, *The people in Washington are smarter than me*. If intelligent people told me, "Communism's bad. It's going to engulf us. To take us in," I believe them. I had to. I was sure it could happen: the Russians could come in a parachute drop. Or a HALO drop or some submarines or space capsules even. (Calley, 1972, p. 222)

Calley and Simpson were placed in a context within which they had been trained to follow orders to kill and not question those orders. They had been conditioned by their culture, society and training, which had created certain mythologies to explain to them why they were sent to Vietnam and why they were to kill the "enemy." They were part of a culture that inculcates lessons concerning the need to use violence to solve whatever problem arises—as was done in the old West by the glorified gunslinger.

These conditions for violence are, consequently, related to the myths and ideologies[4] stressed in a culture or a nation-state that generally function to rationalize or justify the actions of the state.

Every society claims a genealogy, a point of origin that is grounded in mythology and that explains the origin of its people or of the state. Generally, these myths hold that the members of the group or the state descend from divine sources or are protected by divine intervention. This type of thinking, which differentiates the group or the state from all other groups or states, serves as a reason for dehumanizing those perceived as "the enemy," against whom the state wishes to pursue aggressive action. They are not, of course, protected by or descended from the same bloodlines and do not have the same pedigree. The important point is that the myths and ideologies stressed in a culture or state are expressed in the language of the important authority figures and are transmitted, through the process of enculturation or socialization, to the minds of the people living within the bounds of the state. As the people absorb and begin to believe these, they are being conditioned so that when ordered to engage in acts they might not usually consider to be moral, they are willing to obey the orders because of the elaborate system of justification which has been constructed.

As with the example of Calley and Simpson, a similar manifestation comes from Bosnia. In the morning newspaper on November 27, 1992, a Serbian nationalist soldier recounted his memory of what he had recently accomplished.

> We told them not to be afraid, we wouldn't do anything to them, they should just stand in front of the wall. But it was taken for granted among us that they should be killed. So, when somebody said, "Shoot," I swung around and pulled the trigger, three times on automatic fire. I remember the little girl with the red dress hiding behind her granny. (Burns, 1992, p. A1)

He is confessing to the fact that he, along with two companions, executed ten members of a Muslim family from a distance of about ten paces. Even though this particular man felt some remorse and claimed that he remembered Muslims who were kind to him, his memory was forged by Serbian leaders who filled his mind with propaganda. He was, for example, reminded that in the Serbian collective memory Muslims were viewed as a threat as far back as the Middle Ages, when Serbs were defeated by the Ottoman Turks. He claimed that Serbian political leaders told him that the Bosnian Muslims were "planning to declare an 'Islamic republic' in Bosnia" (ibid., p. A13). He was told that Muslims "would also require Serbian children to wear Muslim clothing," and, as he noted, he was told that "we would have to cleanse our whole population of Muslims. That's what we have been told, that's why it has been necessary to do all this" (ibid., p. A13). These are the same type of sentiments and the same form of motivations, the invoking of the same type of memories, with which humanity has been struggling throughout its relatively brief period of consciousness. These sentiments, these myths, do not, however, simply arise within a cultural context. They are created, manipulated and used by those in positions of power and leadership. Hence, they are tied to politics and to power.

Inexorably, then, we cannot escape the fact that at every level genocidal violence involves individuals confronted with choices to be made. Sometimes these choices determine whether one will pull the trigger, sometimes whether one will undertake the initiative to oppose genocide and organize an active intervention to stop the violence. This is the politics of genocide, and what I want to examine is how to build a movement to convince individuals, if you will, to make them choose, to oppose genocide and to participate in a movement to oppose and prevent genocide. It would be a movement that would focus political pressure on political institutions and leaders of those institutions to convince them that pursuing a policy of stopping genocide is a moral, ethical and politically expedient act to undertake.

# PART I

## Genocide and Political Movements

# 1

# Building a Movement to Stop Genocide

There was a time when the United States of America was a very different country than it is today. In the 1950s America was characterized by hidden inequality and racism. It was a time in stark contrast to what was to appear just a few short years later. The changes that occurred in the period generally referred to as "the 60s" were the result of grassroots movements, in particular the civil rights movement and the anti–Vietnam War movement. These participatory movements put pressure on the leaders of the American political system to attempt to make the United States a more just and humane place to live. In particular, leaders were called upon to implement measures to guarantee rights to minorities and to stop the war in Vietnam. These movements were particularly important during the presidency of Lyndon Baines Johnson (LBJ). When Johnson was elected president in 1964 he set an agenda that would transform the United States. The transformation would falter and would proceed in fits and starts but the programs, generally known as "The Great Society," made an America unlike what it was in the 1950s.

The transformation began with cultural movements and then spread to political movements. The first cultural manifestation of change could be seen when the beatniks emerged to challenge some of the traditional mores of the society. This accelerated even faster with the advent of rock and roll. The cultural movements were met with fear, as change generally is, in particular fear of a communist conspiracy manifested in a view of the civil rights and antiwar movements as part of that conspiracy. In fact, there were even those who argued that rock and roll was part of this imagined communist conspiracy.

Political change became more of an overt agenda when John F. Kennedy was elected president in 1960. Of course, there were signs of alteration before that, but these were accelerated by Kennedy's ascendance to office and speeded up even more when John F. Kennedy was assassinated on November 22, 1963. Lyndon Johnson was sworn in as president as he accompanied Kennedy's body from Dallas to Washington, and Johnson took the Kennedy rhetoric and turned it into policy.

## A Brief Introduction to Politics in the 1960s

Six years after the U.S. Supreme Court issued its ruling in *Brown v. Board of Education* (1954), over 99 percent of Southern black schoolchildren still attended state-segregated schools. In the South blacks could not get jobs, and, in fact, in the *Atlanta Constitution* employment ads were segregated by race and gender. "In 1960 black men were offered three jobs in the paper: car washer, custodian and broiler cook. African American women saw six listings for maids, and openings for a salad girl, a laundress, and a babysitter" (Farber, 1994, p. 77). This ad appeared in a city that prided itself on being the "most progressive city in the South." Due to this apparent slow progress the civil rights movement continued to grow.

The movement for civil rights gained energy and exposure on August 28, 1963, when 250,000 people gathered at the Lincoln memorial in Washington, D.C. Dr. King's "I have a dream" speech propelled the movement to the national stage and was followed by important events too numerous to detail in this brief review. Suffice to note that the movement was in full swing and was to witness events such as Freedom Summer, where in 1964 volunteers traveled to the South to register voters. "By the end of the summer, project workers had been arrested over 1,000 times, been shot at 35 times, suffered 30 bombings and 80 beatings; at least six people were murdered in civil-rights related events" (ibid., p. 94). Project workers viewed politics as a key element in their strategy for change so they organized the Mississippi Freedom Democratic Party. This, along with other activities, was designed to put pressure on local, state and national political leaders, and it worked.

In 1964 the Civil Rights Act was passed, and it profoundly changed the American landscape. The act contained

> ten titles and ran to twenty-eight pages. Title II of the act essentially outlawed racial discrimination at all places of public accommodation, including hotels, restaurants, and theaters. Title VII outlawed discrimination in employment. Other titles legally bound the federal government to cut off funding to any program at any level of the government that was racially discriminatory. The act strengthened the power of the Justice Department to bring suit against segregationists, increased the investigatory power of

# Building a Movement to Stop Genocide 23

the Civil Rights Commission, and further involved the federal government in school desegregation. Legal racism, practiced in the South for better than half a century, had now been formally and rhetorically repudiated by all three branches of the federal government. In order to address the nation's most obvious political, social, and moral failure, the federal government had greatly expanded its authority to intervene in the daily life of every American citizen. (Ibid., p. 96)

All American citizens did not react positively to the passage of this act. Many blamed Lyndon Johnson for overturning the old ways of life, and President Johnson lost Louisiana, Georgia, Alabama, South Carolina and Mississippi to Barry Goldwater in the 1964 election. This was the beginning of the turn to the Republican Party in the South, as seven Republican congressmen were elected in the Deep South for the first time since Reconstruction. Lessons to be derived are quite clear as the activity resulting in the passage of the Civil Rights Act of 1964 demonstrates that leaders desiring to change existing forms of behavior must be willing to seize the initiative and face up to any consequences. Leadership takes courage.

Basically, Lyndon Johnson wanted to "use the power of the federal government," in his words, to "build a society where the demands of morality, and the needs of the spirit, can be realized in the life of the nation." He dreamed of creating what he called the "Great Society." To pursue that agenda he would use the power of the state. For Johnson, liberalism meant that the

federal government had the responsibility, power, and ability to reduce inequality, protect historically oppressed minorities, champion American interests and values around the world, and balance the private sector's singular focus on making money with a broad concern for the nation's long-term good. The Johnson administration rivaled the New Deal in the sheer number of bills passed, including consumer protection acts, mass-transit aid, antipoverty programs, health measures, the creation of the National Endowment for the Arts and Humanities, consumer and workplace protection acts, aid to higher education, and path breaking antipollution, conservation, and beautification measures. (Ibid., p. 105)

White House assistant Joseph Califano summed up the prevailing sentiment: "We simply could not accept poverty, ignorance and hunger as intractable, permanent features of American society. There was no child we could not feed, no adult we could not put to work, no disease we could not cure, no toy, food or appliance we could not make safer, no air or water we could not clean" (ibid.). Floods of legislation were unloosed. Housing acts were passed, as were school bills, preschool programs, rent supplements, training programs, medical assistance, legal aid, food and meal subsidies, rat control, delinquency prevention, supplements of social security benefits, expanded welfare programs and food stamps. In 1965 only about 633,000 people received what was minimum aid; ten years later over 17 million people benefitted from food stamps. In 1965 Medicaid and Medicare were passed.

The flurry of activity began to have an effect. Programs such as Aid to Families with Dependent Children (AFDC) grew, and poverty declined from 21 percent of the population in 1959 to 12 percent in 1969. While the antipoverty programs were clearly whittling away at poverty in the United States, the Johnson administration wanted to extend political rights to all Americans and, on August 6, 1965, LBJ signed the Voting Rights Act. While there is no connection, five days after the signing of the Voting Rights Acts the Watts riot occurred. It was the first major riot of the 1960s and was followed by many more. The summer after Watts, 43 urban areas exploded, and in 1967, 167 cities reported riots. While many of them were set off by acts of police brutality, the riots, along with the rhetoric of black radicals, caused, or were an excuse to allow, many whites to turn away from the civil rights movement. Whites were confused, but some backlashed. Vietnam and the increasing frustration and cutbacks in social programs began to have an impact on the attitudes of many Americans so that by 1968, when Richard Nixon was elected president, many of the Great Society programs were no longer popular—in spite of the fact that they were very limited in extent and cost.

The innovations undertaken by Johnson included a psychological as well as a political and economic segment. His basic idea was to give people the sense that there was someone out there who cared and to provide experience in taking action to do something to bring about change. The basic programs included job training, no cash handouts, no tax increases, education, Head Start, early childhood education, Community Action Participatory (CAP), programs to provide economic opportunity, college loans and many others, including antipollution and environmental programs. In the first year of operation all this cost a mere $1 billion, or 1 percent of the federal budget.

These were experimental programs undertaken in the spirit of trying to make the United States a better, more humane place for all of its diverse citizens. The spirit motivating these actions included the idea that even if they may not succeed, at least an attempt was made and we would be able to find out what worked and what failed to achieve the goals of creating opportunity and a more just and equitable country. Basically the idea was to open up the system, to give those on the margins a sense of a positive future, to provide hope.

The relevant point for this exploration is that people were mobilized by a combination of leadership exercised by the president of the United States and a popular, grassroots movement to put pressure on the political institutions to take action to try to change the status quo. A similar set of events occurred in the case of the anti–Vietnam War movement, but in this case presidential leadership was not only lacking, but opposed to the goals of the antiwar movement.

## The Anti–Vietnam War Movement

The anti–Vietnam War movement was modeled after the civil rights movement and motivated by a war that escalated throughout the 1960s. As noted above, 1960 seemed to signal a sudden transformation in America. John F. Kennedy not only raised the sense of new challenges for young people, but also appeared to signal an end to the era of Eisenhower and the older generation. Some viewed Kennedy's election as a sign that a new generation was about to take power.

The anti–Vietnam War movement, Farber argues, was the United States' prodemocracy movement, and while there is great disagreement over interpretation of the impact of this period, three perspectives on the 1960s appear to dominate the discussion (this summary is from Farber 1994).

Arguing from the liberal perspective, the 1960s was a period when millions of Americans refused to tolerate the gap between ideals and reality. Young people in particular demanded that the country live up to the values they had been taught. From this viewpoint many mistakes were made, such as the Vietnam War, but generally, the liberal view was that the system worked and the 1960s was a noble era of reform.

A more conservative view is that the liberal policies of the sixties, in particular the youth revolt, were carried to excess. In fact, conservatives have mounted a sustained assault on the sixties' surge of liberal reform, foreign and social policy, civil rights, federal involvement in social services for the poor, affirmative action, profit-reducing federal regulations, abortion rights and public reluctance to support military intervention overseas. Their basic argument is that the movements, in particular the counterculture, were apolitical and self-indulgent and were caused by post–World War II affluence and permissive child-rearing.

A third point of view is grounded in the experience of those who participated in the movements and asks what can be learned from that period. The argument here is that people need to understand rather than ignore or try to imitate the movements of the 1960s. In addition, the period must be placed in a historical context, and the connections between events need to be understood within that context. Finally, the experiences of the 1960s can provide future movements for human liberation with important lessons about the American political system. It is, in fact, the possible lessons that are of most interest here.

What is now referred to as "the movement" began with two proactive struggles for change—the civil rights movement and the student new left. We have already discussed the first, but it is important to note that *both* were rooted in the post–World War II world of the 1950s and confronted fundamental dilemmas that confronted all political movements in the United States. First, how to effect change on a national scale through movements founded on personal relationships and grassroots organization. Second, what to do when confronted by political leaders who were unwilling to change (Farber, 1994, p. 9; Gitlin, 1993).

Both the new left and the civil rights movements articulated four primary values:

1. Equality or the full inclusion of society's dispossessed
2. Personal empowerment for each person to control the institutions that effect their lives
3. A moral politics grounded on belief in individual growth, compassion for one's fellow human beings and intolerance of injustice
4. The central importance of community as a locus of meaningful engagement in life and politics.

Throughout the period there was a direct belief in the importance of participatory democracy and a vision of citizenship that assumes that individuals are capable of managing their own affairs. This was expressed in the Port Huron Statement drafted by the Students for a Democratic Society (SDS) in 1962. While it was a classic expression of participatory democracy, the antiwar movement went through various stages and factions, all of which are beyond the scope of this discussion. It is sufficient to note that the years 1967, 1968, 1969 and 1970 were the height of the movement, and they were described by Todd Gitlin (1993), a participant in many of the activities, as "a cyclone in a wind tunnel" (p. 242). Gitlin lists the sequence of some of the many events that occurred:

> draft card burnings, the march on the Pentagon, Stop the Draft Week, The Tet Offensive, The McCarthy Campaign, Johnson decides not to run for another term, Martin Luther King killed, buildings occupied at Columbia University, demonstrations in Paris, Prague, and other places, trips to Hanoi by Americans such as Jane Fonda, Robert Kennedy killed, riots at the Democratic national convention in Chicago hundreds of students massacred in Mexico City, protest at the Miss America pageant, Nixon elected president, United States deserters flee to Canada and Sweden, mutinies, "fragging" of officers and others by enlisted men in Vietnam, riots on college campuses such as San Francisco State, Berkeley, Harvard, Stanford, etc., the incident at Peoples Park, police shootouts with Black Panthers, the entire "youth culture" movement including the idea that drugs, sex and

rock and roll were what were important, Woodstock, women's consciousness raising, the Chicago Conspiracy trial, Charles Manson, Altamont, My Lai, Weatherman bombs, Nixon's invasion of Cambodia, students killed at Kent State and Jackson State Universities, a fatal bombing in Madison, Wisconsin, trials, bombings, fires, agents provocateurs, and the presence of numerous grand abstractions, such as "resistance," "liberation," "revolution," "repression." (P. 242)

There were, therefore, many varieties of opposing the Vietnam War, from civil disobedience and resistance to the draft to using violence and supporting the Vietcong and the North Vietnamese. Most depended on some form of public protest. During this period protests grew steadily larger so that on April 26, 1968, up to a million college and high school students took part in a national student strike. At the same time there were those engaging in electoral politics such as supporting the insurgent candidacy of Eugene McCarthy and Robert Kennedy as they opposed Lyndon Johnson for the Democratic nomination for president in 1968.

When Nixon was elected president in 1968 the strategy he pursued took some steam out of the popular movement. Perhaps the final high points of antiwar protest occurred with "The Moratorium" on October 15, 1969, and on November 15, 1969, with "The Mobilization" in Washington. After these there were no plans for a follow up—no idea of what to do. People felt burnt out by frustration and factionalism and tired of the endless disputes and debates. The movement fizzled as the "no longer new left trapped itself in a seamless loop: growing militancy, growing isolation, growing commitment to The Revolution, sloppier and more frantic attempts to imagine a revolutionary class, growing hatred among the competing factions with their competing imaginations" (Gitlin, 1993, p. 381). The Weathermen "were an extension of bad politics" (p. 382) and the movement cast about for justification which it tried to find in a Marxism adapted to its uses. The vanguard concept, leaders of the revolution was trotted out to justify the actions the movement began to disintegrate. "Bring the War Home" was a slogan and the violence became expressive and indiscriminate. Casualties grew and the left was on the way out.

After the invasion of Cambodia and the killing of students at Kent and Jackson state universities, there were massive antiwar demonstrations at colleges across the United States. Many colleges and universities closed early for summer vacation, and the spirit of antiwar protest and student activism never recovered from the summer vacation of 1970. In 1970–1971 there were fewer demonstrations, and fewer still the next year. The media had learned not to give air time to demonstrations and so they became nonevents. Stopping the draft caused many college students to lessen or lose their commitment to ending the war, and the killing of students at Kent State University in 1970 showed that protest could be a dangerous activity. The great irony is that when Nixon resigned because of Watergate and the war was finally terminated in 1975, the movement had won its greatest victory but there was no one around to collect the honors.

However one evaluates the political movements of the 1960s, from whatever perspective, "none of the most vital dreams of the 1960s—whether they were of a beloved community, a color-blind society, a Great Society, a 'higher consciousness,' an end to patriarchy, or freedom for the people of Vietnam—came to pass. But despite the failures, much did change, and most of the changes were for the better, even if they were never quite enough, even if they sometimes brought new difficulties in their wake" (Farber, 1994, p. 263).

The 1960s became a scapegoat. Blaming the 1960s for any and all of the nation's moral and spiritual wounds became a way for many Americans to avoid thinking about how and why many of the problems brought to consciousness by the antiwar and civil rights movements persisted.

Whatever lessons are derived from the political movements of the 1960s, one fact remains clear. They were popular movements, sometimes supported by political and moral leaders and sometimes opposed by them. These movements clearly indicated that if the will is present, a political system can be moved by popular participation to head in a direction it apparently may not be intending to go. If, consequently, there is to be any hope of preventing genocide, we should learn from these attempts, even if some judge them to be failures, and act to build a new movement to stop genocide.

## Building a Political Movement

If, in a rudimentary fashion, we define politics as it is defined in many introduction to political science textbooks (Shively, 1999), as decision and choice, then we are clearly confronted by political choices that may involve ethical/moral dilemmas. How we make the choices we do, and how we might convince people that it is a good idea to make a choice to oppose genocide becomes our task.

Political scientists also argue that there exists a hierarchy of political behavior ranging from the least to the most involved. The least involved takes the least amount of time and energy and is quite passive, while the most active requires vast amounts of time and energy and may have a high burnout factor built in. The range, from lowest to highest, usually looks something like this:

> Observing and keeping informed (using media to follow events)
> Using a website to follow events

Voting

Writing a letter to a newspaper

Writing a letter to a public official

Working in local groups or for a political party

Persuading others to vote or participate

Helping to form a political group

Becoming a candidate

Participating in protest activity

These activities also form a continuum from the more conventional, such as voting, to the more unconventional such as participating in a demonstration or protest. If we take this information and examine the amount of participation in these activities it is clear that the more passive the act the lower the level of participation. There are good reasons for this since most people devote the activity of everyday life to survival, to raising families and to other, more primary activities. In addition, there remains a paradox at the heart of this information. Namely that the very people who most desperately need the assistance of a government, the least advantaged and most likely to be victimized, are the least likely to participate. Motivating participation is, therefore, of great importance. To accomplish this it is first necessary to create a favorable attitude toward participation and political change.

## Political Change

In modern America there are many political movements. There are movements in protest against the World Trade Organization, in favor of stricter gun controls, in protest of child labor in distant countries, against globalization and genetically engineered food, in favor of gay marriage, or against it, against logging in national forests and others. Missing from this and other lists is an organized movement to mobilize people to prevent genocide. Although there are groups, which will be discussed later, devoted to this activity, there is no large-scale, grassroots political activity to change the way Americans view the genocidal behavior that was so persistent in the last century. In order to understand how a movement might be built to oppose genocide it is necessary to start with some basic theories concerning how political change occurs.

Political change remains one of the great unsolved puzzles of political theory. For thousands of years attempts have been made to find some way to describe how and why political systems and individuals change (Marcuse, 1972; Moore, 1970). While it is difficult if not impossible to ascertain precisely what causes change, there are many theories about how and why it occurs. Most begin by attempting to classify change.

While these systems of classification do not necessarily tell the observer how or why change occurs, they do provide a mechanism that may be used to help clarify how we think about the process. Theories order one's thoughts so that events may be more clearly understood, and they help one find some logic in the seeming chaos. Obviously, it is critical to remember that any scheme of categories is, by definition, static. As soon as categories are created, a dynamic, ever-changing set of events, a process, is turned into a rigid set of categories. The first point to remember, therefore, is that political change is a long-term, ongoing process; it does not occur like a bolt of lightening, and it may take generations to see the results. With this in mind, let me attempt some rudimentary form of categorization within which the discussion of change may proceed. I am going to divide political change arbitrarily into two broad types: fundamental change, which might move in several directions, and marginal or incremental change.

Fundamental change is change that occurs infrequently and is the same thing as revolutionary change. Basically, it involves an alteration in the primary organization and operation of the politics, economics and social organization of a nation and a change in the distribution of wealth and power within that context. It is, therefore, very rare and occurs only over long periods of time. Fundamental change is even more complex, however, since it might be proactive or reactive. Proactive change would move the nation or the world closer to ideals of justice and fairness and is devoted to the preservation rather than the destruction of human life.

Reactionary change is the opposite of proactive change. In systems attempting to become more humane, it involves a reaction against the existing system and an attempt to move back to some imaginary pre-existing time when things were supposed to be superior to the present. Reactionary change is not proactive and does not lead to solving the basic social and political problems facing a society or the world. For example, the coming to power of Hitler in 1933 may be viewed as an example of reactive change. In a system that is authoritarian, moving toward justice is proactive.

Marginal change is basically incremental. Slow changes are made in an existing system. This might involve factors such as reform of campaign finance laws or the change of control from one political party to another. This type of change leaves the basic distribution of wealth and power intact and does not alter the organization or operation of politics, economics or the social system. Marginal change may also be proactive or reactive. Basically reactive marginal change is movement toward a more totalitarian system, while proactive change moves toward fairness and justice. The basic policy of most ruling groups or administrations in most systems is to pursue one or the other form of marginal change with the idea being to communicate to the people of that system that real change is taking place. In short, to present the illusion of change in order to maintain the legitimacy of the regime and the loyalty of the population.

Keeping these categories in mind it is now time to turn our attention to an examination of what type of strategy may be used to bring about what type of change. The ultimate goal being to find out how to motivate people to denounce or reject the destruction of human life and support a movement to stop genocide.

Since marginal change occurs most frequently we will look at it first. When people in the United States say that they want to change the way politics operates they are usually told to "work through the system," to "get involved in politics" and to participate in the established institutions. The basic argument of this view is that if you put "good" people in important political positions, that is, if you elect the "right" people to office and they appoint more "good" people who engage in rational planning, this will bring about the necessary changes and move the nation and the world toward justice. There is, however, a basic fallacy in this much too broad view. Marginal change is much more complicated. The basic fallacy is that this strategy ignores the root causes of problems and treats only the surface, leaving intact the basic problems so that they are never solved. In fact, they return again and again as testified to by the repeated examples of genocide in the twentieth century. The advice to "work through the system" for marginal change, therefore, confronts the humanitarian reformer with a very difficult dilemma.

That is, this strategy means that you begin your quest for change by accepting the existing institutions and especially the nation-state. Accepting these institutions that have been responsible for committing genocide throughout the ages in order to create a movement to oppose genocide condemns the reformer to dwell in a world of fantasy, since you cannot depend on a system that is propelled by imperatives of injustice to be just. Real change, if it were to occur, would threaten the status quo, and, in particular, the power of the entrenched interests who, like most others, have no desire to commit political suicide. The basic distribution of wealth and power remains intact since no group will willingly engage in activities designed to bring about it's demise. But this gets even more complicated since one of the only ways to build a movement for change is to manipulate the institutions of marginal change. Marginal change is a worthy goal to be pursued, such as intervention to stop the slaughter of the Kosavar Albanians or to stop the atrocities against the East Timorese, since it demonstrates what might be achieved with a full fledged movement and institutions in place. The strategy of working for marginal change, therefore, will not result in fundamental alterations but may very well result in small steps in that direction. The next task is to ascertain how that might be the case.

## Marginal and Fundamental Change: Some Notes Toward a Strategy of Political Change

Marginal change is important because it might be used as a tool to highlight the contradictions in an existing system. For example, if a state maintains in its' official rhetoric that it supports efforts to end genocide in the world but continues to pursue a policy opposed to that end, working for marginal changes, such as the creation of the International Criminal Court which the United States refused to go along with, points out the contradictions. A contradiction exists when any set of structures or actions produce conditions which are contrary to the stated goals. Marginal change of the type just discussed may raise the level of consciousness of people who support action to stop genocide and may, consequently, motivate them to take more vigorous means to recruit others to their cause. In this fashion, marginal change may act as a catalyst when people's expectations are raised by the anti-genocide, pro-humanitarian rhetoric, and they see that the action is incongruent with the words. This disappointment may actually have one of two possible effects. First, it might conceivably lead to a desire to bring rhetoric into line with behavior and move people toward a goal of preventing genocide. Second, it might also lead to alienation and withdrawal, as people believe there is nothing they are able to do to influence the large and seemingly impervious institutions of the state. The direction it takes depends to a great extent upon whether there exist ongoing political movements to steer the impulses of the people in a positive or negative direction.

Individuals and groups who support action to stop genocide, therefore, must not eschew marginal change, but must build upon it to create a movement that will attract those whose consciousness has been raised by the lack of results and by the continuation of inhumane action. We must see that each proactive marginal change may be used to help erode confidence in the old genocidal system and that this erosion of confidence increases the potential for mobilizing individuals to engage in political action. This means that pressure must be kept on the political and social leaders and consciousness of genocide and genocide-like events must be kept in the forefront of people's attention. If linked with a specific strategy, it is just possible that a movement to stop genocide might sprout from the planting of such seeds.

Marginal change will be a catalyst only if people work to make it effective by using it to point out the contradictions in the current system by pointing out the next steps. This means that, simply because contradictions exist, it is not always the case that they are seen. A sustained effort is necessary to bring them to awareness, or consciousness. Essentially, this means that political organization to support anti-genocidal action and institutions is necessary and that unremitting efforts to raise the political consciousness of individuals, to point out to them the dangers of genocide and how it is in their interest to stop it, are parts of a new anti-genocidal mentality leading to an anti-genocidal movement.

In following chapters I will discuss in greater detail how to build upon an already existing foundation of public opinion that continually demonstrates that American citizens are more compassionate than political leaders have led us to believe and also to point out the specific directions in which such a political movement should move—including anti-genocidal education and the creation of multilateral, international institutions empowered to stop genocide. For now, however, I want to focus on how political movements are constructed.

## Political Organizing

The end goal of political organizing should be to raise political consciousness of how important genocide is and to empower individuals so that they start to see how they might be able to participate in a humanitarian movement devoted to ending this horrible epidemic. A movement to stop genocide would act as a mediating structure between the individual and the modern nation-state. It would, in short, be designed to empower people (Berger and Neuhaus, 1977). Since individuals in the modern era often feel powerless when confronted by the institutions of the modern nation-state or the international state system, institutions they do not control, the idea is to provide the feeling and experience of participation and the sense that they might be able to control those structures or, at least, to provide them the opportunity to participate in organizations devoted to those ends. This requires political organizers, and there is a rather vast, although seemingly forgotten, literature in this area.

Creating a movement to stop genocide is not, at least in theory, different from creating a movement to support civil rights in the United States or to end the Vietnam War or to organize communities to take control of their institutions. To be sure, international issues, events taking place thousands of miles away, appear to be more distant and less relevant to the life of Americans. In fact, there are five basic perceptual factors that seem to render genocide or other international issues less salient to Americans.

> First, as noted above, they appear to be more remote and have no direct impact on everyday life.

Second, there may be no immediate constituents to bring pressure to bear on the government, since the group under attack may not have significant representation in the United States.

Third, as a result of the above, there is less interest in the issues involved.

Fourth, related to the above, there is little motivation to take action.

Fifth, if the events are truly remote and not spectacular there will be little media coverage and, therefore, little awareness of the possibly genocidal actions. There are numerous examples, including the destruction of large numbers of people in places such as the Sudan, Sierra Leone, Sri Lanka and others.

In spite of these complications, however, the principles of organization should be similar.

The premier political organizer in perhaps all of U.S. history was Saul Alinsky. Alinsky created a model for organizers interested in raising political consciousness and motivating political action to follow.

According to Alinsky (1971), there are no rules for bringing about political change, but there are certain rules for political organizers who wish to bring about political change (p. xviii). First, he argues, the organizer must start from where the world is, as it is, not as the organizer would like it to be. Effective organization is, according to Alinsky, thwarted by the desire for instant and dramatic change. Therefore, working for change is a long-term process, and those interested in supporting that process have to curtail their impatience, their desire for instant alteration in a system that has persevered for centuries. Change has to be preceded, he argues, by a passive affirmative, nonchallenging attitude toward change among the masses who, he contends, must be willing to "let go of the past and chance the future." Some of the goals of the organizer, therefore, are to "create disenchantment and discontent with the current values" and to encourage the people to believe in themselves, to believe they have the power to direct their future and to have an impact on seemingly distant institutions. Organizers must therefore establish some control over the flow of events, and this requires positive action. Action means "politics," and since it is impossible to act politically without engaging in some form of manipulation the important point, according to Moore (1970), is "all human society amounts to manipulation of human beings by each other. Everything depends on who is doing the manipulating and for what purposes. Those who resist the status quo also manipulate both each other and the dominant groups. In a rational society . . . the manipulation takes place to reduce human misery" (p. 61). Political organizers must be realists who see the world as it is and who are prepared to use necessary tactics to try to reduce human misery. In the case of genocide it is important to raise several very depressing questions. In fact, it is absolutely critical to ask why people kill each other, why genocide persists and how it is motivated if we are going to have a successful movement to prevent it. This means that it is necessary to enter the forbidden and depressing territory of questions concerning how deeply entrenched in human nature impulses to genocide reside and what if anything might be done to overcome these tendencies. There is a growing body of literature on these questions, and I am going to take the easy way out by ignoring them for the moment as I concentrate on the building of a movement to prevent something that, it is conceivable, might not be preventable. I am, therefore, making a huge assumption that human action to stop genocide is possible, but not that it will necessarily be effective. Rather, it seems to me that, even if we fail, the very least we must do is try.

The basic point is that there are concrete, realistic alternatives to doing nothing. Despite this, there are many people who loudly proclaim that genocide is inevitable, on the one hand, and that only revolutionary change will stop it, on the other. Both become self-fulfilling prophecies condemning the victims of the world to further massacre since they are both prescriptions for paralysis, for inaction. They allow the perpetrators of genocide to triumph without opposition. The fact is that without a movement to oppose genocide, it will inevitably continue, and the first step toward stopping it is a movement directed at raising consciousness of the pervasiveness of genocide and how it might be mitigated.

The first step, the creation of a movement, has been discussed above. This movement must begin by addressing the problem of political consciousness.

## Developing Political Consciousness of Genocide

The form of political organization discussed above has as the primary goal the formation of political consciousness, or, if you will, heightening awareness of why genocide is important and how it has an impact on all people. Along with this should come a desire to do something to stop or prevent genocidal acts. The beginning of political consciousness is probably the feeling that one is a worthwhile human being who has the ability to influence his or her own life, in particular, to feel that one has power to pursue action to affect the institutions that are most directly related to one's own life. In this case, of course, most Americans will believe that genocide occurring in distant lands is not of immediate concern. Consciousness-raising would point out what I call "the practicality of morality"—how a foreign policy based on ethical and moral principles may have positive reverberations for all people, including those who live in apparently safe circumstances far from the atrocities. In order to accomplish this, it is important to provide information and to provide citizens with experiences that demonstrate how they might successfully influence the policy of their government—in this case, to participate in multilateral or regional organizations and institutions with power to stop genocide.

The first step is the appearance of social, moral and political leaders, who pave the way for a change in attitudes. Instead of feelings of isolation, these leaders would stress the common humanity and empathy of all people. They would build on the already existing public sentiment for a more compassionate policy.

The second step is to provide avenues through which action may be manifested, that is, to support existing organizations or to build new ones devoted to stopping genocide. This may include many different kinds of activities. Earlier I listed a hierarchy of political action which ranged from writing letters to participation in demonstrations. All of these avenues may be utilized, but the activity must be designed for primary impact. While there are a number of organizations devoted to the task of preventing genocide, there are few engaged in political organizing with a view toward increasing the consciousness of the American public or the political leadership. Among the diversity of groups one may find nongovernmental organizations, such as Amnesty International, Human Rights Watch, Physicians for Human Rights; Holocaust centers, of which there are many in communities around the United States; institutes and groups affiliated with various universities and groups whose primary focus is on genocide. Among these the Genocide Research Project, a collaboration between the University of Memphis and Pennsylvania State University, maintains a website with a comprehensive listing of resources.

In fact, the list appears to grow every year. Most of these, however, are oriented toward the provision of information and not to a more overt politics of prevention. Others are more active politically and very often devoted to a single important political goal. For example, the Cambodian Genocide Program at Yale University focuses on that genocide and on bringing perpetrators to justice, but it maintains connections to other organizations interested in the prevention of genocide. While I am unable to provide a comprehensive list, some of the main organizations, most of whom have existed for some years and are, therefore, tested in their commitment to the prevention of genocide include the following: the Campaign to End Genocide, Prevent Genocide International, International Alert and Aegis Trust. In spite of the growing number of organizations of all types, however, the prominent questions, largely unanswered, remains, How does one exert influence on the institutions of American government to try to move them to stop genocide?

I have addressed this in detail, and that argument merits restatement.

# Building a Movement to Stop Genocide

Before we examine the more specific actions that might be taken, it is important to reemphasize that activity must be engaged in with a view to the reality of world events. One must not expect instantaneous results. When we ask what we are able to do to prevent genocide in a seemingly genocidal world we must remember that is only one part of the most important question. The rest is not only what one does but, perhaps more importantly, what one does not do! If we all sit quietly as silent observers of atrocity we will have forgotten the awful lessons of the past century. It is often not our actions that speak so loudly to historians, but our lack of action. What is most important is to attempt to convince as many as possible to live their lives preserving rather than destroying human life. In the long and short run we must make the ugliest realities of people's daily lives less ugly. We must first stop the violence and then provide long-term solutions.

There is one last point that must be considered. Most advocates of a movement to prevent or stop genocide forget that the vast majority of people probably fear change more than they wish to see genocide halted. Movements to save life require hard work and must appear nonthreatening. If a more humane international system is the goal, then change must be conceived of as an ongoing process, and, apparently, pressure must come from the bottom up. First, those in positions of political leadership must have their attention focused on the reality of an ongoing, grassroots political movement. Second, the movement has to be aggressive in its pursuit of justice. And, third, the struggle does involve not only politics but also changing the way people interact with each other. It is not sensible, and it is premature, to expect political and economic change if people are unable even to get along with each other.

As we undertake this journey together it is important to remember that this is an ongoing process. Perhaps the best summary of how we might think about such a course of action has been provided by one of the leading thinkers who was most influential in moving young people to take action against what they viewed as an oppressive system in the 1960s. Herbert Marcuse (1972) wrote that the success of any movement to humanize politics at whatever level

> Depends to a great extent, on the ability of the young generation—not to drop out and not to accommodate, but to learn how to regroup after defeat, how to develop, with the new sensibility and new rationality, to sustain the long process of education—the indispensable prerequisite for the transition to large-scale political action. For the next revolution will be the concern of generations, and . . . may take all but a century. (Pp. 133–34)

To be sure, this is not much solace for those whose lives are being lost and that is why we have to think of both long- and short-term strategies.

The first goal is to save life; the second is to bring about permanent change so that those lives will be less likely to be threatened. To accomplish this it is imperative to begin where Alinsky tells us to start, with the world as it is, not as we want it to be. One indication of the "world as it is" may be found by examining what the American public thinks about action to prevent genocide.

# 2

# Genocide and Public Opinion: A Comparison of the Policy-Making Elite and the General Public

The technological innovations of the twentieth century provided the means by which mass killing could take place on a level almost beyond comprehension. Perhaps more depressing than the numbers, however, is the possibility that many of these lives could have been saved if policy-making elites in the major international states, in particular in the United States, had been willing to take decisive action to stop the violence. Pondering the horrible repetition of genocidal events in the twentieth century, it is easy to conclude that policy-making elites have consistently stumbled and procrastinated while they observed the slaughter in action.

At the same time, however, they offered rhetorical reassurance to the peoples of the world that they were, in fact, acting to preserve the very same lives which were so brutally taken. In some cases involving the United States, elaborate excuses were formulated. Sometimes they took the form of arguing that the public was not interested in what was happening in far-off lands and would not, in any case, support intervention to save human life. In this chapter I am attempting to ascertain if that assertion is accurate. I plan to examine public opinion surveys and compare the views of the public with policies actually pursued by the policy-making elite.

To address this I will explore what the public knows and thinks should have been done in the cases of the Holocaust, Bosnia, Rwanda and Kosovo. The basic question, to reiterate, is whether in spite of the policy-making elites' adherence to a hypocritical double standard wherein they talk about human rights but appear reluctant to act, the general public displayed a more humanitarian view that these same elites not only ignored but misrepresented.

## Public Opinion and Genocide

As a country, does the general population approve of the positions adopted by the policy-making elite? Thinking about this question leads one to the obvious conclusions that, if people do not have information about genocidal massacres or if these are not covered by the media, there will be little or no response, no interest and no pressure to stop them from recurring. Data exist which will shed light on these issues.

The Pew Research Center for the People and the Press compiles these types of data.[5] In examining the public's interest in news stories in 1997, they found that overall the public's interest in news fell from 1986 through 1996: in 1986 25 percent of the public followed major news stories "very closely," while in 1996 the number fell to 19 percent. The most closely watched story of 1997, as you might expect, was the death of Princess Diana. News from Washington, that is, stories about policy, did not make the top ten list, and only 49 percent of the public paid very close or even "fairly" close attention to stories on domestic policy. The story ranked second was the dispute with Iraq over the weapon's inspections, but, generally, stories about foreign policy drew little attention.

Only 12 percent followed "Clashes in Bosnia with U.S. troops" "very closely," and only 4 percent followed the "Civil War in Zaire." There was no mention of other situations in Bosnia, no mention of Algeria, no reference to Rwanda. In other words, almost all stories dealing with genocide were of little interest.

In addition, the Pew Research Center also examined what they call "Public Attentiveness to Major News Stories from 1986 through 2000." Over 600 stories were referenced. The overall highest ranking story was the explosion of the Space Shuttle Challenger, followed by 80 percent of the respondents. Prior to the conflict in Kosovo, the highest ranking for any story about Bosnia dealt with Clinton's policies in Bosnia and ranked 231 with 26 percent saying they followed it "very closely." This, by the way, was the same percent that followed "The Trial of Lorena Bobbitt" and a percentage point higher than those following closely the O.J. Simpson case in October 1994. In March 1999, however, 43 percent said they followed NATO air strikes against Serbian forces in Kosovo, and in April 1999, 41 percent said they followed closely NATO air strikes against Serbian forces. This was the highest ranking yet for any situation related to the conflict surrounding the former Yugoslavia and was a far different result from the 5 percent indicating they followed closely the "ethnic conflict in Kosovo, Serbia," in March 1998. One month later, however,

# Genocide and Public Opinion

in May 1999, interest appeared to be waning as the figure declined to 32 percent. The first reference to Bosnia appears in July 1991, and until the action in Kosovo, public attention varied but at no point moved beyond 25 percent. In fact, it generally languishes in the 10–15 percent range. Interest in other genocide-like events remains even lower on the public interest scale.

**Table 2.1**
**Percentage of People Who Say They Follow the "Civil War in Bosnia" "Very Closely"**

| Date | Rank | Percent |
| --- | --- | --- |
| Sept 1992 | 548 | 10 |
| Jan 1993 | 438 | 15 |
| May 1993 | 437 | 15 |
| Aug 1993 | 363 | 19 |
| Sept 1993 | 436 | 15 |
| Oct 1993 | 416 | 19 |
| Dec 1993 | 434 | 15 |
| May 1994 | 382 | 18 |
| June 1994 | 503 | 12 |
| Dec 1994 | 474 | 13 |
| Feb 1995 | 574 | 8 |
| March 1995 | 526 | 11 |
| June 1995 | 300 | 22 |
| Aug 1995 | 413 | 16 |
| Sept 1995 | 428 | 15 |
| Feb 1996 | 326 | 21 |
| March 1996 | 378 | 18 |
| April 1996 | 342 | 20 |
| July 1996 | 410 | 16 |

"Tribal Massacres in Rwanda." May 1994, rank = 504 Percent = 12
"The Civil War in Zaire." May 1997, rank = 614 Percent = 4
"Civil War in Cambodia." May 1990, rank = 617 Percent = 4
"Ethnic Conflict in Kosovo, Serbia." March 1998, no rank Percent = 5

Among the over 600 stories there was only one reference to Rwanda, ranked 504 in May 1994, with 12 percent saying they followed the "Tribal Massacres in Rwanda" "very closely," ranked 614 with 4 percent following closely was "the Civil War in Zaire" and ranked 617 also with 4 percent in May 1990 was the "Civil War in Cambodia."

Overall, the range of interest starts at the high of 80 percent who say they followed the explosion of the Space Shuttle Challenger (July 1986) to a low of 2 percent who say they followed "Tom Cruise's separation from his wife" (April 1990).

What does this mean? The more recent genocides of the twentieth century clearly have been covered by the visual media, CNN and the networks. On the other hand, if my local newspaper is any guide, stories rarely appear where they may be noticed. Moreover, there is an old principle of political science that notes that people are interested in issues only when they appear to have some impact on their personal lives or pocketbooks. If people in positions of opinion leadership and political responsibility do not take the lead in emphasizing that it is important to try to prevent genocide, it is unlikely that the general public will have any inclination to take action to stop abuses of human rights in what appear to be far-off and remote locations. This is, in fact, reinforced by the information gathered since September 11, 2001. The Gallup Poll has noted that there is "little doubt that the Sept. 11 terrorist attacks were the top news story of 2001" and that "Roughly half of all Americans in a December 2001 Gallup Poll mentioned some aspect of the war on terrorism as the most important problem facing the nation" (Gallup, 2002, pp. 1–2.). Moreover, the Pew Research Center tabulated data concerning how closely news stories about the terrorism attacks were followed and found that in mid-September 74 percent said they followed the story "very closely," and 78 percent said they were still following the story in October 2002. When they asked about the U.S. military effort to fight terrorism in Afghanistan the number following that story "very closely" fell to 51 percent. In fact, after the terrorist attacks of September 11, Americans' interest in the news rose sharply. The Pew Center (2002) points out that "just 23% of the public paid very close attention to the typical news story before the attacks, which is comparable to the yearly averages since 1990. But after the attacks, that number more than doubles to 48%" (p. 2). Overall the terrorist attacks dominated the top news stories of 2001 (p. 1).

**Table 2.2**
**Top News Stories of 2001**

| Story | Following Very Closely |
|---|---|
| 1. Terrorism attacks on the U.S. (10/17-21) | 78% |
| 2. Trade Center/Pentagon attacks (9/13-17) | 74 |
| 3. Identifying those who attacked U.S. (10/1-3) | 72 |
| 4. High gasoline prices (May) | 61 |
| 5. Defending against future terrorism (10/1-3) | 57 |
| 6. Release of U.S. air crew from China (April) | 55 |
| 7. Building anti-terror coalition (10/1-3) | 53 |
| 8. Economic effects of terrorism (10/1-3) | 52 |
| 9. Possible U.S. military action (10/1-3) | 52 |
| 10. U.S. military effort in Afghanistan (10/15-17) | 51 |
| 11. Airplane crash near Kennedy Airport (11/13-19) | 48 |
| 12. Reports of Anthrax around the country (10/31-11/7) | 47 |
| 13. Winter weather in Northeast and Midwest (January) | 42 |
| 14. Reports on the U.S. economy (11/13-19) | 41 |
| 15. School shooting in San Diego (March) | 39 |

There can be, in my opinion, no clearer demonstration that the American public is more likely to pay attention when they feel threatened personally and that, consequently, genocides committed in faraway places are less central to their consciousness.

Academics may study and write until their fingers are unable to pound out another word, but without the public's and policy-making elite's highest level of concern and attention, it will have little or no effect. What remains most interesting about all this, however, is the fact that, in spite of the absence of leadership, the public, even if not following the stories closely, was more willing than the policymakers to support interventions to stop the violence. While they may not have followed the stories closely, they expressed concern when questioned about them. This is, in fact, confirmed by other research.

## Public Opinion and the Holocaust

In an interesting essay on "Shoah in the News," James Carroll (1997) points out that in the years 1995–1997 more than 600 stories about the Holocaust have appeared in the *New York Times* alone (p. 1). He notes, "Thousands of others have appeared in other American media," so that the Holocaust is one of the most covered genocides in history. The recent attention, Carroll believes, has taken several forms: confessions of various sorts, challenges not to forget, new information such as the Swiss bank controversy, and old information published again in new places (p. 11). The increased attention results, he thinks, because the end of the century is forcing people to face the truth about, perhaps, the greatest crime of genocide. The main mechanism in the modern era for what he refers to as a "moral reckoning" may be the popular news media (p. 17). Certainly, this remarkable outpouring of attention has increased public knowledge.

Numerous surveys have examined public knowledge about the Holocaust. This is, of course, important, since many believe that the Holocaust is a defining event of the twentieth century. For certain, it is the genocide with which most people are acquainted and the one to which all others are compared. In 1994, a Louis Harris poll found that 94 percent of the people in France, 84 percent in England and a smaller percentage, to be sure, but a majority nonetheless of 62 percent of Americans believed the Holocaust really happened (Singer, 1994).

As summarized by Singer (1994), majorities in the United States also do not believe that "Jews still talk too much about what happened to them in the Holocaust" (62 percent Anti-Defamation League, May 1992) and do not think the Holocaust is a "closed chapter in history." In fact, 73 percent (CBS News 1994) believe "we should make more efforts to discuss it and teach it to young people." Over 90 percent believe "the Nazi extermination of the Jews actually took place (CBS News, January 5, 1994) and think the Holocaust is relevant today even though it happened long ago (63 percent, *Los Angeles Times*, April 1994). Moreover, the American public apparently does not think the Holocaust was an isolated event, since 47 percent responded that they did indeed think there were "situations similar in nature to the Holocaust going on in the world today" (Roper Organization, 1992).

Finally, U.S. intervention to stop the exterminations was overwhelmingly supported by Americans who responded to the question, "If (Adolf) Hitler had not tried to conquer any other countries, but was still exterminating millions of Jews, do you think the U.S. (United States) should have intervened with its allies to stop the holocaust?" Seventy-seven percent said "definitely yes," while an additional 11 percent said "maybe yes." Interestingly, as we shall soon see, American public opin-

# Genocide and Public Opinion

ion also supported U.S. intervention in Bosnia and, to a lesser extent, in Rwanda under similar circumstances where the interventions were multilateral and supported by U.S. allies (see Singer 1994).

Table 2.3
Perceptions of the Holocaust

|  | Percent |
| --- | --- |
| "Jews still talk too much about what happened to them in the Holocaust." | 62% ("disagree") |
| "We should make more efforts to discuss it and teach it to young people." | 73 ("agree") |
| "[There] are situations similar in nature to the Holocaust going on in the world today." | 47 ("agree") |
| "If (Adolf) Hitler had not tried to conquer any other countries, but was still exterminating millions of Jews, do you think the U.S. should have intervened with its allies to stop the holocaust?" | 77 ("Yes")<br>11 ("maybe yes") |

## The Holocaust and Modern Genocides

Even though public opinion was not overwhelmingly clear that the genocides in Bosnia and Rwanda were similar to the Holocaust, respondents did believe that there were some similarities. Thirty-seven percent believed they were similar, but 44 percent said they were "not really" similar (NBC News, *Wall Street Journal* Poll, April 1993). Yet, when the questions were phrased slightly differently and the public was asked, "While they are of different magnitudes, do you think there is a parallel between the Holocaust and the ethnic cleansing that has been occurring in Bosnia," 42 percent said "definitely yes," and 28 percent responded "maybe yes" (Program on International Policy Attitudes, University of Maryland, April 1994).

When the comparisons were more specific and the question stated that "ethnic cleansing through killing Muslims and locking them into concentration camps is essentially a small version of (Adolf) Hitler's genocide against the Jews," 48 percent replied that they thought it very convincing that the United States should take strong steps to stop this genocide and 50 percent "agreed strongly" that the United States should contribute to peacekeeping devoted to stopping genocide, while 28 percent "agree somewhat" (Program on International Policy Attitudes, University of Maryland, June 1996). Again, this is consistent with other research.

## Bosnia and Public Opinion

In an article called "Portraying American Public Opinion toward the Bosnia Crisis," Richard Sobel (1998) points out that a majority of polls showed American support for humanitarian intervention if it was multilateral. In short, Sobel, found that there was "little relationship between citizen attitudes and foreign policy decisions" (p. 17). These findings are, of course, consistent with a basic proposition of political science, that public opinion has little influence on foreign policy decision making unless there is a particularly volatile issue, such as the Vietnam War, which draws public attention. While it is generally conceded that Americans know little about foreign affairs (ibid.) and that their support of intervention to save lives in Bosnia was based on limited knowledge, over time they became more acquainted with the situation and began to support intervention more strongly (ibid.). Sobel's strongest finding was that there was a "disparity between relatively strong public support for multilateral intervention and relatively weak government responses in both the United States and Europe. A second anomaly appears between comparatively supportive public attitudes on multilateral intervention and the reporting of those opinions in U.S. media stories that stressed opposition" (ibid.).

The reasons for these anomalies are presented in detail in Sobel's interesting article and his recent book (Sobel, 1998, 2001). Most important for this chapter is that the American public supported intervention to stop the genocide at the same time that American policymakers were reluctant to intervene and the American media were portraying public opinion as opposed to intervention. While there was very little support for the United States to intervene alone (Sobel, 1998, p. 21), there was strong support for multilateral intervention in a fashion similar to that supported to stop Hitler.

His data lead Sobel to conclude that the opinions of the American public were not accurately represented by the media and were not accurately interpreted by the policymakers. Borrowing a phrase from Lance Bennett (1989), Sobel argues that this is a phenomenon known as the "marginalization of the majority." As summarized by Sobel, this is important because it means that policymakers do not consider public opinion to be an important ingredient in their formulation of foreign policy. As Sobel (1998) notes: "Among 'voices' expressing opinion on controversial subjects, those from institutions like the Congress, the presidency, or the media themselves are considered superior to popular opinion. The relatively passive media will report even biased institutional views over popular attitudes" (p. 27). This is referred to as "popular inferiority," and is not confined to the situation in Bosnia. Other misrepresentations of popular opinion include, as Sobel notes, the supposed turn to the right in American politics during the 1980s, when public opinion actually found continuing general liberal predominance in attitudes, except on crime (p. 28), and the overstated popularity of Ronald Reagan as president when he was actually less popular in his first term than other presidents have been (p. 28).

This raises important questions about fundamental ideals of democracy. Public opinion was misrepresented and ignored while at the same time policymakers complained about how ignorant the public was concerning foreign affairs. As we shall see, the public view of Rwanda was not precisely as clear as that concerning Bosnia but was much more complex than its portrayal in the media or the policymakers.

Table 2.4
Perceptions of Bosnia

| Question | Percent |
| --- | --- |
| "While they are of different magnitudes, do you think there is a parallel between the Holocaust and the ethnic cleansing that has been occurring in Bosnia?" | 42 ("definitely yes") 28 ("maybe yes") |
| "Ethnic cleansing through killing Muslims and locking them into concentration camps is essentially a small version of (Adolf) Hitler's genocide against the Jews." | 48 (very convincing U.S. should take strong steps to stop this genocide) |
| "The United States should contribute to peacekeeping devoted to stopping genocide." | 50 ("agree strongly") 28 ("agree somewhat") |

## Public Opinion and Genocide in Rwanda

American public opinion generally supported multilateral intervention to stop the genocide in Rwanda. When asked if the UN should have "gone in with a large military force to occupy the country and stop the killings," 62 percent of respondents said they "should have" (Program on International Policy Attitudes, University of Maryland, April 1995). Various forms of intervention were supported. Sixty percent supported using UN troops to destroy the government radio stations that were broadcasting propaganda feeding the genocide, and 74 percent supported UN troops setting up "safe havens" (Program on International Policy Attitudes, University of Maryland, April 1995). These questions obviously refer to UN troops as opposed to U.S. troops. When the questioning shifted a bit to focus on U.S. contributions, Americans expressed some reluctance but nevertheless criticized the policy followed by the Clinton administration.

Americans generally (46 percent) believed that the United States did not have a vital interest in Rwanda, although 35 percent did think the United States had such an interest (Gallup Organization, October 1994), and in another poll, 63 percent agreed (ABC News, *Washington Post*, June 1994). Yet, when asked to evaluate U.S. policy toward Rwanda, Americans were very critical. Twenty-eight percent said the American response was "fair," while 29 percent said it was "poor," with only 3 percent believing that the U.S. response was "excellent" (Gallup Organization, October 1994). When asked whether they "approve" or "disapprove" of the way (President Bill) Clinton is handling the situation in that country ("How about... Rwanda?"), 34 percent expressed approval, while 37 percent disapproved and 29 percent had "no opinion" (ABC News, *Washington Post*, June 1994). At the same time Americans, by a slim plurality, favored U.S. armed forces participating as part of a U.N. mission to try to stop the violence in Rwanda, 45 percent compared to 41 percent opposed (Yankelovich Partners, Inc., May 1994), but only 34 percent in the same poll believed the United States should do more to reduce the violence in Rwanda. Moreover, while the public did not think the United States should take the lead in stopping what the pollsters called the "civil war" in Rwanda, 42 percent believed the United States should take an equal part while 46 percent said they should not be involved (Hart and Teeter Research Companies, June 1994), and 51 percent thought the United States "Did not have a responsibility to stop the killing in Rwanda" (CBS News, June 1994).

Even though the American public did not support the United States taking the lead to stop the genocide in Rwanda, they were overwhelmingly (63 percent) in support of sending U.S. troops as part of a humanitarian mission to help refugees (CBS News, July 1994), and 45 percent thought the "United States should have acted sooner in doing something about the situation of the Rwandan refugees" (CBS News, July 1994).

When asked to evaluate President Clinton's response to Rwanda, 61 percent thought he did not have a clear policy (ABC News, *Washington Post*, June 1994) and 45 percent favored the use of U.S. armed forces as part of a UN mission to stop the violence (Yankelovich Partners, Inc., May 1994). Sixty-nine percent of Americans also supported sending U.S. military forces to provide humanitarian aid (Yankelovich Partners, Inc., August 1994), and 54 percent were worried that these forces might "become too involved in local issues and disputes in Rwanda—as some feel occurred in Somalia" (Yankelovich Partners Inc., August 1994). Finally, Americans did not want to send only U.S. ground troops into Rwanda; 61 percent opposed unilateral U.S. intervention (CBS News, June 1994).

## Table 2.5
## Perceptions of Rwanda

| Question | Percent |
|---|---|
| Should the UN have: | |
| "gone in with a large military force to occupy the country [Rwanda] and stop the killings?" | 62 ("should have") |
| Destroyed the radio stations broadcasting propaganda feeding the genocide? | 60 |
| Set up safe havens? | 74 |
| The United States does not have vital interest in Rwanda. | 46 (35 percent say it does) |
| Was American response to Rwanda: | |
| "Fair" | 28 |
| "Poor" | 29 |
| "Excellent" | 3 |
| "Approve" or "disapprove" of the way (President Bill) Clinton is handling the situation in that country? [Rwanda] | 34 "approve" 37 "disapprove" 29 "no opinion" |
| Should the United States participate as part of a UN mission to stop the violence in Rwanda? | 45 "support" 41 "opposed" |
| Should the United States do more to reduce the violence in Rwanda? | 34 "yes" |
| The United States does not have a responsibility to stop the killing in Rwanda. | 51 agree |
| U.S. troops should be sent as part of a humanitarian mission to help refugees. | 63 agree |
| The "United States should have acted sooner in doing something about the situation of the Rwandan refugees." | 45 agree |
| Percent believe Clinton did not have a clear policy | 61 |
| Percent opposed to U.S. unilateral action | 61 |

American public opinion, in other words, did not support intervention in Rwanda as strongly as it did in Bosnia but did support humanitarian intervention even if that meant sending in U.S. troops. The American public seemed to make a distinction between the situations in Bosnia and those in Rwanda, or at least expressed different perceptions of how strongly they supported American intervention. While there are no data to support such speculation, these differences might be accounted for by fact that the ethnic cleansing in Bosnia occurred in Europe in areas similar to where the Holocaust occurred and where Americans identify with the European-based population. Since European people were involved, Americans supported intervention more strongly than in Rwanda. If this is, in fact, the case, then similar attitudes should be expressed when comparing the attitudes toward intervention in Kosovo and East Timor, two of the last examples of near genocide in the twentieth century.

Generally speaking, the American people supported U.S. participation in NATO air strikes against the former Yugoslavia. From March 1999 through May 1999, support ranged, according to the Gallup Poll (Gallup, 1999a, p. 1), from 50 percent to a high of 61 percent in April and 55 percent in May 1999. The Pew Center (April 1999a, p. 1) tracked support for air strikes through May and found support was 60 percent in March, 62 percent in April and only 53 percent in May. On the other hand, there was little support for the use of ground troops. The Gallup Poll asked, "If the current NATO air and missile strikes are not effective in achieving the United States' objectives in Kosovo, would you favor or oppose President Clinton sending U.S. ground troops into the region along with troop from other NATO countries?" Opposition ranged from 57 percent in March 1999 to 65 percent in May, while support ranged from 40 percent in March to 31 percent in May. The same data demonstrate that 34 percent followed the issue "very closely" in April 1999. The question was phrased as follows: "Now thinking about the current situation in Kosovo, would you favor or oppose sending U.S. ground troops, along with troops from other NATO countries to serve in a combat situation in the region right now?" Responses are in Table 2.6.

Table 2.6
Support for U.S. Ground Troops in Kosovo

|  | Favor | Oppose | No Opinion |
|---|---|---|---|
| 99 Apr 26-27 | 36% | 60% | 4% |
| 99 Apr 13-14 | 43% | 53% | 4% |
| 99 Apr 6-7 | 41% | 54% | 5% |

Interestingly, those who favored the use of U.S. troops stated that their reason was primarily "Because the U.S. has a moral obligation to help the refugees." Sixty-seven percent chose this response. They did not believe that the United States had "strategic interests" in the region, with only 8 percent stating that was the case. There was some support for the use of ground troops, and there does appear to exist a reservoir of moral reasoning to support that action.

When compared to the responses from the atrocities in East Timor later in the same year, the Gallup Poll demonstrates that the public was paying "Little attention" and did not support the use of U.S. troops. They noted that around 3 percent "of Americans say they are following the news about the conflict in East Timor closely, which puts it almost at the bottom of a list of news events that Gallup has tracked over the past decade using this measure" (Gallup, 1999b, p. 1). There was little knowledge of the events in East Timor. In spite of this Americans were "not willing to dismiss the potential importance of the situation there out of hand. Fourteen percent say that achieving a peaceful solution to the conflict is a very important foreign policy goal for the U.S., while another 42 percent say that it is a somewhat important goal. Only 33 percent say that such a solution is not important" (ibid., p. 2). Yet, this is lower than the importance attached to other international crisis such as the Palestinian/Israeli situation and the crises in Kosovo, Bosnia and northern Ireland (ibid.). There is little support for the use of American troops in east Timor so that 59 percent of Americans oppose sending in U.S. troops even as part of an international peacekeeping force.

In short, there is less support for the use of U.S. troops in East Timor, as there was in Rwanda as compared to Bosnia and Kosovo. There is a clear European bias in public opinion. It would not be unwarranted here to point out that the African continent has always seemed "peripheral" to American interests, and this perception was probably deepened by the embarrassment in Somalia. In spite of this, American public opinion did follow the situation in Rwanda more closely than those in Angola or Cambodia, but not as closely as Bosnia. When compared to how much they know about the Holocaust and how strongly they supported intervention there, American public opinion was not all that supportive of stopping the violence in Rwanda or East Timor, but was so in Bosnia. What does it mean?

## Genocide and Public Opinion

The conventional wisdom has always held that public opinion has little effect on foreign policy except in situations where the public has a direct interest, such as in Vietnam, where they were being drafted and sent to fight an increasingly unpopular war. Others argue that public opinion does have some effect by creating a "zone of acquiescence"

(Stimson, 1991, pp. 19–21), which defines acceptable policy alternatives between the extremes of the liberal and conservative positions. The data presented above appear to support the first alternative. Indeed, the idea of the "marginalization of the majority," referred to earlier, may be seen clearly in these case studies.

While the majority appears to have been "marginalized," there remain two important questions involving the relationship between public opinion and foreign policy.[6] If opinions are not informed through knowledge and debate, are they a sound basis from which to design foreign policy? And, if people are not well informed, what is being expressed in their opinions? These are important questions to which I see at least two possible responses. First, the idea that public opinion is uninformed as opposed to that of political elites and that the opinions of elites lead to sounder policy is a dubious assumption. While elites may have more information, one must examine the quality of that information and question the goals of the policy pursued. In the case of Kosovo the goal clearly is not to stop the genocidal atrocity, but to degrade Serb forces. Or, according to public rhetoric, to do so without losing the lives of any NATO troops. In short, as Peter Maas (1996) has noted in reference to Bosnia, it is policy designed for good public relations, not to achieve any substantive result that would benefit those suffering in the Balkans. If policy is designed for public relations as opposed to achieving any substantive foreign policy impact, then elite actions are not going to be influenced by public opinion. In fact, the policy-making elite will attempt to manipulate opinion to support the actions they plan to take, which, in turn, they view as in line with their perceptions of the range of opinion displayed by the public.

Second, public opinion appears to become better informed when a situation remains at the center of attention for longer periods of time, but there also appears to be a fatigue factor. So, in reference to Kosovo, the Pew Center points out that 66 percent of Americans "are able to correctly identify Kosovo as the province in Yugoslavia where there is conflict between Serbians and ethnic Albanian compared to only 42% who could do so at the outset of the bombing" (Pew, 1999b p. 4). The fatigue factor begins to become apparent as we note that the percentage of those following news about the air strikes declined from 43 in March to 41 in April and had fallen to 32 in May.

A further question posed by my colleagues was whether the commitment to stopping atrocity would continue to remain strong if the costs of involvement began to rise and, in particular, if it involved the loss of American life? Again, recent data help to answer that question. Support for U.S. participation in NATO air strikes hovered around 62 percent in

April 1999 but began to decline in May to 53 percent. Polls also demonstrated that more people were "very worried that U.S. troops might suffer casualties" (66 percent compared to 55 percent in March) and an even greater increase in concern about the financial costs of sending troops (38 percent compared to 21 percent). Nearly two-thirds (63 percent) were also very worried that American forces could be involved in Kosovo for a long time" (Pew, 1999b, p. 1). The public is less supportive of sending U.S. ground troops to Kosovo (47 percent in favor and 48 percent opposed), but "when the same question is reinforced with the phrase 'to try to end the conflict in Kosovo,' a narrow 51%–42% consensus emerges in favor of ground troops" (ibid., p. 2). Americans do think ground troops will be necessary, and if that is done 72 percent say it is "very important" for Clinton to get Congressional approval. Yet, in spite of these worries, Americans believe it is important to try to stop the atrocities in Kosovo with nearly seven-in-ten (69%) stating that "preventing the killing of Kosovo citizens is a *very important* reason for using U.S. troops in the region" (ibid.).

Finally the question that is unanswerable was the last raised by one of my colleagues. Namely, what specific costs would the American public be willing to bear? What price in American lives would they think stopping the slaughter in Kosovo might be worth—10, 100, 10,000? Where's the cutoff? Most guesses are that the price will probably not be very high because in the late twentieth century we learned that wars are bloodless affairs not meriting sacrifice. Perhaps, as my colleague pointed out in a private communication, this is the fault of the Persian Gulf War, because "it taught the American public that war should be 'easy' and that we should be able to intervene militarily pretty much anywhere, 'win,' and get out, with minimal or no loss of American life. Look at the humanitarian intervention in Somalia—one American body dragged through the streets and the American people screamed to get us out of there." In addition, as the recent polls demonstrate, there appears to exist a strong fatigue factor. Americans, policymakers as well as the public, seem to tire easily and get fed up quickly with ongoing stories. Commitment seems ephemeral. One wonders how support would have played out during World War II in the face of constant media coverage and media allowing Yugoslav officials to present their side. Would we have allowed Goering and Goebbels to appear with Larry King to present their side to provide the illusion of "balance"?

In fact, however, the question is not answerable given the profound absence of leadership. Of course, we must remember that leadership was not successful in rallying the American public to persist in the Vietnam

War or the Somalia intervention. While these are clearly different cases, the precedents linger. There appears an isolationist impulse that runs deeper when American casualties begin to pile up. Yet, in my reading of the mobilization during World War II, a much more trying and difficult time, Americans supported the cause. Of course, the threat was much more obvious; the entire country was mobilized and placed on a continued state of alert, and all the resources were devoted to mobilizing public support for the effort to defeat Germany and Japan. Such all-out mobilization may be very dangerous in these times of weapons of mass destruction and confused loyalties. The enemy is not always clear. Yet, when the United States is attacked directly as on September 11, 2001, polls show that Americans are willing to support almost any action taken by the leadership to pursue the attackers. The Halo Effect, wherein political leadership receives extremely high ratings in times of a crisis, especially a direct threat to the homeland, appears to operate, but at some point there is a questioning of that leadership, particularly if the policies pursued appear to be ineffectual or do not achieve results quickly. At the point of this writing, it is too early to ascertain how that has played out in the current situation.

What is clear is that with leadership, intelligence and knowledge, the public could be moved to support action to decrease rather than increase suffering. In pursuit of these goals one cannot stress too strongly the role of political and moral leadership as well as the role of the media. If there is no leadership building support for a policy to stop the continuing calamities of genocide, and there is no accurate portrayal in the media of these events, public support to bring about a more humane world is unlikely to grow. Therefore, when examining the cases of Rwanda, Bosnia, Kosovo and East Timor, one must consider the possibility that both the media and the policymakers failed either to exercise such leadership or to consider the reality of the public's perceptions. In particular, in the cases of Bosnia, with the massacre of an estimated 250,000 Muslims, and Rwanda, with the slaughter of some 800,000 Tutsis, humanitarian impulses were not only ignored, but manipulated to support a position opposed to humanitarian intervention.

Yet, these data reflect some hope. They indicate that the general public appears more concerned about saving human life than the policy-making elite. Perhaps, if knowledge of this gap comes to public attention, policymakers will be forced to bring their policy in line with public opinion. The American public is ready for moral leadership preparing the groundwork for a new position in international politics, a position that supports saving life rather than allowing the norm of numbing and genocide as usual to continue. In short, there may be some hope that the American public could be persuaded to support a movement to stop genocide. Building on this base of public opinion and proceeding from the perspective of a new vision of morality and responsibility, a movement to stop genocide would have to begin by creating the mechanisms to put pressure on the policy-making institutions.

# 3

# Putting Pressure on U.S. Political Institutions

We saw in chapter 1 how a political movement could be built, and in chapter 2 we saw what the American public actually believed about foreign policy and genocide, and now we are going to examine how to put pressure on the policy-making institutions to change that policy. Basically the primary question is how to put the question of supporting human rights and preventing genocide on the agenda so that these issues will be considered seriously by the political institutions and leaders of the United States. To pursue this question we will first examine the process of agenda setting and then look at the process that might be pursued in order to get such an agenda considered.

### Putting Genocide on the Agenda

When we speak of getting issues on the agenda we mean that the public is concerned and the policymakers are actively considering doing something about the issue. The most comprehensive analysis of how to get issues to be considered by policymakers, how to get them placed on the agenda for discussion, may be found in the work of Cobb and Ross (1997). They begin by pointing out that most people believe that the main reason for success or failure is the differential resources available to proponents and opponents. In other words, those with *the* most resources, in particularly money, are *the* most likely to be successful in placing items on the agenda. This is not, however, always true. They point out that those with the most resources do not always win, and there are resources other than money that might be mobilized. Basically, their argument is that the first step is to transform grievances into issues that appeal to the public. There are three separate steps in this process: naming, blaming and claiming (p. 5).

The first step is to name an issue in such a fashion that appeals to the public. In the case of genocide we have seen how sympathy is built up by repeated media portrayals of cruelty, and this leads to calls for intervention in places such as Somalia and Bosnia. Simply talking about genocide is probably necessary but not sufficient. Unfortunately, the issue must be named in such a way as to create profound public sympathy for the victimized populations. I say "unfortunately," because this means that policy making is influenced by the CNN effect, whereby the media, by portraying the worst excesses of cruelty and violence, create sympathy for the victims and pressure from the public to stop the atrocities. The problem, of course, is that this does not always lead to effective policy making.

The second step is blaming. This involves "transforming a grievance into a political issue. It involves identifying a culprit to blame for the unfair treatment that a target group—the victim—has received" (ibid., p. 6). If the victim group is viewed positively by the public, it will be more likely to receive support. Those who are politically weak and have a negative image will be less likely to receive support. If, therefore, the Clinton administration had built up support for the Bosnian Muslims and had engaged in a campaign to point out to the public that most of the atrocities had been committed by the Serbs, who were also more adequately armed, support for humanitarian intervention might have been even stronger.

The third step, claiming, "involves making specific demands on government" (ibid., p. 6). This includes defining an issue in such a way that the policy to deal with it is supported. According to their analysis there are "five issue characteristics that groups can use to gain backers" (ibid.). The first of these is "ambiguity," which allows the public to create their own meaning, so one would couch the issue in vague terms using symbolism that would resonate to most of the people. Instead of talking about genocide, one humanizes the victims by telling personal stories and pointing out how they are simply trying to protect their families and how they are just like we are. Second is social significance, which means that the issue will have an important impact. The third characteristic, temporal relevance, means the issue has a time dimension and, if not dealt with at this moment, will affect everyone in the future. Fourth is nontechnical issue definition, meaning the public should be able to understand the issue. This means avoiding overly complicated arguments and phrasing the issue in terms to which individuals are able to relate. Fifth is categorical precedence, meaning the "issue is unique and officials cannot simply handle it as they did a past problem" (ibid.). The issue of genocide in Rwanda or Bosnia would have to have been defined as an issue with possible solutions that would be successful, thereby differentiating it from previous cases. All of this is for the purpose of setting an agenda with the issue, in this case, genocide, as the central point of consideration.

Before examining how to get American political institutions to focus on this agenda to prevent genocide, it is important to note that, just as there are methods to place an issue on the agenda, there are ways to keep it from being considered. These, while relevant, are less important for our immediate consideration. In sum, we are talking here about what are referred to as agenda conflicts or "what issues government will act on" (ibid., p. 41). Since the world is so complicated, with so many diverse issues and so many different groups of people attempting to get government to view their issues as significant, the competition to get on the agenda is fierce. Issues and groups compete with each other, and this makes it difficult for nontraditional or new issues to get on the agenda. Those groups who are most successful in presenting the issue of their concern in such a fashion as to appeal to the public, to the long-held traditional views of the public and the policymakers, are the most likely to gain success. In the traditional workings of the institutions of U.S. politics, this means that those with the most power, the most resources, in particular financial resources, usually are the most successful in shaping agendas. How to overcome that and put pressure on the institutions is the next topic

Politics, as noted in chapter 1, involves making choices and decisions. It also involves elite policymakers analyzing public opinion to ascertain whether certain policy actions would be likely to be supported by the public, and it, moreover, involves an accurate perception of the world as it is, not as the particular actor would like it to be. In the case of policymakers, this means that in those decisions there is usually some decision maker exercising power. Power, of course, is ambiguous and difficult to define. In many ways it is very similar to the U.S. Supreme Court's definition of pornography; we know it when we see it manifested in the real world. Power flows from resources including wealth, military technology, knowledge and the resource of popular political movements, numbers of people who may be mobilized to support an issue. A movement to stop genocide—or in this case to put pressure on the political institutions to take action to support stopping genocide—would most likely be a popular movement organized along the basis described in chapter 1, that is, the civil rights and anti–Vietnam War movements but brought up to date and designed to fit the context of the twenty-first century. In order to demonstrate how such a movement might influence the various decision-making institutions, it is necessary to very briefly take a look at the structure of American political decision making. This brief examination is not intended to be an exhaustive analysis of American politics. On the contrary, I intend to focus on what I perceive as the "pressure points," or the "access points" of American politics, the points at which the decision-making institutions might be amenable to influence by a citizen-based popular movement.

This analysis, therefore, will examine the basic institutions of American politics with a focus on how to influence those that might be most relevant to a movement to stop genocide. Any analysis of this sort must begin with a forthright confrontation with the political reality of contemporary political institutions. As Alinsky noted, political organizers interested in political change must begin with the world as it is, not as they want it to be. American political institutions are clearly more susceptible to being influenced by those who have wealth and power than by those without those two resources. This means that it is very likely that the people most interested in a movement to stop genocide will have to mobilize a large movement designed to influence political decision makers. We start, therefore, from the perspective that American politics is not the mythologic democratic polity of civics classes, but is a system that substitutes a mythology of democracy for a reality of power.

## U.S. Politics and Foreign Policy

While the primary focus, of course, is on U.S. foreign policy, it is necessary, in order to understand how foreign policy is made in the United States, to examine the major policy-making institutions. Many policy analysts view foreign policy from two perspectives: the content of policy and the process of policy making. The content is a response to the environment of the international political system, while the process involves the inner workings of the policy-making institutions. In this case, the international political system changed markedly after the collapse of the Communist regimes of Eastern Europe and the end of the Cold War. These are the main paradigms informing this enquiry since most of the genocides of the latter portion of the last century involved failed or failing states and the desire of ethnic/religious groups and their leaders to achieve a nation-state based on ethnic or religious purity.

Prior to examining the policymakers' response to these events it will be necessary to examine the cultural and psychological setting of American politics.

## The Cultural and Psychological Foundations of American Politics

For more than 225 years the United States has been a federal democratic political system. Yet, to really understand policy making, in this case foreign policy making, we have to examine more than the simple rules and institutions. Retracing the political history of a country is similar to examining the development of an individual's political belief system—that is the process of political socialization—except in this case we are looking at a form of collective socialization. One way to understand the context of policy making is to start by trying to understand a person's individual development. Think about the way that you developed your own political beliefs and then try to reconstruct that development. That is, was there a person or set of events that you remember clearly as influencing your views? What sort of events and experiences impressed you? What do you remember clearly, and what appears fuzzy or remains murky? Engaging in this exercise will probably cause you to find that your personal biography is as intricate as the history of a country. You may find, for example, that what you think you remember about your past is a combination of actual recalled experiences, remembered from the point at which you are presently reliving these experiences, as well as events that have been reported to you by others—perhaps parents, relatives or those who knew you when the events supposedly took place. The problems an individual faces in reconstructing his own personal history happen to be the same problems faced by historians attempting to write the history of a country or group of people. Some of the events are agreed upon, others are subject to varying interpretations, and some may never have occurred at all. In short, some are facts, others are assumptions, and some are myths.

All nation-states and groups have what are called founding myths, myths related to their origins. These myths are passed on from generation to generation and ultimately find their way into the dominant ideology of the nation or group. In the United States the founding myth is very prominent and reinforced through rituals and rhetoric. It holds that the United States is a democratic nation founded on the principle of individual liberty and that the country is the single best hope for all peoples in the world. This translates into a belief system that creates the impression in the minds of those socialized to accept the mythology that there are few if any inequalities in the system and that virtually anything American is superior to any other variation, whether it be policy, philosophy or manufactured products.

For example, the existence of economic inequality is explained away by a series of ideological statements, forming a dominant mythology, which are manipulated to hide the reality of policy and politics. While it is simply the case that American politics, like the politics of all nation-states, is rooted partly in fact and largely in myth, the myth may replace the facts if it is repeated and taught over the years. These myths become, through the process of political socialization, the foundations upon which policy is structured. There is, however, one additional effect of this process that must be understood, since it operates to reinforce conformity and to make dissent unlikely. It operates something like this.

People are not born with political ideas. As far as is known, everything we know about politics is taught to us either formally, as for example, through the process of education, or informally, via the process of cultural transmission. We have seen that the process operates to transmit to every individual the norms of the existing culture and political system in order to convince individuals to accept the norms as "natural" and to exhibit "approved of" or "desirable" forms of behavior. By extension, if this process is successful, it operates to control what is regarded as "deviant" behavior. The problem is that all deviant behavior is not necessarily destructive. Some might be constructive, such as peaceful demonstrations during the civil rights movement to secure the elements of democracy for all people, while others might be destructive, for example, individual acts of criminal behavior or terrorism.

The ability to make distinctions is important because the most efficient means of controlling populations and insuring conformity and obedience is to transmit, through the process of political socialization, norms of behavior that are congruent with the dominant ideology in a society. If people can be convinced that these norms are all legitimate, no matter what they are, that, in other words, this is the way they *should* behave, then it will not be necessary for those in power to resort to force to control dissidents. Obviously, if all citizens, or even a large number, internalize and/or accept the desired definitions of "normality," if they conform and obey the "leaders," there will be few if any deviants and no support for those who do emerge to question the policies pursued by political leaders. In short, there will be no major disagreements with the policymakers if all are conforming as opposed to questioning citizens.

## U.S. Foreign Policy and the Constitution

According to the U.S. Constitution the major responsibility for making foreign policy is vested in the president and in the Congress. The president is commander-in-chief of the armed forces, while Congress was given the power to declare war. Of course, there has been no formal declaration of war since 1941, and yet the Untied States has participated in numerous low-intensity and full-scale wars. Presidents attempt to circumvent the constitutional provision allowing Congress to issue formal declarations of war for many reasons. Congress is a slow-moving institution, since it is a collection of senators and representatives from the fifty states, all of whom represent different constituent interests. The president, as a singular figure, is able to act expeditiously and with less possibility of deadlock. Consequently, presidents have resorted to subterfuges such as that used by Lyndon Johnson during the Vietnam War.

Johnson had the Gulf of Tonkin Resolution introduced after a supposed, but now disproved, attack on American warships in the Gulf of Tonkin in 1964. When this resolution was passed, with only two dissenting votes in the Senate, Johnson used it as a substitute for a declaration of war.

The president also negotiates treaties, which Congress ratifies with a two-thirds majority vote in the Senate. Again, formal treaties have become a much rarer occurrence than in the past. They have been replaced by executive agreements, which do not require a two-thirds vote for ratification. Further powers related to the making of foreign policy that are given to the president include the power to nominate high-level government officials such as the secretary of state, the national security advisor and others. Congress has to confirm these appointments, but they owe their primary allegiance to the president and are, for the most part, obliged to carry out his foreign policy.

As far as the regulation of foreign commerce is concerned, the president has no official power but negotiates treaties and appoints trade representatives and members of the cabinet with power over such matters, while the Congress is supposed to regulate, according to the Constitution, interstate and foreign commerce. Finally, the president has the power of the veto, and Congress controls finances and is able to investigate any action undertaken in this area.

As far as the other political institutions, such as the Supreme Court, their role in foreign policy making is rather limited. The Supreme Court does issue decisions in cases regarding the president's foreign policy-making powers on occasion but is, for the most part, not involved intimately in the making of foreign policy. This means, therefore, that a movement to prevent genocide and bring pressure on American policymakers to support such action should be targeted at the president and the Congress.

## The President and Foreign Policy: Exerting Pressure to Prevent Genocide

In order to begin to understand the points at which pressure might be exerted on the president to support action to prevent genocide, it is necessary to begin with the election process. Presidential elections have become popularity contests financed by large contributors and heavily influenced by the media. If American citizens were interested in motivating an American president to support a policy to prevent genocide they would focus on influencing this electoral process. Understandably, this will be very difficult since the amount of funds available to such groups will be much smaller than those collected by corporations, labor unions or other groups interested in influencing the same process in order to pursue other policies. In the absence of financial resources, political organizers must turn to other alternative resources such as the mobilization of large numbers of people willing to act to put pressure on the institutions and to participate actively in voting or influencing the process in some other way, such as volunteering their time. The problem is that such mobilizations have met with limited success in the past. While presidents have been influenced by public opinion, the election of presidents has not been really susceptible to those same influences. Even during the Vietnam War the most outspoken opponents of that war had a difficult time, and none really succeeded in gaining a major party nomination for the presidency. They did cause Lyndon Johnson not to seek renomination in 1968, but this was partially the result of events in Vietnam, in particular the Tet Offensive, as well as action by antiwar protestors.

The primary obstacle is that third parties, that is, political parties other than the Republican or Democratic parties, have a difficult time making inroads in the electoral process. There are both psychological and structural reasons for this difficulty. First, the system of political parties and elections in the United States is structured in such a fashion as to make it very difficult for third parties to participate on an equal footing with the two major parties. In fact, the historical allegiance of most Americans to the Democratic and Republican parties, even though this appears to be weakening, remains and is reinforced by other structural characteristics of the system. In particular, the fact that elections are held within and regulated by the fifty states and that the presidency is decided not by a popular vote but by the electoral college, which means that even if a candidate secured a large number of votes, he would not be able to win unless he won the large and important states. Consequently, the traditional role of third parties in American politics has been to interject issues into the arena, but rarely to win an election. It is even difficult for third-party candidates to get their names on the ballot, since the Democratic and Republican parties collaborate to make this difficult. Usually it requires the signatures of thousands of registered voters and the payment of a substantial sum of money. The system simply is not structured to make it easy for third-party candidates to approximate winning an election. The best that may be hoped for a candidate wishing to mobilize American policy to prevent genocide is that he or she might successfully put that item on the agenda of one of the two major parties. This is, however, unlikely unless large-scale public support is forthcoming.

It is perhaps easiest to visualize the process by dividing it into four distinct stages at which pressure might be exerted.

First, the positioning phase of presidential politics involves potential candidates attempting to gain name recognition so that they will be recognized by the public and the political elites as viable candidates. This often involves the hiring of high-priced consultants whose responsibility it is to get the potential candidate's name before the public as often and in as favorable a set of circumstances as possible. At this point it would be important for those wishing to move American policy in the direction of genocide prevention and participation in the type of policies discussed earlier to make it known that they will not vote for a candidate who does not support those policies and that they will, in fact, refrain from voting for a candidate whose policies are the opposite. Hence, if a candidate is not willing to publicly declare support for multilateral international action to prevent the abuse of human rights, it is the obligation of those supporting such action to make it known through the media and through other action, such as political demonstrations, that they will support an alternative candidate. It would also be helpful to attempt to influence contributions to campaigns, since fundraising is a primary activity at this stage of presidential politics, by attempting to boycott products and companies that either participate in the sale of weapons or other products that support the killing of innocent people and to attempt to pressure other companies to make it known that they support action to prevent genocide. Such action has worked in the past, notably in the case of the boycotts of lettuce and grapes organized by the United Farm Workers Union during the 1960s.

The second stage of presidential politics is that of the primary elections. Similar activity must be organized at this stage by those wishing to stop genocide. It used to be the case that candidates received the nomination for president without running in primary elections. It was the presidential campaign of John F. Kennedy in 1960 that demonstrated how important primary elections could be, and since that time the number of candidates running and the number of primary elections have both increased. Primaries are smaller versions of the general election, and since they are held in numerous states it is difficult to mobilize action to cover all the possible bases. It most likely would be most efficacious to concentrate on the early primaries and those in the largest states. Hence, the New Hampshire primary would be significant, as it was in the 1968 election, when Senator Eugene McCarthy, supported by a cadre of young campaign workers, ran in opposition to the incumbent president, Lyndon Johnson. McCarthy did not defeat Johnson, but he came close, and the fact that Johnson did not do as well as expected of a sitting president led him to withdraw from the contest. Most important, however, the election demonstrated that the Vietnam War was an important issue. Not understood at the time, moreover, was the additional point that not all voters who voted for McCarthy held the same position on that issue. Some wanted to end the war by withdrawing U.S. troops, while others wanted to end it by increasing military action. Positions on issues of genocide prevention must be thought out thoroughly and communicated to the public in an unambiguous fashion so as to mobilize the necessary participation.

The last two stages are the national nominating conventions and the campaign. Similar strategies are to be pursued at both. One strategy attempted in the sixties was to try to get the two major parties to discuss the issue of the Vietnam War at their conventions. To accomplish this, organizers began at the party caucuses in those states which used that mechanism to nominate delegates to the national convention. People opposed to the Vietnam War started by attending the local district conventions and trying to get the issue of their concern discussed and passed on to the next level and, ultimately, to the state convention and the national convention. This was often opposed by the political elites as a diversion from what they viewed as the main issues. It is, therefore, incumbent on those who wish to see U.S. policy move in the direction of genocide prevention to make their case convincingly so that it appears that preventing genocide is, as argued earlier, in the interest of all and that it is in the interest of the United States to assume a leading role supporting the preservation of human rights in international politics.

Finally, if a movement to prevent genocide has not been successful prior to the national election campaign, it is unlikely that it will generate much influence after the campaign is already in progress. The hard work must be accomplished prior to the campaign so that the issue is on the agenda and is discussed during the campaign.

Once a president is elected and after taking office it becomes increasingly difficult to exert pressure on the executive branch of government. Foreign policy is usually under the direction of a complex bureaucracy including the secretaries of state and defense, the national security advisor and others. They are, for the most part, isolated from public pressure and the organization of public opinion, and public demonstrations of disapproval of policy is the primary alternative. Congress, however, is more susceptible to pressure but often less central to the making of foreign policy.

## Foreign Policy and the U.S. Congress

The first fact to remember about members of the U.S. House of Representatives and the U.S. Senate is that their primary interest is in getting elected and staying in office. Realizing that this is their main concern, the question then becomes, how does one influence decisions? Congress is allocated certain specific powers in the U.S. Constitution. Among these are the power to levy taxes, the power to borrow and spend money, the power to regulate interstate and foreign commerce, the power to declare war and others. The behavior of individual members is affected most directly by the desire to maintain themselves in power and by a series of formal and informal rules of the game, the violation of which may draw sanctions from the leadership. The main informal rules include apprenticeship, legislative work, specialization, courtesy, reciprocity and institutional patriotism.

Apprenticeship simply means that longevity is rewarded. The longer one remains in office, the more likely he will be given positions of leadership. Consequently, the most powerful members of both houses are those with the longest terms in office. This most likely means they are more difficult to influence, since they have built up support from important groups within their district or states and usually run from safe districts. It is sadly the case that most congressional elections are not highly competitive, and this further insulates members from public pressure. Given the existence of these basic institutional constraints, the existence of external and internal access points has to be examined. That is, at what points in the process might pressure be applied to members to influence them to support a policy to prevent genocide?

The first points involve elections. I have already noted that most elections are not highly competitive, often with no real opposition to an incumbent candidate, and incumbents generally win most congressional elections. This means that once again those without large financial resources must organize mass public support to put pressure on members. It is simply impossible to escape the fact that public pressure is the weapon of those without large amounts of money. If this fails, then the member must be threatened with loss of his position, and this too requires public organization of large numbers of voters.

The internal access points involve the legislative process. It is difficult to exert pressure in this way, since the rules of the institutions and the fact that most policy is made in committees and influenced by senior members of the congress direct the supporters of action to prevent genocide back to the organization of public opinion. In the long run, those without significant corporate positions and without access to large amounts of money are left with few political resources. They must rely primarily on numbers, organizing the public, and time, hopefully the mobilization of volunteers, and of course, publicity. The public is simply at a disadvantage as compared to the organized interest groups when it comes to influencing either the executive or legislative branch of government.

That is why, therefore, even if public opinion polls reveal significant public support for an issue, it often does not manifest in policy. The policy-making institutions are, to some significant degree, insulated from public support. The Madisonian system of checks and balances was, of course, designed with the intent of striking a balance between public influence and elite decision making without public interference. Policy-making elites are more likely to ignore public opinion unless it is accompanied by large-scale indication that this will have negative consequences on their reelection campaigns.

Moreover, there are significant reasons that international policy and issues are perceived as less salient, or less important, to citizens than local, state or national issues. First, the events are taking place in remote locations far away from the United States, and appear to have less direct impact. Second, there is no immediate constituency supporting action in most cases. Third, there is less interest, and fourth, less motivation to do anything. Fifth, media coverage is likely to be lower unless the events are spectacular or involve extraordinary violence.

In truth, as noted above, the public, while not powerless, is at a distinct disadvantage when compared to those who are able to contribute large amounts of money to political campaigns. This is nowhere more evident than in the policies, domestic and foreign, pursued under the presidential administrations of Bill Clinton and George W. Bush. Since my interest here is in foreign policy related to genocide, I will confine my analysis to that portion of the policy-making process. To be succinct, both administrations were devious and blatantly opposed to humanitarian intervention to prevent genocide. While they talked about supporting human rights and stopping genocide, in reality they overtly opposed multilateral action to prevent genocide. In this sense, therefore, they are striking examples of the kinds of policy that must be opposed by those who wish to see a movement to prevent genocide. They are striking case studies in what should not be done.

# PART II

## Guilty Secrets: Genocide and the Failure of U.S. Foreign Policy During the Clinton and Bush Administrations

The depressing topic of genocide is made more depressing by the fact that it has been part of the repertoire of human behavior since humans first crawled out of the swamps and has become more and more common as the centuries progressed. If that is not bleak enough, we can descend into even greater darkness by pointing out that our likelihood of stopping this scourge of death is a long shot and that the United States, the lone remaining "super power" in the post–Cold War world, has been reluctant to participate in action to prevent this repetitive epidemic of mass murder. Genocide is as old as humanity and as new as the most recent headlines.

Bosnia, Rwanda, Kosovo, East Timor! The names of the genocides or near-genocides of the 1990s trip off the tongue and linger in the memory. Since 1990 the world has witnessed a succession of genocides or "genocide-like" events so that at the end of the last destructive century and the start of the new one, genocide remains in the forefront of human consciousness. Books have been written, debates have been engaged, and numerous proposals describing how and why it occurs or how to stop it have poured forth from the fervent minds of academics, journalists and others. Missing from much of this literature is a basic description of how leadership from the most significant power in the post–Cold War world might have prevented or, at the very least, mitigated the worst aspects of these horrible events.

My basic thesis is that, in spite of the rhetoric, when directly confronted by genocide, American leaders of the foreign policy-making institutions have been unable, incapable or unwilling to take action to stop and, ultimately, to deter human destructiveness. In fact, there are, I contend, chilling parallels among all the recent cases that cannot be explained away. The absence of action to stop the spiraling violence, coupled with the rhetoric to spin the impression that decisive action was being undertaken, was characteristic not only of President Clinton's policy toward genocide, but of U.S. policy historically, which is being pursued by the present Bush administration as well.

It is no secret—in fact, it is a general principle of political science—that once we get beyond the rhetorical idealism of talking about foreign policy that guarantees human rights, there are really two factors that drive U.S. foreign policy: first, national interest based on considerations of power and sovereignty, and second, presidential and partisan interests based on the latest public opinion polls and the next election. When humanitarian considerations come into play they are usually the result of television exposure. Consequently, most of the rhetoric is simply that and does not necessarily lead to any specific policy initiative. It should come as no surprise, then, that the United States, along with other nation-states, does not have the prevention of genocide as a main goal of foreign policy.

U.S. policy appears to be based on an ethic of apology instead of action. Rather than stop genocide, the United States apologizes for the slaughter years after it has taken place. Somehow, this is supposed to exonerate, or perhaps excuse or justify, the lack of action to save lives. One writer has noted, "It seems as if apologies are becoming a regular part of business and politics" (Szechi, 2000, p. 1). He questions whether it is "really possible for anyone to apologize meaningfully" (ibid.), especially to people who are now dead? And he answers that the "key problem with symbolic apologies is that in a quiet way they release us from the obligation to know why the world we live in is the way it is" (p. 2). Indeed, he argues that every nation and business has probably done something of which they are, or should be ashamed. Yet, we cannot change the course of history and apologizing may make us feel better "and implicitly release us from any obligation to understand what happened" (ibid.). It is far better, he believes, and I agree, to "study the history of our nation's and our community's relations with the rest of humankind. That way we may be able to avoid having our children and grandchildren apologize to the rest of the world for something we are doing right now" (ibid.). But, the proclivity for apology as a replacement for accepting responsibility and understanding policy continues.

Robert McNamara, secretary of defense in the Kennedy and Johnson administrations and one of the architects of the failed policy in Vietnam, is the foremost practitioner, closely followed by former President Clinton.

McNamara said that he is "sorry" for the Vietnam War, but he believed he had a higher obligation to be loyal to the president (McNamara, 1995). This is characteristic of the attitude of policymakers when faced with the decision between making a moral choice or following orders, and it had been evident at least since the decisions in the famous Nuremberg trials. But while McNamara apologizes and refers to the Vietnam War as a "tragedy," Vietnamese leaders such as General Giap, reject this view. For them the war was not a tragedy at all. Rather, as he notes, "Maybe it was a tragedy for you.... You wanted to replace the French; you failed; men died; so yes, it was tragic, because they died for a bad cause. But for us, the war was a noble sacrifice.... So I agree that you missed opportunities and that you need to draw lessons. But us? I think we would do nothing different, under the circumstances" (Mirsky, 2000, p. 56). McNamara's apology is an attempt to justify his actions and to set himself up as having been aware of the problems at the time, but also as having been hemmed in and unable to take the necessary action to avert the tragic situation. In short, it is an attempt to deny his responsibility for the death and destruction. This, sadly, is characteristic of leaders in failed policy and demonstrates that, as the particular policy was being pursued, they were blinded by partisan political interests and unconcerned about the human implications of their actions. Years after, when the policy has been revealed as an immoral failure, the apology is forthcoming as a rather lame attempt to explain away and justify their role in formulating and carrying out that policy. This has become a dominant feature of U.S. foreign policy making, and Vietnam has become the paradigmatic case.

Therefore, I am going to start by examining the influence of what has come to be known as the "Vietnam syndrome" and show how it influenced U.S. policy in Bosnia. Following that, I will look at what happened in Rwanda, Kosovo, East Timor and the attempt to establish the International Criminal Court before concluding with some ideas about how to prevent genocide and how to build a movement to support that action.

Before we get to the analysis, however, a caveat is necessary. I do not mean to imply or argue that the United States has a unique capability to intervene in and prevent or deter every humanitarian disaster that occurs. We cannot fall into what D.W. Brogan called the "illusion of American omnipotence," the "illusion that any situation which distresses or endangers the United States can only exist because some Americans have been fools or knaves" (Brogan, 1952, p. 21).

Former Senator J. William Fulbright had another name for this syndrome. He called it the "arrogance of power," the idea that there is no problem the United States cannot solve. Yet, the missing element is the will to try. Absent a vision of domestic and foreign policy, there are no goals to be pursued, and, hence, leadership is not necessary because there are no apparent objectives, no destination to which the nation and the world might be transported. Simply flow with the tide. The problem, of course, is that if you flow with the tide, you will be washed out to sea and, perhaps, swept away by currents beyond your control or understanding. Absent diplomatic leadership and a system that attempts to foresee such possible humanitarian disasters, there will be little likelihood that the political institutions will be successful in controlling or preventing genocidal violence. As Alan F. Kuperman noted in *Foreign Affairs* (2000, p. 117), "intervention is no substitute for prevention."

Inexorably, then, we come back to the questions with which I began, why the reluctance to intervene and how does one decide what, if any, action to take? Of course, these are extremely difficult questions that must be answered within the overall context of a coherent foreign policy. Both were distinctively lacking in the 1990s and in the historical context of U.S. policy toward genocide in the twentieth century. While it is often the case that alternatives are not always clear and in some cases one must choose between the lesser of two evils, this does not necessarily mean that one of the alternatives is not distinctly more preferable. Context must be examined and a decision made to protect the most innocent. Unfortunately, in this post–Cold War era, we are left with the horrible reality that the only way to stop the loss of innocent life is to kill or injure other innocent life—which is pretty damn depressing. Given that the real world is not always congruent with the way we would like it to be, foreign policymakers must be in a position to adjust to unpleasant and unforeseen circumstances and make difficult evaluations. U.S. foreign policymakers were limited in their ability to do this as a result of two particular past experiences, Vietnam and Somalia, which cast shadows over, and exerted tremendous influence on, the making of U.S. foreign policy in the post–Cold War world.

# 4

# The Failure of Prevention: Bosnia

In what is, I think, one of the first post–Cold War novels, *Our Game*, John Le Carre (1995) has one of his characters summarize Western policy toward genocide: "All through the Cold War it was our Western boast that we defended the underdog against the bully. The boast was a bloody lie. Again and again during the Cold War and after it the West made common cause with the bully in favour of what we call stability, to the despair of the very people we claimed to be protecting. That's what we're up to now" (p. 204). He goes on to provide an accurate description: "planned apathy is the kindest description I can think of: act natural and look the other way while the ethnic cleansers do their hovering and restore what politicians call normality" (p. 229).

If "looking the other way" became the norm, we should be able to find empirical evidence by examining initiatives taken or not taken to stop genocide in the post-Holocaust period. The case of the former Yugoslavia is a telling example, since any American initiative in Bosnia was stymied by what had by then become known as the Vietnam syndrome. Before we examine specifically how it operated, a brief background of the conflict is necessary.

## A Brief History of the Conflict[7]

Forty-eight years after the extermination and concentration camps were liberated, genocide was ignored by the major world powers, neither punished nor prevented until they were forced to act. In what used to be Yugoslavia, torture, murder, rape and starvation became everyday occurrences. Estimates of the total number of people massacred approach

250,000. Huge numbers of refugees were created, and 30,000 to 60,000 Muslim women were estimated to have been raped as a systematic policy to humiliate Muslim families. Rape was used as a political weapon. While estimates of numbers vary, they are all outrageously large. As noted, the Bosnian government estimates that "as many as 50,000 or even 60,000 women have been raped and claims to have partially documented 13,000 cases of Muslim women violated by Serbs" (Leber, 1993, p. 3). A European commission of inquiry reported that 20,000 women had been raped, and a Michigan law professor who represented the Bosnian victims estimated more than 50,000, with another 100,000 women and children killed (Halsell, 1993, p. 9). Documented cases showed that rapes had been committed on children as young as 3 years of age and on women as old as 84. Halsell, who interviewed Muslim women in Bosnia, recounted examples almost too horrible to repeat. One woman described what she witnessed in a camp for 150 women and children: "I saw Serbs raping children—girls as young as six and eight years old" (p. 8). Another woman, a nurse, describes her detention in a "rape camp": "I was one of 1,800 women kept as prisoners in Brocko. There were 600 women in my room. I was given a number—31. When they called your number you had to go. One woman told me she was gang-raped by 50 Serbs" (p. 9).

While the Serbs were not solely responsible for all the atrocities, they were the primary perpetrators. Atrocities ran the gamut of the traditional horrors found in most genocides. The destruction of towns, villages and homes, forced evacuation, ethnic cleansing of populations, bombing, shooting, beatings, killings, forcible imprisonment, inhumane treatment, use of detention or concentration camps, massacres and any atrocity of which the human mind is capable of conceiving.

As the winter of 1994 approached, the UN-designated "safe havens," in particular the Bihac area, were under attack and the United States and NATO appeared to be unwilling to take decisive action. U.S. politicians blamed the UN for not being effective, for not being able to stop the violence, but the UN was never designed to undertake that role and without the United States or other great powers' monetary or military contributions is ineffective—as we will see once again in the case of Rwanda. So the slaughter continued, and it became necessary to ask the same question about Yugoslavia that was asked concerning Nazi Germany: How did what used to be a civilized and sophisticated European multiethnic nation degenerate into a state of hatred and depravity as great as that of any genocide of the twentieth century?

The three groups, Serbs, Croats and Muslims, share a common South Slavic ethnic background. They speak similar languages but are divided by cultural, religious, political and ideological differences. The Bosnian Muslims are Europeans. They are not the stereotyped Muslims of Serb

# The Failure of Prevention: Bosnia

propaganda. For the most part they lived in cities and engaged in the common urban occupations such as artisans, teachers, doctors, small businessmen, while some were farmers. They were, for the most part, pacifists and wore regular clothing. Generally, they viewed their religion as a national identity and viewed themselves as secular Europeans.

Croatia flourished from the tenth to the thirteenth century, while Serbia prospered in the thirteenth and fourteenth centuries. Croatia became Catholic, while Serbia adopted the Independent Orthodox religion. A third force also arose. There always have been contending schools of Christianity, and a derivative sect of the Manicheans called Bogomils took root among the Slavs. They were similar to the Albigenses of southern France who were in favor of a "purer, simpler monotheism" (Meyer, 1993, p. 61). This group was denounced as heretics by both the Orthodox and Catholic churches, and the Bogomils were not regarded as Christians. They were, in fact, sold as slaves and treated harshly.

In 1389, at the Battle of Kosovo, the Turks defeated an army of Serbian nobles, and in 1415 the Ottoman Turks "offered the Bogomils military protection, secure titles to their lands and freedom to practice their religion—if they counted themselves as Muslims and did not attack Ottoman forces" (ibid.). Conversions to Islam occurred, but hundreds of thousands of Serbs moved to escape Turkish oppression and were welcomed by the Austrians, who used them as a cushion from Turkish invasion.

In 1875, Bosnian Christians, Serbs and Montenegrins with the support of Russia revolted against the Turks, and the Austro-Hungarian army took advantage of the opportunity and invaded Bosnia. Bosnia and Hercegovina were annexed by Austria in 1908, and this angered Serbia and its Russian ally. Yugoslavia was formed in 1918, when the Austro-Hungarian and Ottoman Turk empires that had dominated the Balkan region collapsed in defeat. Serbia, Macedonia and Montenegro were composed mainly of Orthodox Christian populations that had been within the Turkish sphere, but had significant Albanian Muslim, Hungarian and German minorities. Slovenia and Croatia contained mostly Catholic populations and had been part of the Austrian empire. Croatia also contained Orthodox Serbs. Bosnia-Hercegovina had a mixture of Croatian Catholic, Orthodox Serb and Muslim populations.

In the period between World War I and World War II, the multiethnic state of Yugoslavia experienced internal conflict between the groups, and there were high tensions between the Serbs who wanted greater centralization and the Croatians who wanted greater autonomy. Within ten years the parliamentary government broke down, and the Serbian monarchy set up a royal dictatorship.

Hitler and Mussolini gave the Croats the chance they had waited for when Germany invaded Yugoslavia on April 6, 1941. Partition followed in which Serbia was kept under German military administration. Croatia and Bosnia-Hercegovina were formed into a German satellite state. Officials of this puppet government belonged to the violent pro-Nazi movement of Croatian ultranationalists known as the USTASHA Party, led by Ante Pavelic. The partition and German occupation soon led to resistance, civil war, ethnic cleansing and genocide.

The civil war was multisided. The Yugoslav communists under Josip Broz Tito led a Partisan resistance against the German occupiers and their collaborators. Tito advocated restoration of a multinational Yugoslavia united in class struggle and Marxist revolution. The Serbian nationalists, called Chetniks, wanted a "Greater Serbia." They fought against the anti-Serb, pro-German USTASHA, but they also slid into collaboration with the Italians and Germans against Tito's partisans. The USTASHA fought for a "Greater Croatia," alongside the Germans against both Chetniks and partisans. But the lines were not always rigid. Sometimes communists and Chetniks fought Germans and USTASHA, and Chetniks and USTASHA cooperated against communists.

Ethnic cleansing and genocide intensified the horrors of the Nazi occupation and the civil war. In Serbia the German army shot all male Jews and Roma (Gypsies) in the fall of 1941 and murdered Jewish women and children in a gas van sent from Berlin in the spring of 1942. Bulgaria rounded up more than 7,000 Macedonian Jews and turned them over to the Germans, who deported them to the death camp at Treblinka in March 1943. In Croatia and Bosnia-Hercegovina, the USTASHA regime murdered most of the Jews and Roma, especially in the notorious concentration camp at Jasenovac. Some Jews managed to flee to the protection of the Italian zone along the coast or joined the partisans. Over 7,000 Croatian Jews who had not been immediately killed by the USTASHA death squads and were unable to reach safety were turned over to the Germans and deported to Auschwitz. The USTASHA regime paid the Germans thirty Reichsmarks per deported Jew to cover the cost of their transportation. Altogether some 60,000 Jews and 27,000 Roma perished in Yugoslavia during World War II.

The murder of Jews and Roma was only one aspect of this ethnic cleansing. Germans expelled many Slovenes as they tried to "Germanize" the territory, and many other Yugoslavs perished as prisoners in German concentration camps such as those at Sajmiste and Banjica. Italy also imprisoned many Slovenes and the Chetniks and murdered and expelled Muslims and Croatians in regions under their control. They had plans for far more extensive ethnic cleansing on the road to "Greater Serbia," if it had been within their power.

Croations also had plans for a greater Croatia and in pursuit of that goal committed some of the most deadly massacres when the USTASHA attacked the Serbian population in Croatia and Bosnia-Hercegovina. The

USTASHA wanted a "Greater Croatia" that was also pure of "foreign" elements. Thus, in addition to murdering Jews and Roma, the USTASHA regime aimed to eliminate the numerous Serbian communities within its borders—nearly two million people constituting 30 percent of the population—through a combination of ethnic cleansing, forced conversion and mass murder. Some 300,000 to 400,000 Serbs were murdered outright; hundreds of thousands were driven or fled over the border into German-occupied Serbia. German-led antipartisan sweeps through regions of Serbian settlement within the boundaries of the USTASHA state killed others and sent many to camps. In the end, over one million Yugoslavs lost their lives in World War II from all causes, more than half of them as victims of genocide. With the dissolution of Yugoslavia in the 1990s, they returned to their genocidal past as each group reawakened and exploited the memory of the old hatred to motivate new atrocities.

## Genocide in Modern Europe

The most recent conflict was related to the collapse of Communist rule in the former Soviet Union and Eastern Europe and to the triumph of nationalism over democracy. Yugoslavia was composed of six federated people's republics and two autonomous regions (Vojvodina and Kosovo). They were governed from the Serbian capital of Belgrade. Four of the six republics had non-Serb majorities: Slovenia, Croatia, Macedonia and Bosnia-Hercegovina, and they began to move to gain independence.

Serbia and Montenegro stated that they would not allow non-Serbs to rule over Serbs and "in 1991 Serbian troops, wearing the uniforms and supported by the heavy weapons and aircraft of the former Yugoslav army, set out to 'free' Serbian towns and villages in Croatia and Slovenia" (Curtiss, 1993, p. 8). The leader of the Serbs, Slobodan Milosovic, was a Serb communist who "gained power by using the traditional mechanisms of propaganda. He controlled the media and used them to stir up nationalist hatred. Milosovic manipulated the stirred-up nationalism and the expansionist demand for a greater Serbia, which became respectable when Serb intellectuals wrote in a 1986 memorandum that the Serbs were the losers in Tito's Yugoslavia. His main tactic was to stage large public rallies and manipulate the elections. Milosevic was successful in using television to stir up the public, and extreme nationalist authors wrote much of the propaganda. These appeals to Serbian nationalism heightened the discontent among Serb minorities in Croatia and Bosnia-Hercegovina and motivated the rising nationalism of other groups. The Serbs then used techniques first pioneered by the Nazis to ethnically cleanse the areas they conquered. Sealed freight cars deported Muslims to camps where they experienced conditions similar to and reminiscent of those in the concentration camps of World War II. Gutman's (1993) dispatches made very clear the similarity between these camps and those of an earlier era. He drew parallels to Auschwitz (p. 36) and quoted survivors who pointed out that some of the camps were indeed death camps (pp. 44, 50), while others were rape camps (pp. 64, 68, 69).

The first year of fighting between Croatians and Serbs killed 10,000 people, with a million Serbs and Croats driven from their homes. Serbia occupied a third of the territory that was assigned to Croatia. The ceasefire freed Serbian troops and after the European Community recognized the Republic of Bosnia on April 6, 1992, with the United States following, and the next day, Bosnian Serbs began the siege of Sarajevo. The world now began its vigil and watched as the slaughter continued and escalated. Neither the United States nor the UN, nor NATO, nor the European countries, nor Russia was willing to take action to stop the genocide.

The Europeans classified the conflict as a civil war, not an international conflict, and openly supported the partition of Bosnia, all the while ignoring the carnage. The partition was the process that evolved into the Vance-Owen Plan. Before the war "4 million Bosnians were divided into 109 municipalities, of which only 32 had an absolute Serb majority" (Cohen, 1993, p. 40). Under the European plan, the Bosnian Muslims' territory was to be given to the Serbs. But the Vance-Owen Plan never got off the ground. In its place a new plan was proposed in June/July 1993 to divide Bosnia into three sections, with the Croatians and the Serbians gaining the largest amount of territory and the Bosnian Muslims relegated to a series of "safe havens," which were actually similar to Native American reservations. In either case the Muslims lost whatever territory they once controlled, and the demise of Bosnia became a fait accompli.

The world was left with the apparently accurate perception that genocide and atrocity were legitimate means to secure policy goals. If a leader or group is interested in securing territory, uniting a previously fractious people, or pursuing some other political goal, using genocide as the means to achieve these or other ends was justified, since the international community did not appear likely to take action to stop these "crimes against humanity." There was no politics of humanitarian intervention. U.S. policy saw intervention to save Islamic lives as problematic unless they lived on top of huge strategic oil reserves. In fact, the reluctance to intervene was praised as the advocates of *realpolitik* justified U.S. policy by appealing to the Vietnam syndrome.

The basic argument was that intervention would propel the United States into a quagmire like Vietnam. In other words, U.S. policy appeared to be that the United States would participate in humanitarian intervention in three circumstances, most of which had little to do with

## The Failure of Prevention: Bosnia

the humanitarian part of the intervention: economic self-interest (Persian Gulf War), pursuing a Cold War policy of containment (Vietnam, Nicaragua), and as a not too costly means to achieve domestic and international political goals (Panama, Grenada, Somalia). Humanitarian intervention to save thousands of Muslim lives was beyond the pale of U.S. foreign policy. The Bosnian Muslims were, to use Helen Fein's concept, defined as being outside the "universe of moral obligation," and when a people is defined as being outside that universe, as with the Jews of Europe, the Armenians by the Turks, the Kulaks by Stalin, the Ibos in the Biafran War, the intellectuals and other Western-tainted people by the Khmer Rouge, they become targets for extermination. So in the post–Cold War world we were left with a new, but very old-world era of ethnonational violence and no leadership intent on developing mechanisms to prevent the continuous slaughter of innocents well into the late twentieth century.

This lack of U.S. leadership to save life was justified by invoking the Vietnam syndrome and attaching to it the experience of the United States in Somalia. What happened in Somalia was the collapse of the government, which was replaced by warlords who proceeded to engage in brutal repression of the people as they fought each other. Anarchy ruled in the streets and people were starving. As images of the cruelty appeared on television, the United States asked the UN to sanction an intervention, which it did by passing UN Security Council Resolution 775. A military force of 24,000 troops went to Somalia to

> protect relief workers, in order to feed the people. In May 1993, the operation was given over to the UN through UN Operation in Somalia II (UNSOM II). In June, twenty-four Pakistani soldiers serving the UN force were killed, and the mission was expanded to go after the warlords, particularly General Aidid in the Mogadishu area. In October, eighteen U.S. soldiers were killed in an ambush. Not long after these incidents, participating nations, most important the United States, announced their intention to leave the country. (Simon, 2000, pp. 21–22)

Somalia was, consequently, added to Vietnam as an indicator of why humanitarian intervention was not practical.

### U.S. Policy in Bosnia and the Vietnam-Somalia Syndrome

After the Persian Gulf War, President Bush declared the Vietnam syndrome to be "dead." What he meant was the United States would once again use its power on the stage of world politics but would do so selectively. The Vietnam syndrome may have been dead, but there remained the same obsession with "credibility" that pushed the United

States into the Vietnam War and kept them from getting out when the policy proved to be clearly counterproductive. The new twist was that, once committed, the United States *must* fight to the end. The idea that any initiative could be abandoned instead of being followed relentlessly forward to its conclusion was dismissed because it assumed that such a retreat would be harmful to the nation's prestige—more harmful than carrying on with a policy that might be plainly misguided or foolish or contrary to the nation's interest—as was the case in Vietnam. Any initiative now committed prestige and credibility, and, once they were committed, control was effectively abandoned and there could be no turning back. The result of this type of thinking meant that nothing short of full-scale commitment could even be contemplated.

This was clear in Bosnia, where the United States neither acted nor threatened military force to stop the atrocities taking place because of the perception that the slightest sign of intervention would send the United States down the slippery slope to another Vietnam—which the American people would not support. So the United States did nothing. In fact, of course, there was no evaluation on a case-by-case basis. All events at the time were compared to Vietnam. The United States would commit either all the way or not at all.

The practical impact of such a position is to severely limit the international community's ability to prevent genocide or to defend human rights. Military victory is the only reasonable goal.

The evidence that this thinking was applied to Bosnia becomes clear when we realize that the United States was aware of the concentration-like camps set up by the Serbs as early as June 1992. In fact, Secretary of State Eagleburger admitted, "All of us were being a little bit careful ... because of this issue of whether or not it was going to push us into something that we thought was dangerous" (Danner, 1997b, p. 58). Hence, even when the pictures of the camps were broadcast on television Bush continued to maintain his reluctance to intervene. "I don't care what the political pressures are. Before one soldier ... is committed to battle, I'm going to know how that person gets out of there. And we are not going to get bogged down into some guerrilla warfare. We lived through that once" (ibid.). Then secretary of state Eagleburger noted that "Vietnam never goes away," and this was obviously the case for the Bush administration.

Former U.S. ambassador to Yugoslavia Warren Zimmerman pointed out that when any change in Bush's passive policy was proposed, "the ghost of Vietnam" could be felt in the room:

> the "lesson" drawn from Vietnam was that even a minimum injection of American forces could swell inexorably into a major commitment and produce a quagmire. The second objection ... was the view that had prevailed

## The Failure of Prevention: Bosnia

during the successful prosecution of the Gulf War: there should be no US military intervention unless the objectives were clear, the means applied to [them] would bring certain victory, there was an "exit" strategy (the earlier the better).... Pervading all these reasons was an almost obsessive fear of American casualties ... (Ibid.)

Essentially, this meant that unless victory was certain there could be no intervention. General Colin Powell reinforced this view during the time he was Head of the Joint Chiefs of Staff when he declared that no limited force should be used in Bosnia: "As soon as [politicians] tell me it is limited, it means they do not care whether you achieve a result or not. As soon as they tell me 'surgical' I head for the bunker" (ibid.). Leaders, according to Powell, had to start with a clear idea of what the political objective was and then decide whether it was to "win or do something else." For Powell, the most important thing was to get "decisive results." He also thought that the opposite of "win" is not "lose" but "to fail to achieve decisive results." As Danner notes: "If a military action does not prove 'decisive,' it has failed. And if a proposed mission cannot be virtually guaranteed to produce such results, it should not be attempted" (ibid.). Apply this reasoning to the United States' entry into World War II and you achieve a fair picture of the implications. Without certainty that Hitler could be defeated, no action should be taken. Or, better yet, without certitude that intervention would save the Jews of Europe, none should be undertaken. As a result of the Vietnam analogy, political leaders allowed the military free reign to define "results." Of course, it is not the military's job to define "results," and it is possible for a president or the public to decide that a result other than winning a war might be decisive—such as saving lives. Given these legacies of the Vietnam syndrome it is not surprising that no action was taken.

I saw this in operation for myself when, in the winter of 1993, I was invited to present a seminar to the Policy Planning Staff of the State Department on whether the events that were transpiring in Bosnia constituted "genocide." The circumstances of that invitation are less important than the result, which was a determined intention by the U.S. government not to classify the atrocity as genocide.

In my presentation and accompanying paper I traced the history of the term starting with the Armenian genocide, including the Holocaust, and the coinage of the term by Raphael Lemkin, through the 1948 International Convention on the Prevention and Punishment of the Crime of Genocide, the Khmer Rouge atrocity and the massacres in Indonesia, among others—in short, cataloguing the sad record of twentieth-century atrocity. The question I was asked to address was straightforward: "Were the events in Bosnia genocide?" After my trip through the historic record, I concluded that, indeed, it constituted genocide under the Convention and that there was an international legal and moral duty to intervene. I even outlined a set of strategies to be pursued.

But the U.S. government was in denial. Those who listened to my obviously unpersuasive presentation appeared to be divided between "legalists," who argued that the Bosnian tragedy could not be genocide because it was a civil war and, therefore, we had no obligation to intervene, and "moralists," who took a diametrically opposite position. But there is more.

I was also given a set of documents, official state department reports that catalogued some of the more horrible atrocities. These reports were the result of UN Resolution 771, September 22, 1992, which called upon states to collate information relating to violations of humanitarian law. The U.S. government, transmitted to the UN Secretary General its initial report on information concerning violations of humanitarian law and grave breaches of the Geneva Conventions on the territory of the former Yugoslavia. As noted in the report, "the report details allegations of wilfull killing, torture of prisoners, abuse of civilians in detention centers, deliberate attacks on non-combatants, wanton devastation and destruction of property, and others including mass forcible expulsion and deportation of civilians (ethnic cleansing)." It went on to note: "We are working actively with others on a resolution to create a UN commission to look into these charges, to establish the facts, and to prepare for possible prosecution of individuals found guilty of those crimes."

The report never mentioned the word "genocide." Instead it stated that the "United States has focused on the violations identified in the Resolution and other grave breaches as defined in Article 147 of the Fourth Geneva Convention (Geneva Convention Relative to the Protection of Civilian Persons in Time of War of August 12, 1942)." Having defined the events in the former Yugoslavia as a war, in this case a civil war, the United States was under no obligation to intervene as it would have been if it had defined the events as genocide.

This first report then proceeded to document incidents of "Wilfull killing," "Torture of Prisoners," "Abuse of Civilians in Detention Centers," "Deliberate Attacks on Non-Combatants," "Wanton Devastation and Destruction of Property," and "Others, Including Mass Forcible Expulsion and Deportation of Civilians." It also provided details, including dates, names of victims and perpetrators and descriptions of the acts committed, for over fifty incidents. The initial report was followed by others using the same format (see *U.S. Department of State Dispatches*). The report on December 28, 1992, also contained a statement from Secretary Eagleburger presented at the International Conference on the Former Yugoslavia, in Geneva, Switzerland, December 16, 1992.

In this report, the secretary, after discussing the situation, talks about authorizing and enforcing a no fly zone and reexamining the arms em-

# The Failure of Prevention: Bosnia

bargo. He also calls on the UN to "begin identifying the individuals who may have to answer for having committed crimes against humanity," noting that, "We have, on the one hand, a moral and historical obligation not to stand back a second time in this century while a people faces obliteration" (923). He even cites specific names and dates of atrocities committed, but he never uses the term "genocide."

This continued refusal to use the term "genocide" persisted throughout the transition from the Bush to the Clinton administration.

During the 1992 election campaign candidate Clinton denounced Bush's inaction. This motivated General Powell once more to express his opinion in the *New York Times* suggesting that military force must be matched to political objectives. He noted that President Bush was aware of this and that history has not been kind to talk of surgical bombing or limited attack. Lurking beneath this was, of course, Vietnam. As former Ambassador Zimmerman noted, "the Pentagon's tactic was never to say no, simply to raise the objections which made the proposal seem unworkable" (Danner, 1997b, p. 58; also see Zimmerman, 1999). Danner goes on to point out that even though the officers "never got very good answers to [their] incessant questioning of what was the precise military objective and what political end would be served by achieving it . . . it is also true that Bosnia proved the United States incapable of managing a complex war requiring a limited use of force for limited objectives." Bosnia also demonstrated that the United States was incapable, or unwilling, to participate in or take the lead in forming a multilateral response to atrocity. This was to be repeated in Rwanda. Yet, in spite of these restrictive interpretations, the United States finally participated in a NATO intervention. Why?

## Why Intervention?

Finally, in the fall of 1995, NATO, under the leadership of the United States, brought the respective presidents of the three groups, Milosovic (president of Serbia and Montenegro), Tudjman (leader of the Croats) and Izetbegovic (leader of the Bosnian Muslims), together at Wright-Patterson Air Force Base in Dayton, Ohio. On November 22, 1995, the thirty-second anniversary of the assassination of President John F. Kennedy, they accepted a cease-fire agreement. Why?

By this time it was becoming obvious, written in major newspapers and shown on television, that the long period of nonintervention and U.S. ambivalence was moving the international community closer to a possible breakdown of any semblance of international order. Internationalism of any sort, including multilateral peacekeeping, was under attack, especially in the U.S. Congress, which refused to allow American troops to be under the command of non-American commanders. The fact that it took so many years before the remaining super power would be moved to generate leadership to stop one set of atrocities (Rwanda is another and in some ways even more disgraceful matter) allowed the world to see the impending breakdown with a degree of clarity. The UN mission was on the verge of failure, largely because of a lack of U.S. support and aid—the United States was for many years the largest debtor nation to the UN because the United States refused to pay its assessed dues. The massacres at Srebrenica in the summer of 1995 finally may have pushed the leading powers to a position where they hoped to avoid further humiliation.

The reported massacres at Srebrenica were another chapter in a long story of cruelty, but these seem finally to have pushed the United States over the edge (Honig and Both 1996). Reportedly, between 5,000 and 8,000 Muslims were killed and buried in mass graves. According to accounts of survivors, the atrocities followed what was now an all too predictable model. As 25,000 refugees fled the area on July 11, 1995, along with 300 Dutch UN peacekeepers who were unable to defend them, the massacres began on July 12. While the majority of women and children were taken to safety, the men were forced into trucks and partly finished houses near Srebrenica, or transported to warehouses in empty school buildings close by. Descriptions from survivors convey the horror they experienced as the massacres continued throughout the night and for several days. The most poignant description is in chapter 3, "The Masscare," of the definitive work by Honig and Both (1996, pp. 48–67).

While no one is sure precisely how many people died in the fields and woods surrounding Srebrenica, it does seem to have impressed the international community. NATO was clearly threatened and the UN was being ridiculed. Because of these factors, Clinton finally acted and a very important question is why he did so one year prior to the American presidential election scheduled for November 1996? If the intervention had failed, or if there were large numbers of American casualties, the reaction against Clinton would have been negative. If, on the other hand, there was some semblance of "success," Clinton would have, for the first time in his presidency, demonstrated that elusive capacity known as "leadership." In fact, it appeared that Clinton learned a lesson that many American presidents had discovered: sometimes it is easier to find success in foreign policy, as compared to domestic policy.

The Clinton administration, therefore, suddenly had taken initiatives not only in Bosnia, but in Haiti and in the Middle East, and was expressing strong support for the Anglo-Irish negotiations. Clinton's popularity increased in 1996, as he pursued these initiatives and as he appeared to confront the suddenly less popular Republicans on the budget. While the risks were considerable, the gains probably outweighed those risks when one realizes that these were the first "successes" that the administration was able to claim and they came one year prior to the election. In addition, there were also certain realities within Bosnia.

## Bosnian Realities

There is little doubt that any successful nation building or institutionalization of the peace to make it a permanent fixture of this troubled landscape was going to take time. The notion that American forces might be withdrawn quickly, and that in a short time they would have succeeded in bringing stability to the area, was an illusion. Too many people died; too many hatreds were stirred up; too many ambitious leaders saw too many opportunities. Yet, these same realities also played a part in bringing about an agreement.

Assuredly, the move toward a cease-fire was at least partly motivated by the new military success of the Croations in the Krajina region of Croatia. When the cease-fire finally was signed the Serbs occupied about 49 percent of Bosnia, down from the previous 70 percent they had controlled before the military successes of the Croats and Muslims. This is precisely the percentage they were to be given by the agreement. It was, therefore, easier because it would no longer be necessary to convince the Bosnian Serbs to give up territory.

Reaching an agreement was also felt to be, at least at that moment, in the interest of three of the four involved parties. Milosovic clearly saw the agreement as an opportunity to have the economic embargo lifted as well as a chance to undermine the leadership of Radovan Karadzic, whom he viewed as a rival. Milosovic was certainly more interested in an agreement than the leaders of the Bosnian Serbs, the only party not to derive some immediate relief from the agreement, since they lost territory they had conquered by force of arms and were relegated to a smaller area. Moreover, their two primary leaders, Karadzic and Mladic, had been indicted by the war crimes tribunal and, under the terms of the agreement, were banned from holding any office in the new Serbian Republic of Bosnia. Mladic had been implicated directly in the ethnic cleansing of the Croats in Krajina and was an unadulterated advocate of an ethnic Serbian state. In November 1994 he told the German magazine, *Der Speiegel*: "Our aim remains the unification of all Serbian lands. Borders are drawn with blood" (Zimmerman, 1995, p. 4).

The Croatians, after gaining back some territory, viewed the agreement as an opportunity for consolidation, a chance to rearm and reevaluate their present position. They also, of course, were assured that the United States would support and continue to arm them. Retired U.S. military personnel were in Croatia providing training and support (Curtiss, 1995, p. 103).

The Bosnian government was the weakest of the parties because it had been unable to get arms. The country had no outlet to the sea, and this made the arms embargo more effective. It was in their short-term interest to halt the violence, at least for a brief period. After years of fighting and suffering, it was time for a pause. In addition, the United States seemed to be willing and committed to training the forces of the Bosnian Muslims in an attempt to even out the playing field. This presented a certain danger, since it put the United States in the position of not appearing neutral.

The Croations were forced into an alliance with the Bosnian Muslims but harbored ambitions of their own, and their president was known as a fervid nationalist. There was no love lost between Croats and Muslims, and many observers feared that, given the opportunity, the Croatians would turn on the Muslims if they perceived it to be to their advantage.

The territorial arrangement seemed likewise difficult. The border areas of the settlement appeared likely to become flash points of conflict, and the NATO troops are still in place. In addition, there was fear concerning how the different parties would react in the long run. Some observers feared that there might be a kind of "Somalian" law, that after a period of time even peacekeeping forces wear out their welcome and are viewed as an occupying force.

The significant military power of the United States and its NATO partners appears to have turned out to be more than a match for those who might have wanted to disturb the peace. The Vietnam analogy simply did not hold. The Bosnians were not only not the South Vietnamese; the Serbs were not the North Vietnamese. As Zimmerman (1995) notes: "Far from being intensely committed fighters for their country or their ideology, they are an army with poor morale engaged in a sordid landgrab" (p. 6).

All this means that the intervention should have signaled a move to a more encompassing idea of national interest than the isolationist impulses that dominated the U.S. Congress. In the post–Cold War era, when it is necessary to control the more egregious examples of ethnonational violence, it is necessary to view multilateral intervention as in the national interests of more powerful democratic states, especially if that intervention is aimed at supporting weaker democracies. If such support is not overt and forthcoming, the lesson to small vulnerable countries may be that there is no international order and that their real friends lie elsewhere. This neglect or withdrawal into isolationism will also weaken the strong democracies by giving the "appearance of hypocritical self-interest that begins to gnaw at their moral (and thus their political) credibility" (Judt, 1995, p. 37).

Perhaps the most telling phrasing of these questions appeared in *Love Thy Neighbor* by Peter Maas (1996), a moving book about Bosnia where he asks how you might explain U.S. policy to a Bosnian Muslim:

## The Failure of Prevention: Bosnia

> When the Bosnian looks at you, with anger and fear and incomprehension in his eyes, and asks why America, the America that loves democracy and human rights and just built a Holocaust Museum that receives millions of visitors every year, won't stop genocide in Europe at the end of the twentieth century, what do you do? Shrug your shoulders in neutrality, pretend like you don't know? What would you say to the Jew in Berlin? "Sorry, I can't take sides." (P. 115)

Maas proceeds to note that Clinton's "rare displays of resolve were deceptions" (pp. 266–267) when, as he points out, "The other jobs that needed to be done—such as arresting war criminals, protecting refugees who wanted to return home, and overseeing the unification of Bosnia—were largely ignored" (p. 272). Maas concludes by taking us back to the analogy of appeasement.

> Finally I want to explain that appeasement does not work. Forget all the moral objections to it, about the humiliations it has brought to our governments and to ourselves; just think of the practicalities. Clinton and his counterparts in Western Europe generally had their way against the "laptop bombardiers." They did nothing for more than three years and watched as more than 200,000 people were killed. It took a few weeks of bombing in the late summer of 1995 to let the Serbs know that there was surprisingly, a limit to the forbearance of our leaders, that they really should settle for half of Bosnia, which they did. Our leaders could have demanded far more in the name of justice, could have done far more in the name of justice, but chose not to. In their desire to stop the war on terms acceptable to Milosovic, they abandoned their promises never to reward ethnic cleansing. They appeased. They also overlooked an important lesson of history. Peace is not guaranteed by a thick treaty or enforcement troops; it is guaranteed by justice. (P. 272)

This was never clearer than the genocide in Rwanda in 1994.

# 5

# A Second Failure of Prevention: The Rwandan Genocide

If Bosnia was viewed as peripheral to U.S. strategic interests, then Rwanda, as well as other African nations, is literally seen as even more completely removed from U.S. perceptions of their national interests. In spite of the fact that there have been repeated abuses of human rights and large-scale extermination of human life, the United States, along with the other major world powers, continues to view Africa as peripheral. Most of the events remain remote, since they are rarely given much coverage in the media and since American citizens have relatively little knowledge of the continent. In countries such as Sierra Leone and Sudan genocide has occurred, and the U.S. Holocaust Memorial Museum Committee on Conscience issued one of the only "Genocide warnings" it has issued, along with the unveiling of a display, on the Sudan on November 15, 2000. The commission estimated that two million people had died in the Sudan, that four million had been displaced in the past seventeen years of civil war and that the "Primary responsibility for the devastation belongs to the Sudanese government" (Committee on Conscience, 2000). Yet, this is not a new phenomenon since it was in Rwanda that one of the largest and quickest genocides of the twentieth century took place.

The countries of Rwanda and Burundi are twins, and the roots of the conflict in Rwanda go back to the fact that both were Belgian colonies. The colonial power structure supported one tribal group, the Tutsi minority, over another, the Hutu majority, and made the Tutsi heirs to power. In Rwanda, a Hutu party took power in a democratic election in 1962–1963 precipitating massacres of Tutsi in the countryside. Tutsi refugees fled to Burundi and Uganda. The refugees in Uganda formed a guerilla movement that liberated Uganda from the dictator Idi Amin and became the basis for the Rwandan Patriotic Front (RPF).

In Burundi a Tutsi-dominated government ruled until 1993. Prior to that time Hutu resistance and government genocides occurred from 1965 to 1993. The first steps toward democracy were reversed after the assassination of the first Hutu president in October 1993. Army officers drawn from an elite Tutsi group led a coup that overthrew the first democratically elected president of Burundi, Melchior Ndadaye. President Ndadaye was the first Hutu to hold the position. Burundi, which is 85 percent Hutu, was governed by a Tutsi elite that still controls the military. Genocide-like events had taken place periodically, the largest in 1972, when the government organized violence against the Hutus and took an estimated 100,000 lives—some estimate the toll as high as 250,000 Hutus. A report by the Carnegie Endowment for International Peace criticized the United States and, in particular, President Richard Nixon and Secretary of State Henry Kissinger for "indifference, inertia, and irresponsibility" (Leitenberg, 1994a, p. 33). Various attempted coups by Hutus and rumors led to further massacres against the Hutus by the military in 1965, 1988 and 1991. Other massacres against Tutsi were organized by relatively unorganized Hutus in 1988. The violence in Burundi continued, and the International Commission of Inquiry into Human Rights Abuses in Burundi estimated that 25,000 to 50,000 people were killed in October 1993 massacres. Nothing was done. The previous genocides organized by the military governments resulted in 1972–1973 in about 100,000 deaths and in 1988 around 20,000. In Rwanda similar events were taking place.

In Rwanda the largest genocide occurred in 1994 and was precipitated by the downing of an airplane on April 6, 1994, carrying the presidents of Rwanda and Burundi. The plane was shot down as it approached the airport in the Rwandan capital. It took less than an hour for roadblocks to be thrown up and killings to begin. The response clearly was planned as the first victims were "members of the political opposition, both Hutu and Tutsi. The killings were at first confined to the capital, but the response of the United States and other Western countries was only to evacuate their own nationals" (ibid., p. 34).

The attack against the plane was attributed to the RPF, the paramilitary group organized by Tutsi refugees in Uganda who were seeking to regain power in Rwanda. The RPF had invaded Rwanda in 1990 in response to reports of massacres against Tutsi. Negotiations with the RPF concluded in 1993, leading to a transitional government. The government of Rwanda never implemented it, and the last deadline was April 5, the day before the plane went down.

This area of Africa, known as The Great Lakes, is commonly seen as

## Second Failure: The Rwandan Genocide

a mess of ethnic hatred and hostility. Knowledgeable observers, however, point out that the ethnic hostility is manipulated for political purposes. The two groups, more accurately the Bahutu and Batutsi, have virtually identical cultures. They have intermarried and have extensive contact. Ethnic divisions exist, but as one expert put it, "A privileged clique of extremist military and political leaders is ruthlessly determined to block negotiated reforms that would loosen their exclusive grip on power. They have demonstrated time and time again ... that they are willing to kill members of their own ethnic group to achieve their naked political ends.... Rwanda's ruling party, the National Republican Movement for Democracy (MRND) and other extremist politicians have repeatedly stalled the implementation of last August's peace agreement" ("Genocidal Massacres in Rwanda Follow Invasion and Extremist Coup," *ISG Newsletter* [spring 1994], p. 6).

In Rwanda there was a group equivalent to the Ku Klux Klan or the Attachees in Haiti, the Coalition for the Defense of the Republic, which opposed the peace process and expressed anti-Tutsi propaganda. Hours after the presidential plane crash, members of the presidential guard, all Hutus, killed moderate government officials and leading opposition figures such as the acting prime minister, the president of the Constitutional Court, and so forth, even though many were also Hutus. In short, politically powerful extremists within the Hutu ethnic group were killing politically moderate Hutus.

The genocide in Rwanda was helped along by arms from the former Soviet Union, South Africa, Egypt and France. France had taken over the role as the primary supporter of the Hutus from Belgium since Belgium cut off lethal aid in 1990. Rwandan government ministers were being received in Paris even as the massacres continued.

As in Bosnia, the genocide did not begin without warning. Human Rights Watch warned about the possible massacres at least thirteen months before the genocide took place. The UN Human Rights Commission kept the report confidential because they had too many African countries on the public list of human rights violators, and they did not want to appear racist. There is no doubt that the international community failed to act as it did in Bosnia. Two recent reports make the magnitude of that inaction very explicit (Des Forges, 1999; Organization of African Unity, 2000).

After the massacres began, the Canadian commander of the UN observer force asked the secretary general to provide him with new rules of engagement so he could protect civilians. The request was rejected. Even though the Organization of African Unity (OAU) criticized the decision to withdraw UN troops no action was taken to stop the genocide. The African members of the Security Council did favor action, but the United States was opposed. As one observer noted, "Rwanda became the first application of President Clinton's admonition in an address to the United Nations on September 27, 1993, that the UN must learn 'when to say no.' In that speech, Clinton argued in a replay of his position on Bosnia, that the UN needed to ask 'hard questions' before sending peacekeeping forces to any additional sites, and it must recognize that it 'cannot become engaged in everyone of the world's conflicts' " (Leitenberg, 1994a, p. 37). The United States then agreed to a UN resolution authorizing the sending of force only after Secretary General Boutros Boutros-Ghali reported that the conditions established by the United States had been met. These were spelled out in Presidential Decision Directive 25 (PDD-25) issued in May 1994, which listed seven factors that the U.S. government would consider if required to vote on peace operations in the UN Security Council, six additional and more stringent factors to consider if the participation of U.S. forces was involved, and three final factors if the U.S. forces might be engaged in combat, sixteen considerations in all.

The reluctance to act was, as in Bosnia, a product of the U.S. experience in Vietnam and Somalia. In spite of this hesitation, the secretary general continued to try to raise a force to intervene, but was stymied and on May 25 announced his defeat because he failed to raise contributions of military force from the members of the UN. "During all these weeks, the US government had also instructed its spokesmen 'not to describe the deaths there [Rwanda] as genocide, even though some senior officials believe that is exactly what they represent' " (Leitenberg, 1994a, p. 38). On May 27 President Clinton met with the secretary general and said the United States would not commit forces, and on Memorial Day the president addressed the American public and stated: "we cannot dispatch our troops to solve every problem where our values are offended by human misery, and we should not." He said the very same thing in a second address at the Naval Academy: "We cannot solve every such outburst of civil strife or militant nationalism simply by sending in our forces" (p. 39).

Leaders of fourteen African states said the situation was a scandal and offered to send troops. The U.S. Department of Defense, however, even disputed the level of repayment it should receive from the UN for sending fifty armored personnel carriers. "In mid-June it was still demanding that it be reimbursed $15 million for the shipping costs to and from Rwanda, and for things such as spare parts. Estimates of those killed had by this time reached 500,000 to perhaps 800,000. The fifty U.S. vehicles did not arrive until mid-July" (ibid., p. 39).

A cholera epidemic now began to sweep through the area, and President Clinton asked for $320 million in emergency relief funds and on July 22 proposed sending 4,000 U.S. troops mainly to the refugee camps in Zaire. Britain, Australia and Canada committed small contingents for

## Second Failure: The Rwandan Genocide

a humanitarian assistance mission. This was all done four months after the troops and money might have prevented the disaster that had already occurred.

During all this Clinton maintained that any U.S. troops deployed to Rwanda would not engage in peacekeeping, and administration officials reinforced that view. Interviewed on MacNeil-Lehrer on July 27, and reported on NPR July 31, Secretary of Defense William Perry said that the United States had

> "unique capabilities" for airlift and logistics—but not for peacekeeping: "It would not be the best use of our forces." It was on this occasion that Perry also provided the US government estimate of four million Rwandan refugees. Four days later, while visiting the refugee camp in Goma, Perry explained that "The United States does not have combat forces here, therefore we are not providing peacekeeping" [National Public Radio, July 31, 1994].

Obviously, the combat forces were not there because they had not been ordered there by the president or by Secretary of Defense Perry. However, at the very moment that Perry was speaking, 2,000 first-line U.S. Marine and Army personnel had been ordered to fight forest fires in Washington State. "The armed forces of the United States, the world's most thoroughly equipped, trained and ready military force, was suddenly incapable of performing peacekeeping duties, and was only uniquely capable of logistics" (Leitenberg, 1994a, p. 40).

In September 1994 the Senate authorized $170 million of the $320 that President Clinton had requested. The Senate also wrote into the legislation "the provision that all U.S. forces had to be withdrawn from Rwanda by October 1 unless Congress specifically approved a longer stay."

The budget drawn up by the UN for its force was $100 million, but was not approved. U.S. responsibility would have been 30 percent of the total peacekeeping budget or about $30 million. As of November 7 the United States had spent

> $237 million in support of humanitarian assistance in the Rwandan emergency. That is roughly eight times more than its peacekeeping assessment would have been. In addition, had a peacekeeping mission been deployed, many or most of those killed might have been saved, and a massive refugee exodus possibly averted. Estimates are that emergency assistance to Rwanda by all OECD [Organization for Economic Co-operation and Development] states—the United States included—may exceed $1 billion for calendar year 1994. (Leitenberg, 1994a, p. 42)

Ambassador Stephen Lewis of Canada, a member of the panel investigating the genocide in Rwanda, concluded that the "role of the US government in blocking a more effective UN intervention force throughout the genocide was 'an almost incomprehensible scar of shame' on American foreign policy. 'The United States knew exactly what was going on,' he said" (UN Department of Public Information, 2000, p. 2). The report, as other analyses of the genocide, goes on to point out that an international military force would have been able to "deter the killers" (OAU, 2000, section 10.8). They quote General Romeo Dallaire, commander of the UN Assistance Mission to Rwanda, who noted that "The killing could have been prevented if there had been the international will to accept the costs of doing so" (ibid., p. 6). A report to the Carnegie Commission involving thirteen senior military leaders and prepared by Colonel Scott Feel of the U.S. Army concluded that, "A modern force of 5,000 troops . . . sent to Rwanda sometime between April 7 and April 21, 1994, could have significantly altered the outcome of the conflict . . . forces appropriately trained, equipped and commanded, and introduced in a timely manner, could have stemmed the violence in and around the capital, prevented its spread to the countryside, and created conditions conducive to the cessation of the civil war between the RPF and the RGF" [Rwandan Government Forces] (ibid., p. 9). Instead, the UN, led by Belgium and Britain and the United States, which refused to acknowledge that a full-fledged genocide was in fact taking place, reduced the number of troops to 270. The in-depth analysis of this report, along with the report by Human Rights Watch, provides more than ample justification to conclude that saving lives in Africa was a low priority.

In fact, some people argue that the Rwandan and Bosnian situations demonstrate the force of racism in foreign policymaking. Others argue that strategic interests were not involved. One might credibly ask whether the response would have been different if it were Christians in Bosnia who were being cleansed ethnically and if it had been whites in Rwanda who were being hacked to death? Whether the resistance to intervene to stop genocide was caused by racism, perceptions of strategic interests, or domestic politics, the fact remains that hundreds of thousands, perhaps millions, of lives could have been saved if the UN, led by the great powers, in particular the United States, had taken the initiative to use military force to separate the combatants and save those lives that had been lost. Yet, the remaining years of the twentieth century produced two additional crises (although there were in actuality many more, these were the two most directly involving the United States) that demonstrated in a rather rudimentary and hesitant way that some lessons had, in fact, been learned but that the United States remained a reluctant participant and an even more reluctant organizer in multilateral undertakings of humanitarian intervention.

# 6

# Lessons from the Late Twentieth and Early Twenty-First Centuries: Kosovo, Clinton and Bush

The blood hardly stopped flowing in Bosnia and Rwanda when the world was confronted with two crises that would test the resolve of political leaders to preserve human life and prevent genocide. Milosovic was once again on the move, this time in Kosovo, and the Indonesian government was continuing its massacres in East Timor. But the same reasons the world hesitated in Bosnia and Rwanda made interventions in these situations equally difficult, if not unlikely. In spite of the precedents, however, action was taken in both cases, and it is important to see precisely what occurred.

The violence in both Bosnia and Rwanda was explained away, if not justified, as the result of hundreds of years of "ethnic hatred," or, in the case of Rwanda, hundreds of years of "tribal hatred"—interesting, isn't it, that in African countries the hatred is tribal while in European countries it is ethnic. These oversimplified explanations allowed the rest of the world, and in particular the Western developed countries, to ignore the reality of politics in the twentieth century and provided a rationalization for their lack of response in the face of the continued slaughter of innocent people. For in both situations the violence was manipulated by political leaders to achieve certain goals related to power. These types of political games, played by many leaders throughout the ages, have had particularly deadly consequences for millions of innocent people.

It is in this fashion that the toll is magnified since memory of the past is reconstructed to write out of existence or change the record of past atrocities. It is much more convenient to create ideologies of denial and myths of intractable conflict than to take positive action to rectify the situation. Or, as we shall see in the case of the Clinton administration, to apologize for what you did not do and take credit for what you should have done even though you did not do what you claim.

If the violence in Rwanda was the result of a legacy of colonial domination and the manipulation of boundaries, and if the violence in Bosnia was the result of ambitious political leaders manipulating and reawakening ethnic hatred, then something could be done about those situations if those leaders fomenting the violence had been confronted by a system of multilateral institutions designed to stop the violence and to keep the peace. If, on the other hand, as our contemporary mythology would have us believe, these are the result of hundreds of years of ethnic or tribal hatred, nothing can be done and humanity is able to wash its collective hands and reassure itself that it bears no responsibility and no guilt. The context of the late twentieth century, then, was a context of extreme ethnonational violence in pursuit of political goals. This became even clearer as the century wound to a close and Milosovic set out once again to ethnically cleanse a province in the former Yugoslavia.

## Kosovo and NATO

Kosovo is a province in the former Yugoslavia. The majority of the population, 90 percent, is made up of ethnic Albanians, who until 1989 were granted a fair amount of autonomy within the former Yugoslavia. When Slobodan Milosovic took over, he removed the autonomy, bringing Kosovo under direct control of the Serbs. This move was strongly opposed by the Kosovar Albanians. While the fighting raged in Bosnia, Kosovo remained relatively quiet until 1998, when open conflict erupted between Serbian military police and a group known as the Kosovo Liberation Army. They wanted to unite Kosovo with Albania. Milosovic attempted to stop this move and sent Serbian police to prevent it from taking place. During 1998 around 1,500 Kosovar Albanians were killed and 400,000 people were forced from their homes.

The conflict soon turned into a "systematic program to ethnically cleanse the Serbian province of Kosovo of its roughly 1.7 million ethnic Albanian residents" (U.S. Department of State, 1999, p. 1). Since March 1998, Serb forces expelled over one million Kosovars from their homes and engaged in practices commonly associated with the definition of genocide found in the UN Convention on the Prevention and Punishment of the Crime of Genocide. These included summary executions; forcible rape; destruction of homes, villages, mosques and churches; looting and burning. The U.S. Department of State, as it did with Bosnia, issued a report (May 1999) that catalogued and defined the most egregious abuses of human rights.

This report notes that the term "ethnic cleansing" was first used in Bosnia-Hercegovina in 1992 and since then has become quite common. The report defines it as "the systematic and forced removal of the members of an ethnic group from a community or communities in order to change the ethnic composition of a given region. In Bosnia, many ethnically cleansed towns and regions were eventually re-occupied by members of another ethnic group" (U.S. Department of State, 1999, p. 1).

Cleansing began in Kosovo in February and March 1998, when the Serbian Ministry of Internal Affairs Police and paramilitary units attacked the villages of Likosane and Cirez. This resulted in the death of twenty-five Kosovar Albanians, some of whom were thought to have been summarily executed. The scope and pace of the Serbian efforts at ethnic cleansing increased in late March 1999. The UN High Commissioner for Refugees estimated that over 700,000 Kosovars were forced to flee from their homes. As in Bosnia, the United States documented the crimes involved in this forcible cleansing, including lurid details and descriptions. The abuses were divided into seven categories. The first, "Forced Expulsions," announced that

> Serbian forces appear to have driven the vast majority of Kosovars from their homes, trapping many within Kosovo, while pushing even larger numbers over Kosovo's borders. The Serbian authorities claim that the refugee crisis is the result of popular fear of NATO air strikes is belied by the regime's deployment of its military forces in the weeks prior to its rejection of the Rambouillet settlement. Refugees consistently report that they fled their homes not because of any concern of NATO air strikes, but because Serbian forces threatened them at gunpoint. (Ibid., p. 3)

The refugees escaped to Albania, Macedonia, Montenegro and Bosnia and Herzegovina, which placed these areas under extensive pressure as they had to deal with this sudden influx of refugees.

The second category of abuses of human rights documented by the U.S. Department of State involved "Looting and Burning" of more than 600 settlements, "including over 3000 villages burned since April 4" (ibid.). While Kosovar homes were being burned, Serb homes were left intact when Serb civilians painted a Cyrillic "S" on the door so that Serb forces would pass them by. Mosques and religious sites were also attacked, as were schools in at least fourteen villages and towns. At this point the report contained a list that was confirmed by photos taken from the air.

The third category is "Detention," which involves reports that Serbian forces separated military-aged men from their families and placed them in mass detention sites, such as a detention center at a former cement factory that was used to hold 5,000. There were other centers documented in the report. These, of course, are similar in nature to the camps set up by the Serbs in Bosnia and to the concentration camps made famous by the Nazis.

Four is "Summary Execution," of which refugees have provided accounts from at least seventy towns and villages. Executions were not only random, but reports indicated that "Serbian authorities appear[ed] to be targeting Kosovar intellectuals, professionals, and leaders" (ibid., p. 3).

Five is the category of human rights abuse first included as a crime against humanity during the Serb rampage through Bosnia and now included as a war crime, "Rape." Rapes of ethnic Albanian women were reported and gang rapes were included in many of the accounts. The report believes that "there may be many more incidents that have not been reported because of the cultural stigma attached to this offense in traditional Kosovar society" (ibid.).

Six is "Violations of Medical Neutrality," which means that Serbian forces attacked physicians, patients and Kosovar medical facilities. The Serbian forces killed, tortured and detained Albanian doctors and looted and destroyed clinics, health centers, pharmacies and other medical facilities run by Albanians; a list of facilities is included in the account.

Seven is "Identity Cleansing," which means the Serbs were taking documents that verified the identities of Albanians and, therefore, would not allow them to return to their homes and villages.

Generally speaking, the report documents a sad history of ethnic cleansing in Kosovo, which, even allowing for some possible overstatement for propaganda value to justify the NATO air strikes that were forthcoming, compiles a rather unforgiving account of Serb actions in Kosovo. Most notable is the list of atrocities and war crimes including the location and date on which they occurred.

The list runs nine pages and is only partial. Space precludes inclusion of all the accounts, but the flavor may be tasted by recounting two of the better known incidents. As narrated in the U.S. Department of State (1999) report:

> Serbian forces appear to have completed military operations in the city [of Pristina] and began expelling residents and internally displaced persons (IDPs) as of April 4. According to refugee reports, ethnic Albanians were forcibly expelled first from their homes and then from Pristina via train. Approximately 25,000 ethnic Albanians were sent by rail from Pristina to Macedonia on April 1, and over 200,000 reportedly were detained pending transport. According to refugee reports, most of these IDPs were without food, water, medicine, or shelter. Several refugees claim Serbian forces

used loudspeakers and distributed pamphlets to warn ethnic Albanians to leave town or be killed. A Kosovar claimed to have seen three truckloads of dead bodies accompanied by three or four armored vehicles in a graveyard in Pristina on April 2. (P. 4)

In the town of Suva Reka on March 25, Serbs reportedly killed at least thirty Kosovar Albanians by burning them alive in their homes and burned 60 percent of the buildings in the town. The entire ethnic Albanian population of the town was forced to leave as was the case in many other towns throughout Kosovo.

It was precisely these types of incidents and reports that finally led NATO to undertake counteraction against Serb forces that were attempting to cleanse Kosovo of ethnic Albanians. While the NATO action was clearly necessary it was not without controversy.

## NATO Air Strikes and the Role of the United States

As the Serb escalation continued the UN called for a cease fire in August 1998 and in September the Security Council voted in favor of a cease-fire resolution and warned the Yugoslav government that "additional measures" would be taken if it failed to comply. NATO began to take the first steps toward intervention. Heavy fighting continued and in October Western nationals were advised to leave Yugoslavia as NATO prepared for air strikes. U.S. envoy Richard Holbrooke engaged in diplomatic negotiations with Milosovic and Yugoslavia agreed to allow 2,000 troops as a monitoring force into Kosovo. This averted air strikes for a time, but in November and December more fighting occurred, and in January 1999 NATO sent two senior military officers to warn the Yugoslav authorities that air strikes were likely if they did not end the violence.

NATO was not intended in its original form to be a force to counter genocide or protect human rights. It was formed after the Second World War and the original purpose was to fight the Cold War against the former Soviet Union. It was not intended as a means to stop atrocities on a more limited scale. NATO was tested in Bosnia and, because it did not act to stop the massacre of an estimated 250,000 people, was thought to be on the decline. Kosovo received so much attention because of the precedent set by Milosovic in Bosnia as well as for the fact that the United States and other NATO members were worried that the conflict in Kosovo might spill over into neighboring countries such as Greece and Turkey. The fear was that they would join the conflict on opposite sides, and since both were members of NATO, this would have had a serious impact on the southeastern portion of the alliance. There was the additional worry that another serious violation of human rights occurring in the face of NATO inaction might spell doom for the alliance.

During the time of the ethnic cleansing in Kosovo the attention of the government, people and president of the United States had been elsewhere. Americans were diverted by the impeachment trial of the president. Milosovic appears to have taken advantage of the diversion by continuing attacks on Kosovo (Margolis, 1999, p. 2). When Clinton's attention was finally focused on Kosovo, NATO air strikes began in March 1999. There were several important points that need to be kept in mind to evaluate why they were initiated and what their impact turned out to be.

First, as early as October 1998, President Clinton ruled out the use of ground troops. National Security Advisor Sandy Berger stated that U.S. troops would be sent to Kosovo only if there was a peace agreement, and White House Press Secretary Joe Lockhart noted that "President Clinton ruled out the possibility of using U.S. ground troops in a combat situation in Kosovo" (McQuillan 1999, p. 1). Following the usual pattern, the Clinton administration vacillated on the deployment of American ground forces. After stating that none would be used, on February 4, 1999, U.S. Defense Secretary William Cohen said Washington might commit a "relatively small" contingent of U.S. ground forces, but only if a firm peace agreement was reached (CNN, 1999, p. 3). This reflected the debate going on within the corridors of the U.S. defense establishment, as some generals doubted that the use of air power would be sufficient to stop the ethnic cleansing. The *Washington Post* reported that U.S. military leaders doubted that air power alone would stop the massacres. They also "complained about what they saw as the lack of a long-term vision" and "questioned whether U.S. national interests" were involved (Graham, 1999, p. A1). The *Post* further reported that the generals wanted the administration to use economic sanctions and other "non-military levers to compel Belgrade to make peace in the rebellious Serbian province before resorting to air strikes" (ibid.). They did not think U.S. national interests were involved and they thought there was a lack of vision concerning a long-term solution for problems of the Balkans. The generals also challenged the administration view that the conflict would leak over to other areas, the "domino theory," which was being advocated by Secretary of State Albright. They agreed to go along unanimously with the air strikes even though the newspaper reported that "Twelve days after the bombing campaign, the military leaders remain doubtful that air strikes can satisfy the larger political objectives put forward by Clinton and other NATO leaders: stopping the violence in Kosovo and driving Yugoslav President Slobodan Milosovic back to the bargaining table" (ibid., p. A2). The generals also thought the American public was not adequately prepared to accept a prolonged operation, and they expressed frustration at the incremental nature of the bombing campaign, which they blamed on the "requirements of conducting war by consensus among all 19 NATO nations" (ibid.). Moreover, they were reluctant to recommend ground forces, since they thought this might escalate into an open-ended commitment of U.S. troops and stressed, at the same time, that if a decision were made to send ground forces, the force should be very large.

They apparently saw parallels between the view that the violence in Kosovo would escalate into the neighboring states as "uncomfortable echoes of the thinking that drew the United States into the ill-fated Vietnam War three decades ago" (ibid., p. A3). As I noted earlier in reference to Bosnia and Rwanda, the Vietnam syndrome remained very much alive and well, at least in the minds of the American military leaders. Yet, the military leaders did not dissent when they were given the NATO plan and they paid lip service to the notion that the operation could accomplish its stated objectives, which, by that time, had been limited. The narrowly construed objectives were "to degrade Serbian military capability to conduct repressive actions against ethnic Albanians in Kosovo" with no mention made of stopping the Serbian assault (ibid.). Yet, as the paper reported, "For all their skepticism about air power, the chiefs never gave serious consideration to sending in ground troops, at least not U.S. Troops" (ibid., p. 3).

President Clinton had been warned by CIA Director George J. Tenet that Serbian forces might accelerate their campaign of ethnic cleansing when the air strikes commenced, and U.S. military leaders pointed out that air power alone would "not be sufficient to stop it" (Graham, 1999, p. A1). NATO supreme commander, General Wesley K. Clark made the same statement in public, but Clinton and his senior White House advisers "pressed on with their planning for an air campaign" (ibid.). According to the *Washington Post*, "Clinton never believed he had a viable alternative. The use of NATO ground troops, never a likely option, was expressly ruled out by the White House in October, when NATO military analysts produced a study that concluded it would take as many as 200,000 NATO troops to protect Kosovo on the ground" (ibid., p. A2). The use of ground forces was killed, therefore, because of the high number. The Clinton administration seized upon this high number as a means to reject the use of ground forces, arguing that the "administration would have been defying public opinion both here and in other NATO countries, and criticized for risking a military quagmire" (ibid.). Given this perspective, the only alternative was air strikes, since not to act would have opened the administration to accusations of allowing another humanitarian disaster to occur.

Additional reports indicate that Clinton knew the use of air power might not stop the massacres so "his speech included another aim: 'if necessary, to seriously damage the Serbian military's capacity to harm the people of Kosovo and, possibly, all of Yugoslavia'" (ibid., p. A3). The U.S. military appeared to have given a mixed message with some arguing for the use of ground forces, but most apparently against it. Clearly, the Clinton administration was unwilling to take a vigorous leadership role to prepare the population of the United States and NATO for the use of ground forces. Taking the middle, some might say easy, way out, they decided to use air power and forego the use of ground forces.

This is an all too common form of policy making. Officials create a form of self-fulfilling prophecy by outlining options in such a fashion as to eliminate all but the one they wish to pursue, in this case stating that the use of ground forces would go against public opinion on the one hand, and on the other noting that some action must be taken. Therefore, they are left with only one possible course of action—the one they wished to pursue in the first place. Excuses replace leadership as a middle course is pursued and results end up equally inconclusive.

When the air strikes commenced, they were supported by many Asian and European leaders, but Indonesia, Russia, China and India called for an immediate halt. Most importantly, Russian president Boris Yeltsin stopped his country's cooperation with NATO and called an emergency meeting of the U.N. Security Council. Leaders of the European Union called on Milosovic to stop the violence, which would stop the air strikes, while anti-NATO protesters demonstrated in front of British Prime Minister Tony Blair's residence. During the controversy the air strikes continued and U.S. spokesmen denied that ground forces would be used. In fact, Pentagon spokesman Ken Bacon said that "ground forces would be introduced into Yugoslavia only as peacekeepers after an accord was in place" (AP, March 30, 1999). The NATO operation moved on to what they referred to as the "second phase," which included the targeting of tanks, artillery and other heavy weapons, transport vehicles and mobile command centers. They also attacked "a number of special police and army barracks in and around Kosovo and are targeting staging areas used by the Yugoslav government forces" (ibid.). In spite of the claims, experts continued to note that the bloodshed on the ground could only be stopped by the use of ground forces.

During this period refugees gave accounts of continued mass killings, which, at the time, could not be verified, since foreign journalists had been expelled from Kosovo. Britain's defense secretary also accused Milosovic of recruiting two men suspected of war crimes in Bosnia and Croatia to assist in the oppression of the ethnic Albanians—General Ratko Mladic and Zeljiko Raznatovic, also known as Arkan. In the summer of 2001, this was confirmed when witnesses began to come forward to tell their stories after Milosovich had been turned over to the International Criminal Tribunal for the Former Yugoslavia meeting at The Hague.

The NATO air campaign was viewed as decisive by some observers, but others criticized it as desultory. One observer noted that "It took NATO's massive air campaign a full 16 days to deliver the same number of strikes as did the U.S. on a single day of the Gulf War against Iraq. Only 15% of aircraft launched carry war loads; the rest fly support" (Margolis, 1999, p. 1). He went on to note, "If NATO can't defeat 7 million Serbs, what can it do?" (ibid.). Amidst debates over whether the bombing was effective in reducing the massacres on the ground, and amidst controversy over the targets hit and missed, and amidst the controversy over the use of expensive high tech weapons and high-flying aircraft to minimize NATO losses, finally in early May, Russia and NATO agreed to a strategy for peace in Kosovo. This came after forty-three days of bombing. The draft of the peace plan called for deployment of an international force in Kosovo. Milosovic maintained he would only accept an unarmed force. NATO also demanded the withdrawal of all Serb troops. Finally, on June 10, 1999, after seventy-seven days of bombing, NATO stopped the air campaign. On June 10, the UN Security Council passed a resolution that welcomed Yugoslavia's acceptance of the agreement, including withdrawal of its military, police and paramilitary forces. The resolution passed the Security Council by a vote of fourteen in favor and one abstention (China). The Security Council then announced it would deploy an international civil and security force to Kosovo under the direction of the UN. The force was known as KFOR, short for Kosovo Protection Corps.

KFOR officially came into existence on September 21, 1999, and was to undertake the following:

> Provide a disaster response capability, including for major fires and industrial accidents or spills.
>
> Conduct search and rescue.
>
> Provide humanitarian assistance in isolated areas.
>
> Contribute to rebuilding infrastructure and communities.

KFOR was not to have a role in "defense, law enforcement, riot control, internal security or any other task involved in the maintenance of law and order" (KFOR Online, 1999).

As of this writing, KFOR remains in Kosovo. While the debate continues over whether the NATO intervention was successful in saving lives, the defeat of Milosovic in the October elections, his apparent loss of power and his extradition to the International Criminal Tribunal for the Former Yugoslavia (ICTY) are probably attributable to the actions taken to place the Serbian state and its dictator in the position of a pariah among nations. Whether the intervention could have been handled in a different, and perhaps more strategically successful, fashion to save more lives is a different question.

Timothy Garton Ash in *The New York Review of Books* (2000b) pointed out that an in-depth evaluation of this type of operation was difficult, since most of the official records remained secret. In retrospect, however, it is very clear that the conflict in Kosovo involved both violations of human rights and a "struggle between two peoples for control of the same piece of land" (p. 52). As Ash notes, "most violations of human rights have political causes," and this was no exception (ibid.). In fact, of course, as in Bosnia, NATO and the United States, as Ash notes, "huffed and it puffed" as it gave one after another "last warning" to Milosovic. As he continued to drive Kosovars from their homes and to destroy villages the Clinton administration and NATO hesitated. Clinton was diverted by the Monica Lewinsky affair. When Richard Holbrooke was sent to negotiate with Milosovic in October 1998, he was instructed "not even to suggest putting U.S. troops on the ground in Kosovo" (p. 53). Milosovic was recalcitrant and the ethnic cleansing of Kosovo resulted, in the winter of 1998–1999, in 300,000 homeless. Whatever finally moved the United States and NATO to intervene they did so, and the operation itself raised questions concerning the credibility of the alliance.

In the beginning of the war NATO foundered, and Ash raises the question of why the "most powerful military alliance in history, with member states representing some two thirds of the worlds economic and military strength, with four million men and women under arms, and combined defense spending of around $450 billion, seemed to be losing to a small impoverished Balkan country with a defense budget of scarcely $1.5 billion and about 110,000 active-duty soldiers" (p. 53). He answers his own question by noting that NATO misjudged Milosovic, believing that he would give in sooner than he did and not anticipating the escalation of the ethnic cleansing, in particular, the "speed, scale and brutality of the mass expulsions" (ibid.). The rhetoric held that the war would be short, and there was fear of alienating what Ash calls the "two big Cs: the US Congress and the Coalition" (ibid.). The Greek, Italian and German allies would not support the effort if they were told that the war would be long and Congress had been particularly adverse to U.S. interventions. The problem of making war by coalition and Congress became readily apparent when the NATO bombing started on March 24. Incorrect targets were chosen and intelligence underestimated the extent to which Milosovic would speed up the mass expulsions. Generally speaking, as Ash notes, there was a failure of Western political intelligence, with both a large and a small I: astonishingly, the Defense Intelligence Agency did not even include Kosovo in its February 1999 survey of world trouble spots. The CIA's signal contribution was to suggest the Chinese embassy as a bombing target believing it to be the headquarters of Yugoslavia's Federal Directorate of Supply and Procurement. For the small i: Western leaders, trying to prevent 'another Bosnia,' learned a wrong lesson from Bosnia. They thought Milosovic had been bombed into accepting the Dayton agreement in 1995. They forgot that it had first required a large ground offensive by Croatian troops. (P. 58)

Additional errors included the suggestion, caused by the American "obsession with achieving 'zero casualties,' that high altitude bombing could stop ethnic cleansing on the ground. If one of President Clinton's goals was to "deter an even bloodier offensive against innocent civilians in Kosovo" (ibid.), the bombing campaign had the opposite effect. Actually, Ash thinks there were two bombing campaigns: one aimed at "preventing Serbian forces in Kosovo from doing further harm to the Albanians, and the strategic one, aimed at Serbia proper. NATO won the second, but lost the first" (ibid.).

NATO claimed that it inflicted huge damage on the Serbian forces alleging that it destroyed 120 Serbian tanks, 220 armored personnel carriers and 450 artillery and mortar pieces. Ash, quoting what he calls a "suppressed US Air Force report" notes that "NATO verifiably destroyed just fourteen tanks, eighteen armored personnel carriers, and twenty artillery pieces" (ibid.). Even if the larger numbers were accurate, the problem was that there was an increase in ethnic cleansing during the bombing. Ethnic cleansing is a low tech operation carried out with machetes, hoes or cigarette lighters to burn houses, and you cannot eliminate these by high altitude bombing.

This failure is the reason that administration spin doctors descended on the media like a plague of locusts after the conclusion of the Kosovo bombing and the agreement between NATO and Milosovic. The buzz was louder than the insects and the message was self-serving and self-congratulatory.

On May 10, in a televised speech, President Clinton celebrated the achievement of "victory for a safer world." Noting that the aggression of the Serbs had been "turned back," and that the Serbs should rise up against Milosovic or "we will provide no support for reconstruction of Serbia," he added that "we are ready to provide humanitarian aid." The president was shameless. He could glibly fabricate on virtually any subject and turn any action to self-serving purposes even if that action was less than successful.

In this case it is worth considering what NATO action in Kosovo wrought. It did not establish a precedent, which would mean that the world was prepared to respond to atrocity, because atrocities and violation of human rights were ongoing in particular in Africa. What, therefore, sort of "victory" had been achieved? Did NATO stop the cleansing? Did they preserve the living places of the Kosovar Albanians? About the only long-range positive impact has been the defeat of Milosovic. Even this, however, does not mean Yugoslavia will be a more democratic society with a stronger, less violent civic culture? Answered in the negative, these questions raise considerations beyond the immediate concern for Kosovo and have grave implications for any doctrine of humanitarian intervention. They point to the outrageous fact that the lives of people in far-off places are fair game for rhetorical manipulations to make the policy pursued by the United States appear successful and humanitarian even when they were not successful and not undertaken for humanitarian reasons. Ignored were basic questions concerning the direction of American foreign policy and what direction that policy would take when confronted by new examples of genocide.

## The Short, Unhappy Life of Humanitarian Intervention Under the Clinton Administration

As the bombs finished falling on Kosovo, Bill Clinton proclaimed his unflagging support for humanitarian intervention. He told NATO troops in Macedonia: "Never forget if we can do this here . . . we can then say to the people of the world, whether you live in Africa, or Central Europe or any other place: if somebody comes after innocent civilians and tries to kill them en masse because of their race, their ethnic background or their religion, and it's within our power to stop it, we will stop it" (Truehart, 1999, p. B4). Two and one-half months later, when the people of East Timor were being slaughtered for voting overwhelmingly for their independence, he changed his tune. In East Timor the United States decided that the human rights violations were outside their sphere of interest and, consequently, encouraged the Australian government to lead an intervention, which was authorized by the United Nations and requested by the Indonesian government.

While the United States issued rhetorical warnings, the main U.S. priority was to maintain good relations with the Indonesian government. Indonesia is a mineral rich nation of 230 million people strategically located. There exists a long-time relationship between the U.S. military and the Indonesian military that goes back to the Cold War, when Indonesia was viewed as a strong anti-Communist ally. In fact, the United States reportedly had no intention of pushing the Indonesian government to stop the massacres. Samuel Berger, President Clinton's national security advisor said, "Because we bombed in Kosovo doesn't mean we should bomb Dili" (Becker and Shenon, 1999 p. 3). He went on to note: "Indonesia is the fourth-largest country in the world. It is undergoing a fragile but tremendously important political and economic transformation, which the United States strongly supports. The resolution of this crisis matters not just for East Timor but for Indonesia as a whole" (p. 4). American corporations also have large investments in Indonesia and were reluctant to jeopardize them by any intervention. Arguments against U.S. intervention in East Timor in particular and against participation in humanitarian intervention in general, went even further as additional objections were raised. For example, Ronald Steel argued that the reason the United States intervened in Kosovo was because of the tottering nature of the NATO alliance. The Kosovo intervention was "meant to prove that NATO was still relevant in post–Soviet Europe" (Steel, 1999, p. 1). This does not apply outside of Europe, Steel argues, which implies that humanitarian intervention is not only the exception rather than the rule but appears to be reserved for Western or European locations. Steel does argue that it will occur "where it can be done relatively cheaply, against a weak nation, in an area both accessible and strategic, where the public's emotions are aroused, and where it does not get in the way of other political, economic or military needs" (p. 2). However regrettable this may be morally, the practical dimension remains dominant. As nations deteriorate and others seek self-determination, which may result in repression and human rights violations, Steel notes that "People have the right to seek their own independent state. But others will come to their defense only where they believe their own self-interest is involved. That is where the line is being drawn today in East Timor and, we might add, elsewhere" (p. 2). This was the very foundation of U.S. policy.

Indeed, Steel is correct; this was the very foundation of U.S. foreign policy under the Clinton administration, and it had tragic consequences in Bosnia, Rwanda, Kosovo, Sierra Leone and, if truth be told, East Timor. What is most relevant here is the rhetoric of the United States as it observed the continuing violations of human rights throughout the world.

Not only did the president and his advisors insist that the United States could not be the "world's policeman," but the president himself went to the UN and reneged on his promise to support humanitarian intervention if and when innocent civilians were being slaughtered because of race, ethnicity or religion. He proclaimed in his annual address to the General Assembly that there were "limits to what the United States can do to counter violence in a world where more than two dozen ethnic or regional conflicts continue to aflict civilians and combatants alike" ("Clinton Defends," 1999, p. A4). The president went on to note: "I know that some are troubled that the United States and others cannot respond to every humanitarian catastrophe in the world. We cannot do everything" (ibid.). Then he made the death of humanitarian intervention official, after eleven weeks of life, by invoking the "never again" phraseology of the aftermath of the Holocaust in a negative fashion when he proclaimed: "It is easy to say 'Never again,' but much harder to make it so" (ibid.). We should not, he noted, promise "too much," because this "can be as cruel as caring too little" (ibid.).

The president, interestingly, neglected to talk about "doing" as opposed to "saying" and "caring." It is, of course, in the "doing" that the reality of policy becomes apparent. Clichés such as not being the "world's policeman" are simply masks to divert attention from the reality of what is actually being done, and what action is not being taken. Of course, no country can be the "world's policeman," but the United States, and others, could, if the will were present, take the initiative to strengthen the preventive mechanisms available to the UN. Such initiatives appear to be far removed from consideration.

One might say that the Clinton administration's support for humanitarian intervention died before it was tested. Or, alternatively, the first crucial test dealt a killing blow to the rhetorical assurance of a president who hesitated to stop the massacres in Bosnia, who forbade the use of the term genocide in discussions of Rwanda and who countenanced only minimal intervention to save lives in Kosovo by eschewing the use of ground troops, which was the only possible way to save Kosovar lives.

Humanitarian intervention in the Clinton administration died a quick and painful death. Hypocrisy became the watchword, the very motto, of President Clinton and his advisors. The rhetorical excesses continued throughout the last years of the Clinton administration, as administration spokespersons organized to attempt to create the impression that the Clinton foreign policy toward human rights violations had been one of success and had set important precedents that would now result in defending human rights throughout the world. But this is questionable.

The Clinton foreign policy has been called by one observer a policy of "underachievement and squandered potential" (Haas, 2000, p. 136). Clinton, he argues, took office in a situation in which the United States had unprecedented advantages and opportunities and did little with it. In fact, he thinks that the "measure of Clinton's tenure is less what he said and did than what he failed to say and failed to do" (ibid.). This means the Clinton era was marked by symbolism as opposed to substance with a foreign policy, actually with all policy, emphasizing "short-term crisis management over long term strategizing" (p. 137). This is, of course, characteristic of most administrations at whatever level. The idea of managing crisis until one's successor takes office is not unusual. So if one does examine the Clinton foreign policy the achievements are meager and the failures many.

Achievements included the North American Free Trade Agreement (NAFTA), the World Trade Organization (WTO), an arms control agreement that ensured that the Ukraine, Belarus and Kazakhstan gave up nuclear weapons to Russia, persuading the Senate to ratify the Chemical Weapons Convention and the negotiations with North Korea, Northern Ireland and in the Middle East (ibid., p. 137). Some of these failures were discussed above, including Somalia, Bosnia and Rwanda. The Clinton administration never successfully explained the basis for the policy it pursued and never made clear why, for example, they stayed out of Rwanda and allowed the massacres to take place but intervened in Haiti. Also never clearly articulated were reasons for lack of action in Bosnia and East Timor and why they decided to intervene in Kosovo as they did. As Haas summarizes Clinton's foreign policy legacy, "Clinton may not leave a legacy in foreign affairs, but what he will leave is a void: no clear priorities, no consistency or thoroughness in the implementation of strategies, and no true commitment to building a domestic consensus in support of internationalism" (ibid., p. 139).

During the 1990s the United States, along with the so-called "international community" failed miserably to deal with numerous human rights crises, including the genocide against the Tutsis in Rwanda, the ethnic cleansing of the Bosnian Muslims by the Serbs in the former Yugoslavia, the use of famine as a form of war in the Sudan, the slaughter of civilians in Algeria, Russian repression of Chechnya's independence, the civil wars in Liberia, Somalia and Burundi and the terror imposed on Sierra Leone and by the rebels and the Taliban in Afghanistan. U.S. policy, as Douglas Lute notes (1998), "lacked leadership, had no comprehensive plan, focused too much on military resources, and failed to anticipate or develop a follow-on strategy to cope with longer-term issues" (p. 21). These criticisms lead to suggestions to make sure such errors do not occur in the future. Basically, many observers agree, noting that without coordinated leadership and a well-prepared contingency plan, errors of the past are likely to be repeated.

With the election of George W. Bush as president in 2000, the question is, will the new Bush administration do any better?

When he first took office, President Bush appeared to have even less inclination to support multilateral action to save human life than the previous administration. All that was changed dramatically when, on September 11, 2001, terrorists hijacked four U.S. airliners and directed two into the World Trade Center in New York City and one into the Pentagon, with the fourth crashing in a field in Pennsylvania. The tragic events presented the new administration with an opportunity to divert the attention of the American public and the world from the continuing resistance to participate in international initiatives to preserve life and focused attention on a new initiative which they called the "war on terrorism." All other international commitments became secondary to this effort, and the previous recalcitrance and isolationism of the new administration appeared to have been forgotten as they set about organizing an international coalition to fight terrorism. But this coalition was formed, as the previous coalitions to fight the Persian Gulf War and to support action against the former Yugoslavia during the Kosovo intervention, to support U.S. interests and to fight wars in which the Untied States was directly involved. In spite of the appearance that the United States was supporting human rights and was more willing to participate in multilateral operations, the war on terrorism has little or no relationship to any overall policy to guarantee human rights to peoples around the globe. A brief review of the Bush administration's actions prior to September 11, 2001, will clearly illustrate why this is the case.

## George W. Bush and the Prevention of Genocide

John Heidenrich (2001), who is at least somewhat sympathetic to the new administration, notes that President George W. Bush had been hesitant to declare U.S. participation in multinational efforts to prevent genocide. He quotes Bush as stating, "We should not send our troops to stop 'ethnic cleansing' and genocide in nations outside our strategic interest" (p. xiii). However, he evades the main point of U.S. participation in and support for such efforts by then stating that "Such a policy is not necessarily unreasonable since U.S. troops should not be sent everywhere and anywhere to fight every injustice and right every wrong." This expression is very similar to that just noted by the Clinton administration after Kosovo and suffers from the same weakness. Supporters of action to prevent genocide have never argued that the United States must right every wrong or stop every injustice. As we shall see in the next section, there are specific policies that may be pursued that render this observation moot. He then corrects this misapprehension by noting that the problem "remains that a hesitance to intervene with U.S. troops must not become an excuse to, in effect, do nothing—if only because, when left to fester, today's problems of 'nonstrategic' human security too often become tomorrow's much larger problems of national security. To preclude such crises, the United States needs to promote early constructive efforts to prevent genocide" (p. xiii).

As I have repeatedly noted, the problem remains that the reality of U.S. policy does not measure up to the rhetoric of either scholars or others who make such pronouncements. The problem that this book attempts to confront is how to change that rhetoric into realistic policy of preventing genocide. This was clearly not the policy followed by the Bush administration prior to September 11.

The fact that U.S. policy, under the influence of the Bush administration, has not moved in this direction is clear from an examination of some of the foreign policy endeavors undertaken by that administration. For example, during the month of July 2001, a UN conference on small arms met to attempt to cut down on the more than 500 million estimated small arms in the world. Estimates held that more than half of these have been acquired illegally through arms dealers who maintain a profitable trade in peddling small arms. These arms fuel many of the conflicts around the globe, including many of the genocides discussed above. The conference proposed marking weapons so they could be traced, prohibiting arms designed for military use from private ownership and measures that would control the illegal sale of arms but would not effect the legal trade and manufacture of such weapons.

The UN defines small arms as "revolvers and self-loading pistols, rifles, sub-machine guns, assault rifles, light machine-guns, heavy machine-guns, mortars, hand grenades, grenade launchers, portable anti-aircraft and anti-tank guns and portable missile launchers" (Reuters, 2001, p. 2). It does not include hunting rifles or pistols. The UN defined the problem as the vast supply of small arms that are very inexpensive to purchase.

The United States opposed any regulation, because the Bush administration argued that such regulation infringes on the right of U.S. citizens to own guns. The opposition was led by Representative Bob Barr, a Georgia Republican, and the National Rifle Association (Leopold, 2001c). The fact that the National Rifle Association could exercise such profound influence on an international agreement that might cut down on the flow of small arms to those wishing to use them to commit genocide indicates how difficult it will be to convince political leaders to participate in multilateral initiatives to save life in the absence of any direct perception of U.S. interest, or more accurately, a perception of a direct threat to the property or commercial interests of the United States. Large and well-funded groups with a constituency base of active supporters exercises an undue amount of influence on policy decisions. Unfortunately, there is no such organization devoted to the prevention of genocide.

Other episodes where the Bush administration has balked at participation in multilateral agreements and attempted to pursue a direction at odds with the majority of the world nations include U.S. rejection of an accord to the Geneva-based negotiations to develop a "protocol" that would allow inspections to help enforce the 1972 Biological Weapons Convention, which was designed to stop the proliferation of germ weapons and which outlaws biological arms. The United States participated for six years in the Geneva negotiations that were oriented toward making cheating more difficult. The protocol allows inspections that, the *Washington Post* points out, "could be conducted at any suspect facility by a newly created international body, and would provide a channel for the United States to pursue compliance concerns with problem states. It also envisions regular, benign, 'visits' to monitor bio-defense and industry facilities declared by States" (Brugger, 2001, p. 7). The Bush administration, however, opposed the protocol because it claims it "would not likely detect cheating" and would "harm U.S. bio-defense efforts and leave U.S. industry vulnerable to espionage and undermine U.S. export controls" (ibid.).

The *Washington Post* pointed out that the treaty was designed not to help detect cheating but to deter states from deploying these types of weapons and to make it harder for cheating to occur. The claim that the protocol would be a threat to U.S. bio-defense programs and industry is questionable, since it actually "provides more protection for U.S. industry and defense effort than a treaty banning chemical weapons which, the United States has already joined and which covers some of the same facilities as the protocol" (ibid.). Once again this stance reflects the apparent trend toward unilateralism on the part of U.S. foreign policymakers during the Bush administration.

The apparent unilateralism, or perhaps isolationism, the tendency to do whatever it wants no matter what policy the rest of the world wishes to pursue, has caused an image problem for the United States, which, while it may not be congruent with reality, does exist in the minds, in particular, of Europeans who view the United States as wishing to go its own way. Moreover, the problems are further aggravated by additional differences such as those over the death penalty, the image of an American society "plagued by guns and violence, gorging on genetically modified 'Frankenfoods,' and beholden to unchecked capitalism" (Blinken, 2001, p. 35). These images are further aggravated by the Bush administration's position on the Comprehensive Test Ban Treaty, pursuit of national missile defense, reluctance to join in the global land-mines ban, refusal to ratify the international criminal court, the attempt to pullout of the Kyoto Protocol on global warming and the apparent U.S. fixation on so-called "rogue" nations such as Iraq. All of this gives the outward appearance of "selfish unilateralism" (p. 36).

Of course, to any observer who has followed the direction of United States foreign policy during the Clinton and Bush administrations closely this should have come as no surprise. It was, in fact, clearly signaled during the presidential election campaign of 2000, when soon-to-be National Security Advisor Condoleezza Rice made very clear the new administration's priorities. In an article in *Foreign Affairs* (Rice, 2000) she made clear that national interest would not be replaced by humanitarian interests (p. 47). She tried to make it appear as though the United States would not abandon humanitarian concerns when she later noted that this "does not mean that the United States must ignore humanitarian and civil conflicts around the world. But the military cannot be involved everywhere. Often, these tasks might be better carried out by regional actors, as modeled by the Australian-led intervention in East Timor" (p. 53). This is the same bogus argument referred to earlier. Since no observer of any intelligence has argued that the United States should intervene "everywhere," the basic argument is for an essentially narrow interpretation of U.S. interests. And this has come to pass as the Bush administration proceeded to attempt to form a foreign policy in line with these and the other restrictions outlined by the new Secretary of State Colin Powell.

The problem for the Bush administration has been that there appears to be a conflict between Powell, who is slightly more internationally oriented, and National Security Advisor Condoleezza Rice and Vice President Dick Cheney, who, along with Secretary of Defense Donald Rumsfeld, are more prone to unilateralism. In fact, President Bush appears to be moving away from the minimum internationalism of the Clinton administration. The Bush administration appeared, prior to September 11, 2001, to be almost contemptuous of international cooperation. The *New York Times* (July 29, 2001) pointed out that the "administration's record in this regard is dismal" (p. 1). Even before taking office, the administration declared it would not seek Senate ratification of the treaty creating the international Criminal Court. Not many months later they announced they were withdrawing from the Kyoto Protocol on global warming. In May, Bush said he was "ready to set aside the constraints of the Antiballistic Missile Treaty in order to test and build missile defenses" (ibid.). If this were not sufficient, the assault on international agreements continued during the summer of 2001 as the administration insisted on weakening a UN agreement to reduce the illegal traffic in small arms and pulled out of efforts to negotiate enforcement provisions for the convention banning biological weapons. They have also put off Senate ratification of the 1996 nuclear test ban treaty and the 1993 nuclear weapons reduction treaty with Russia.

And during August and September the United States withdrew from the UN Conference on Racism that was held in Durban, South Africa, because it did not agree with the language in resolutions condemning Israel or asking for an apology and reparations from countries benefitting from slavery.

Instead of attempting to strengthen these or to fix the problems, the Bush administration does not participate. This negative approach has harmed international efforts since the United States is a key participant in most of these efforts. This also has a negative impact on U.S. influence and prestige and the manner in which the United States is viewed by the rest of the world.

This is a self-defeating strategy, since the United States will no longer be looked to for moral leadership in the international sphere and because it appears as though the United States has no interest in other countries' issues. While these are all significant issues I want to take those most directly related to the prevention of genocide and examine them in greater detail—In particular the battle over ratification of the international criminal court.

## International Criminal Court

It is common among genocide scholars to point out the danger to the human person in the last century and equally shocking to point out how few killers have been punished or held accountable for their acts. Michael Scharf (1997) notes, for example, that "During the Twentieth Century, four times as many civilians have been victims of war crimes and crimes against humanity than the number of soldiers killed in all the international wars combined" (p. xiii). As for accountability he notes, quoting Jose Anala Lasa, "A person stands a better chance of being tried and judged for killing one human being than for killing 100,000" (p. xiv).

Most scholars agree with the idea that there are four or five ways to deal with past transgressions of a nation-state or group: forgetting, trials, truth commissions, history lessons or purges of those responsible. Punishment by a duly established court is rapidly becoming, along with truth commissions, the most agreed upon. The goal of any attempt to deal with past crimes against humanity is always said to be to make sure that these are not repeated. Punishment is supposedly the best guarantee. In actuality, the best guarantee, as Jason Epstein (1999) has eloquently noted, is most likely fear. History appears to have demonstrated, at least to him, that "human beings submit to reason only after they have submitted to fear. Only when all of us learn to fear our violent nature will we be safe from one another" (p. 64). Fear provides protection when those who attempt to commit any of the acts joined together under the rubric of crimes against humanity, war crimes and gross violations of human rights or genocide, know that they will be apprehended and punished. For this to be effective, the pursuit of the perpetrators will be dogged and unrelenting, and there should be mechanisms to prevent their escape. Fear and guilt reinforced by institutions with the power to implement them are the hopes for the future. Truth commissions, which are the next most popular, are less effective if they do not include punishment. If punishment is not part of the recounting of the past, it is unlikely that there will be any deterrent value. Truth commissions have been tried or talked about in diverse locations such as Guatemala, Burundi, Indonesia, Kenya, Mexico, Peru, Nigeria, Ghana, Indonesia, East Timor, Sierra Leone, Argentina and, of course, South Africa. In some cases it was suggested that the commissions would establish truth and be followed by trials that would ensure justice. Generally, the trials do not follow.

The International Criminal Court would cover all the missing holes by providing an institution to try and punish those accused of the crimes we have been discussing. The court is based on the assumption that ending the lack of punishment, or creating an institution to punish genocide, would deter its commission. Even if the court is able to accomplish a small part of this agenda, it is worthwhile, but there are obstacles often not discussed. As identified by David Wippman (2000), these include:

First, the problems with the definition genocide in the UN Convention which narrow the crime to such an extent that it limits the applicability.

Second, problems of enforcement, including who is to capture and try perpetrators of genocide.

Third, the ability of a court to deter criminal behavior is not necessarily established. The ICTY was in operation during the ethnic cleansing in Kosovo but did not deter Milosovic. Moreover, data from domestic criminal courts indicates that the presence of a system of punishments, including the death penalty in the United States, is not necessarily a deterrent to homicide. Consequently, as Wippman notes, "even the best treaty that might have emerged from the Rome negotiations would not likely have had as much of an impact on the incidence of genocide as advocates have suggested, though it could have reinforced applicable norms and created an institution better suited to the prosecution of genocide and related crimes than any existing international institution" (p. 87).

As all treaties, this one reflects political compromises designed to gather the largest number of supporting votes. The treaty was adopted by a vote of 120–27 with 21 abstentions. Important debates raged over the jurisdiction the International Criminal Court would be granted. Some wanted a form of automatic jurisdiction over what they viewed as the core crimes of "genocide, crimes against humanity and, war crimes, so that all treaty parties would be subject to the Court's jurisdiction over those crimes without any need for further state consent" (Wippman, 2000, p. 87). This was supported by nongovernmental organization (NGOs) which also supported a form of "universal jurisdiction," which means that the court could prosecute these crimes no matter where they had been committed. "Nongovernmental organizations strongly opposed any provision that would require either UN Security Council approval for prosecutions or the consent of particular states, such as the state of nationality of the accused. Further, NGOs vigorously supported an independent, self-initiating prosecutor able to commence prosecutions on his or her own authority (including on the basis of information supplied by NGOs), without having to rely on referrals by individual states or by the Security Council" (p. 93).

The debate over universal jurisdiction is illustrative of the U.S. position. Ironically, Henry Kissinger is one of the leading opponents of universal jurisdiction, which is ironic because he is thought to be one of the individuals likely to be arrested and held for trial as a result of his policies while he was secretary of state during the Nixon-Ford administration (Hitchens, 2000). Kissinger's arguments are essentially the old justifications for the continued preeminence of sovereignty over human rights enforcement. Kissinger argues that the concept of universal jurisdiction has "not been subjected to systematic debate, partly because of the intimidating passion of its advocates" (Kissinger, 2001, p. 86). He further argues that there is a "danger" in "pushing the effort to extremes that risk substituting the tyranny of judges for that of governments; historically, the dictatorship of the virtuous has often led to inquisitions and even witch hunts" (ibid.). Kissinger is particularly worried about allowing "national prosecutors to bring offenders into their jurisdictions through extradition from third countries" (ibid.). His second concern is over the International Criminal Court. Kissinger is trying to argue that the concept of universal jurisdiction has weak precedents in international law, being of "recent vintage" (ibid., p. 87). He argues that this is a dangerous precedent that is being pursued primarily by the "parties of the European left" (ibid., p. 88) and, while it is important to bring violators of human rights to accountability, it must be controlled by a "system of checks and balances that includes other elements critical to the survival and expansion of democracy" (ibid., p. 91). He further thinks prosecutors are allowed too much discretion, and because of these weaknesses the United States should "go no further toward a more formal system than one containing the following three provisions" (ibid., p. 95). First, it should be the responsibility of the UN Security Council to create a

> Human Rights Commission or a special committee to report whenever systematic human rights violations seem to warrant judicial action. Second, when the government under which the alleged crime occurred is not authentically representative, or when the domestic judicial system is incapable of sitting in judgment on the crime, the Security Council would set up an ad hoc international tribunal on the model of those of the former Yugoslavia or Rwanda. And third, the procedures for these international tribunals, as well as the scope of the prosecution, should be precisely defined by the Security Council, and the accused should be entitled to the due process safeguards accorded in common jurisdictions. (Ibid., pp. 95–96)

It is immediately apparent that Kissinger intends to lodge primary responsibility in the hands of the UN Security Council, which means that sovereignty remains the primary stumbling block in the path of human rights enforcement. His proposals would ensure that nothing would be accomplished if, for example, Kissinger himself were to be apprehended and indicted, since the United States or one of the other major powers would be able to use its veto in the Security Council to stymy any action. In short, enforcement of human rights and anti-genocide laws would be directed only at those non–great powers without a veto in the Security Council. In addition, Kenneth Roth (2001) points out that Kissinger's objections are "little better than a return to impunity" (p. 150). He notes that Kissinger ignores specific precedents, including the capture and trial of Adolf Eichmann by Israel in 1961, and notes that "the exercise by U.S. courts of jurisdiction over certain heinous crimes committed overseas is an accepted part of American jurisprudence, reflected in treaties on terrorism and aircraft hijacking dating from 1970" (ibid.). There are other criticisms of Kissinger's position, but the main point is that he apparently is attempting to make sure that he is not caught in the web of universal jurisdiction and that the United States is immune from prosecution of any of its citizens, in particular members of the armed forces. As Roth notes, however, "As a nation committed to human rights and the rule of law, the United States should be embracing an international system of justice, even if it means that Americans, like everyone else, might sometimes be scrutinized" (p. 154).

The fact would remain, however, that even if institutions to stop genocide and try perpetrators were established, it is highly likely that the cycle of violence would continue. Therefore, strategies to prevent genocide must include both long- and short-term policies. In the long run, the only way to prevent genocide is to change the socialization process. In the short term, the violence must be halted and perpetrators apprehended, tried and punished. How to accomplish this and build a movement to support these types of actions are the remaining tasks.

For, as just noted, the Clinton and Bush administrations hesitated to pursue or support multilateral policies designed to prevent genocide. Prevention has been sacrificed to a narrow definition of U.S. self-interest as the realities of the new century brought a newly perceived threat to the forefront. Preventing terrorism and apprehending those who launched the attacks on the United States became the first priorities, while preventing genocide, or even acknowledging that it lingered as a continuing threat, was removed from the centrality of consciousness. The remaining section of this book examines what policy may be pursued to stop the repetitious horror of modern genocide.

# PART III

# Genocide and the Politics of Prevention

## Introduction: Preventing Genocide in the Post–Cold War World

In 1945, when the extermination and concentration camps were liberated, the United States emerged as the dominant power in international politics.[8] While unsuspecting people were confronted by scenes of unimaginable horror, they reacted with appropriate shock, but inappropriate claims of ignorance, as the victors proclaimed that justice must be carried forth and the world must never again see such horrible sights. Many believed that genocide would not again be manifested in a world that had witnessed such destruction. How unrealistic and naive! We did not read the signs and allowed ourselves to be lulled out of vigilance by the shows at Nuremberg and Tokyo, by the 1948 passage of the UN Convention on the Prevention and Punishment of the Crime of Genocide and perhaps by our own rhetoric. If we had been more discerning readers of our history before and after the Holocaust we might not have been fooled. In the euphoria of the moment, however, it did seem inconceivable that fifty years later genocide would be rewarded in Europe.

But why? In 1933 genocide began and was, for the most part, unopposed even though only eighteen years earlier Turkey was exterminating the Armenian people. It too was hardly noticed—except as a model by the Nazis. And, who was punished for the killing of Khmer by Khmer in Cambodia or for the massacres in East Timor or take your pick of the numerous genocides or political massacres? The optimism was clearly uncalled for, especially in light of the direction U.S. foreign policy toward genocide would take in the future.

Throughout the last century, the United States demonstrated a clear hesitancy, if not outright reluctance, to participate in humanitarian interventions to stop genocide. Aware, for example, of the events surrounding the Armenian Genocide and the Nazi Holocaust, the United States never acted in the latter case until the Japanese attack on Pearl Harbor and then not primarily to stop the slaughter of the European Jews. In the former case, action was not forthcoming. In more recent times, U.S. foreign policy has been similarly timid. If, in fact, genocide is to be controlled, the United States, as I have argued, must take a more active leadership role pursuing a foreign policy designed to prevent genocide. The basic element of that policy must include support for multilateral action of the type described below.

Pondering the tangibility of mass death in recent history, I wrote in the conclusion of my recent book that genocide could be prevented if specific long-and short-term steps were taken, and while I still believe that is true, I now think further modifications are necessary to bring policy in line with a new reality of the post–Cold War world. I argued that in the short term it was most important to end the violence in order to create the conditions under which steps might be taken to bring about reconciliation and peaceful coexistence. To accomplish this I said that three interrelated steps were necessary: (1) develop a policy to bring together the international laws of war and the UN International Convention on the Prevention and Punishment of the Crime of Genocide; (2) develop an "early warning system" and instruments of humanitarian intervention to recognize and curtail future genocides and political massacres; and (3) formulate mechanisms to capture and punish instigators of genocide and political massacres demonstrating to the world that violence is not an acceptable means to achieve political ends.

In the long term, I continued, if human life was to be preserved, world views had to change from chauvinistic nationalism to cooperative internationalism. Throughout history, with increasing ferocity and deadliness in the twentieth century, genocide was perpetrated by the modern nation-state that collectively made few if any moves to prevent or punish that crime. Since nationalism had been the psychological foundation upon which international perceptions were currently constructed, it must be modified by instituting a process of political resocialization from one that emphasizes nationalism to one that emphasizes internationalism. The mechanism to inculcate this new perspective, I argued, will be changing the orientation of political education so that it emphasizes international human rights and what I called "covenanted internationalism."

Finally, I thought that, while the implementation of these will not necessarily guarantee the end of ethnonational violence and genocide, without them there could be no possibility that the world would be likely to move from an era of unprecedented violence to an era of peace and justice.

In addition, I assumed that nation-states would recognize that it was in their own interests to stop the violence because of what I called the "practicality of morality." Simply stated, action to halt and prevent genocide and political massacres was practical because, without some semblance of stability, commerce, travel and the international and intranational interchange of goods and information were subjected to severe disruption. Therefore, according to my argument, it was in the interest of all to end that disruption and create an environment of peaceful interchange. In short, I thought moral imperatives were supposed to be, in the new post–Cold War environment, the most practical way to pursue our common national interests.

The first thing I want to do is review each of these arguments, since they continue to have at least a modicum of relevance, and then to point out where I made errors of fact and judgment and correct those to try to ascertain how to formulate a policy to prevent genocide.

# 7

# A Foreign Policy to Prevent Genocide: The Practicality of Morality

The failure of American foreign policy in Bosnia, Rwanda and, to a lesser extent, in Kosovo and the international nation-state system's hesitancy to take action in these instances is not only immoral but impractical as well. Foreign policy, in this age of reawakened ethnonational violence, must be dominated by the "practicality of morality." Action to halt and prevent genocide and political massacres is practical because, without some semblance of stability, commerce, travel, and the international and intranational interchange of goods and information are subjected to severe disruption. It is, therefore, in the interest of all to end that disruption and create an environment of peaceful interchange. In short, moral imperatives are, in this new post–Cold War environment, the most practical way to pursue our national interest and to lay the groundwork for the creation of a life-preserving ethic.

To reiterate, if we are to navigate the uncharted paths of the post–Cold War environment it will be necessary to take three broad steps to develop a coherent strategy to prevent genocide in the post–Cold War world.

First, we must devise a multilateral strategy to curtail and prevent genocide and political massacres. This will be facilitated by assembling a coalition of support to halt the violence by developing a policy to bring together the international laws of war and the UN Convention on the Prevention and Punishment of the Crime of Genocide.

Second, we must develop an "early warning system" and instruments of humanitarian intervention to recognize and curtail future genocides and political massacres.

Third, these actions should result in the punishment of instigators of genocide and political massacres, demonstrating to the world that violence is not an acceptable means to achieve political ends.

## International Law and the Prevention of Genocide and Political Massacres

If prevention is ever to become a reality it is essential to create, under the auspices of the UN, a set of institutions that have the power to act to prevent mass killing. These should be based on international law and on a reformulated and strengthened UN International Convention on the Prevention and Punishment of the Crime of Genocide. William Schabas (2000) recently reviewed the major international legal precedents that apply to genocide. My brief account is simply derivative of his more comprehensive text, but I did outline my ideas several years ago and they appear to remain relevant.

Roger Smith (1992b) is no doubt accurate when he argues that international law sets norms and expectations for state behavior but will accomplish little until "governments redefine 'national interest' to include prevention of genocide" (p. 232). Remedies in international law exist that may be used to bring perpetrators of genocide to justice.

Until recently, however, international law has been virtually powerless to stop the large-scale destruction of human life and the primary reason is that international politics is dominated by the nation-state and the idea of sovereignty. In fact, international law is often defined as "the body of rules that nations recognize as binding upon one another in their mutual relations" and is the result of consensus among nations (Slomanson, 1990, p. 1). That is, international law is what the nations of the world agree it is. Nations observe international law when they "believe their national interests are best served by observing rules established by international consensus" (ibid., p. 8). Any program to stop the violence has to confront the nation-state's claim to sovereignty within its borders and its right to use force to go to war to defend its perceived interests.

This cannot be accomplished unilaterally. It will require the kind of coalition building and support inducement manifested in the Persian Gulf War and the recent "war on terrorism," but with a broader definition of interests; that is, attempting to assemble a coalition of support for the policy of bringing together the UN Convention on the Prevention and Punishment of the Crime of Genocide and invoking international laws defining crimes of war as procedures to punish perpetrators and demonstrate to the world that international violence is not to be tolerated by the world community. There are precedents for such action.

## The Nuremberg Principles

At the conclusion of World War II, the victors decided that it was necessary to punish the losers and to demonstrate to the world that certain actions would not be tolerated by the international community of nations. In pursuit of this goal thousands of war crimes trials were held following World War II. Trials were conducted by the International Military Tribunal at Nuremberg (IMT), the International Military Tribunal for the Far East (IMTFE) at Tokyo, the U.S. Military Tribunal at Nuremberg (NMT), the U.S. military commissions sitting at various places in Europe and Asia, the general Military Government Court and Intermediate Government Court of the American Zone in Germany, British military courts sitting in various places in Europe and Asia, the French permanent Military Tribunal sitting in various places in France, the French Court of Appeal and the General Military Government Tribunal of the French Occupation Zone of Germany, the Australian Military Court sitting at Rabaul, the Canadian Military Court sitting in Germany, the Netherlands Temporary Court-Martial and Special Courts, the Norwegian Court of Appeal, the Supreme Court of Norway, the Chinese War Crimes Court and the Supreme National Tribunal of Poland (Tutorow, 1986, p. 5). Before the UN War Crimes Commission was phased out, it reported the following number of war crimes trials: United States 809, United Kingdom 524, Austria 256, France 254, the Netherlands 30, Poland 24, Norway 9, Canada and China 1.

In addition to the war crimes trials, thousands of denazification proceedings were conducted in Germany. The denazification laws were not designed to "punish Germans who had been Nazis, but to remove them from, or keep them out of, positions of postwar leadership. The accused were classified as either major offenders, offenders, lesser offenders, or followers" (ibid., p. 7). The number of cases under these laws was huge. Thirteen million people in the American zone alone had to register, and approximately three million were found subject to classification and over 930,000 defendants eventually were tried by denazification tribunals. West German courts also prosecuted 12,982 defendants as war criminals between 1945 and 1963. While records are haphazard, a "German government publication reported on January 7, 1964 that in the American Zone alone 1814 people had been sentenced, 450 to death; in the British zone 1085, 240 to death; and in the French zone 2107, 104 to death. More than half of those receiving the death sentence were actually executed" (ibid., p. 8). In addition to all this activity, there were numerous trials for which records are difficult to find. Information on trials in Eastern Europe and the former Soviet Union had been virtually impossible to come by but may now be more available. Carefully staged "show" trials of Nazi leaders were held in Czechoslovakia and Poland, and there were a number of trials for acts committed in the concentration and death camps. The major cases involved six camps: Dachau, Mauthhausen, Flossenburg, Nordhausen, Buchenwald and Muhldorf.

All told there were close to 88,000 war crimes cases "opened in West Germany between 1945 and 1983" (ibid.). The most important and well known were the trials now often referred to as the Nuremberg Trials.

After the Nuremberg Trials the judgment of the court was incorporated into international law by the UN General Assembly, which adopted resolution 95 (1) which made the Nuremberg principles[9] part of international law.

> Under this principle, a nation that wages aggressive war commits the supreme international crime, punishable by any nation able to bring that nation's planners to justice. Its leaders incur criminal responsibility—arising directly under *international* law—for their conduct that causes the state to be liable under international law. They may thus be tried and punished for their participation in the unlawful use of force against other states. (Slomanson, 1990, 413)

Nuremberg clearly established that an individual can be the subject of international law. Although the idea of trying an individual for war crimes was first applied in the Versailles Treaty following World War I, when the Allied and Associated Powers arraigned William II of Hohenzollern, formerly the German Emperor, for a "supreme offense against international morality and the sanctity of treaties," he was never brought to trial. It was the Nuremberg judgment that established the precedent that an individual could be tried for violating international law.

The Nuremberg Tribunal specifically rejected the notion that international law covers only the actions of states and cited the case of Ex Parte Quirin (1942, 317U.S. 1,63 S. Ct. 2), in which individuals were charged, during World War II, with landing in the United States for purposes of spying and sabotage. As a result, the tribunal concluded that "crimes against international law are committed by men, not by abstract entities, and only by punishing individuals who commit such crimes can the provisions of international law be enforced" (Falk, Kolko, and Lifton, 1971, p. 101).

The liability of the Nazis was based on the theory that there "was a direct relationship between the individual and international law. The defendants claimed that they had no obligations under international law: their only duty was to the Nazi state which, in turn, would bear responsibility under international law" (Slomanson, 1990, 338).

The tribunal disagreed: "individuals have international duties which transcend the national obligations of obedience imposed by the individual state [to which they owe allegiance]. He who violates the laws of war cannot obtain immunity while acting in pursuance of the authority of the State if the State in authorizing action moves outside its competence under international law (ibid., p. 338).

The Nuremberg Trials were not, however, the only precedent. After the original trials of the high-ranking Nazi officials, President Truman turned the remaining war crimes trials over to the Office of Military Government in Germany. Twelve trials were held over a period of three years. One hundred and eight-five defendants were indicted and several were given death sentences, which were later commuted, while others received prison terms.

The Nuremberg Military Tribunals were based on a series of laws passed by the Allied Control Council, which finally turned over the power to try cases of war crimes to the German judiciary on November 25, 1949.

The Nuremberg Military Tribunal generally "followed the guidelines laid down by the IMT, but there were several significant differences" (Tutorow, 1986, p. 12). One involved the definition of crimes against peace, which was broadened to "include initiations of invasions which were not resisted, for example, those of Austria and Czechoslovakia" (ibid.).

A second difference toughened the definition by stating that anyone who was a member of an organization defined as a criminal organization by the IMT charter was a war criminal. If this had not been modified to state that the accused had to have personal knowledge of the criminal purposes and acts of the organization it would have applied to about two million Germans (ibid.).

A third difference was that the NMT was staffed completely by American judges.

These cases reaffirmed the Nuremberg Principles, which were given another classic expression in the Einsatzgruppen Case: "Nations can act only through human beings, and when Germany signed, ratified, and promulgated the Hague and Geneva Conventions, she bound each one of her subjects to their observance" (ibid.). These cases also reaffirmed the principle that crimes against peace had a basis in international law and rejected the defense of superior orders.

Surprisingly, these hundreds of cases and thousands of defendants were not the only war crimes trials to take place after World War II. An equal or greater number of cases were heard in the Far East.

## War Crimes Trials in the Far East

The two most important trials were the Trial of General Yamashita in the Philippines and the Tokyo War Crimes Trials that opened on May

3, 1946. These trials, especially the Yamashita Trial, were much more controversial than the Nuremberg Trials. When the War in Europe ended, the Allies turned their attention to Japan. The Potsdam Declaration of July 26, 1945, declared, "We do not intend that the Japanese shall be enslaved as a race or destroyed as a nation but stern justice shall be meted out to all war criminals, including those who have visited cruelties upon our prisoners . . ." This "stern justice" had already been meted out in the trial of General Yamashita, who was convicted of permitting his men to commit atrocities.

Yamashita was the commanding general of the Fourteenth Army Group of the Imperial Japanese Army in the Philippine Islands. On September 3, 1945, he surrendered and became a U.S. prisoner of war. He was charged with violating the law of war. On October 8, 1945, he pleaded "not guilty" and was tried before a military commission of five army officers appointed by order of General Styer. The trial took place eight weeks after Japan's surrender and preceded the Tokyo War Crimes Trials.

The trial was conducted by a court that consisted of five generals. As described on appeal to the U.S. Supreme Court, Yamashita was specifically charged with permitting "members of his command" to "commit brutal atrocities," including "a series of acts, one hundred and twenty-three in number," which were considered to be a "deliberate plan and purpose to massacre and exterminate a large part of the civilian population of Batangas Province, and to devastate and destroy public, private and religious property therein, as a result of which 25,000 men, women, and children, all unarmed noncombatant civilians, were brutally mistreated and killed, without cause or trial, and entire settlements were devastated or destroyed wantonly and without necessity" ("In the Matter of Yamashita," 1945, quoted in Falk, Kolko, and Lifton, 1971, pp. 142–43).

The specific charge against Yamashita was that

> while commander of armed forces of Japan at war with the United States of America and its allies, he unlawfully disregarded and failed to discharge his duty as commander to control the operations of the members of his command, permitting them to commit brutal atrocities and other high crimes against people of the United States and of its allies and dependencies, particularly the Philippines; and he . . . thereby violated the laws of war. (P. 142.)

The atrocities had taken place during the battle for Manila in February-March 1945 and Yamashita was not in touch with those committing the acts. In spite of this, he was convicted and sentenced to hang. His lawyers asked the United States Supreme Court to review the case and in a

6-2 decision the Court refused, noting that the decision could be reviewed only by military authorities (Ives, 2001, p. B2).

The U.S. Supreme Court concluded that "the allegations of the charge, tested by any reasonable standard, adequately allege a violation of the law of war and that the commission had authority to try and decide the issue which it raised" (Falk, Kolko, and Lifton 1971, p. 146).

It is obvious why the *Yamashita* case has fallen into obscurity. The trial was of questionable constitutional validity, and it created precedents the United States and other nation-states would rather not face. If these actually were incorporated into international law it would have meant that any officer whose men commit any atrocity would be responsible for their actions. It may, in fact, be the only precedent of its kind.

The Tokyo War Crimes Trials, which convened on May 3, 1946, were similar to the Nuremberg Trials. There were eleven nations[10] and eleven justices who tried twenty-eight defendants. Many of the defendants had been generals in the Imperial Army or held other high office. There were also civilian defendants and, of course, the former Prime Minister Tojo Hideki (Minear, 1971). The defendants were charged as individuals or as members of organizations with crimes against the peace, conventional war crimes and crimes against humanity. Since the charges are important as precedents it is necessary to specify them in a bit more detail.

"Crimes Against Peace" involve murder and "conspiracy to commit murder," accusing the defendants of conspiring to "kill civilians and members of the armed forces of certain nations by the initiation of unlawful hostilities in violation of the Hague Convention of 1899" (Tutorow, 1986, p. 15). The charge of "Crimes against Humanity" accused the defendants of "conspiracy to *permit* [italics added] the armed forces of Japan to violate the laws and customs of war and of criminal failure to take adequate steps to secure observance of these laws and customs" (ibid.).

The prosecution began the case by outlining the structure of the Japanese government so that responsibility could be ascertained. The trial would last two and one-half years and when an opinion was finally rendered on November 4, 1948, the opinion was 1,218 pages long and had taken seven months to prepare. Generally, the verdict was "guilty." Seven defendants were sentenced to death by hanging, and the sentences were carried out on December 28, 1949. Sixteen were sentenced to life imprisonment, one to twenty years in prison and seven years in prison for another. All prisoners were finally released on April 7, 1958.

As with the Nuremberg Trials, the Tokyo Trials were only the most famous. All together there were around "5,700 Japanese tried on conventional war crimes charges and 92 percent of these men were executed" (Minear, 1971, p. 6). There were a far greater number of defendants tried in other Asian trials. The important fact to keep in mind is that the European and Asian trials constitute a record of applicability and demonstrate that, if the will is there, the precedents exist to hold individuals responsible for violations of the laws of war or other crimes under international law. There are in fact literally uncounted numbers of documents and records of the various trials.

The official record of Nuremberg alone was published in forty-two volumes, *Trials of War Criminals*. For the IMT Nuremberg trials about 100,000 documents were collected and about 10,000 were used. The word-for-word transcript covers over 17,000 pages. These trials were based upon a common set of precedents and on international law as it existed at the time. That is not, however, to say that there were no critics of the war crimes trials.

The critics made essentially three broad objections. First, some claimed that the neutral and defeated nations should have been included on the various tribunals. Second, some argued that the laws under which defendants were tried were "*ex post facto* or nonexistent laws, and they argued further that no laws defining war crimes existed until after World War II" (Tutorow, 1986, p. 22).

Third, some argued that the standards used in the war crimes trials were not as rigorous standards of justice as those used in the domestic law of most nations. In particular, the specific argument was that in most nations a unanimous jury is required for a death sentence and in the war crimes cases individuals were sentenced to death in one case at Nuremberg with a vote of 3 to 1, and in Tokyo 6 to 5 with dissents written in the Tokyo trials (ibid., pp. 22–23).

These objections not withstanding, the precedents have been set, massively documented and incorporated into international law. It may be debatable whether there were war crimes before Nuremberg and Tokyo; it is no longer debatable and remedies exist in international law.

### International Law and War Crimes

Most international law relating to laws of war are the result of treaties, custom, judicial decisions, national manuals of military law, and the writings of legal specialists on the subject. The basic idea is that, since it appears unrealistic to believe war will be abolished, the next best thing is to attempt to control the worst effects of warfare by trying to maintain the idea that there are standards of civilization by which conduct is to be judged. While participants in war do not always adhere to the laws regulating warfare, certain basic ideas have gained widespread acceptance. For example, prisoners of war are not to be killed and must be treated humanely; hospitals are not to be targets; noncombatants, persons not taking an active part in the conflict, for example, children, are not to be harmed; and torture is not to be allowed.

States and armed participants comply with the laws for a variety of reasons. These include the role of world public opinion, which might condemn gross violations, the fear that if the laws are violated there will be military or other reprisals—including political consequences such as the loss of friends and allies, and possible judicial consequences such as war crimes trials, which, while they may not have enforcement sanctions, could very well brand the perpetrators as pariahs in the world of international politics. Even when international law does not appear to be effective, it provides standards of behavior to be considered in the policy-making process.

This basic idea that war is governed by rules appears to have existed in almost all societies, but it was only in the second half of the nineteenth century that laws to regulate war were codified. Since that time, the international agreements regulating war have taken the form of declarations, conventions and protocols.[11]

These precedents established the concept that international law applied to individuals as well as nations. Using them as a foundation, it should be possible to create institutions to prevent future genocides and to punish perpetrators. This, in turn, may contribute to creating the environment within which the life-preserving ethic may flourish and begin to create a new form of memory—memory of the common struggles to implement international law to protect the rights of all individuals.

There remain, however, certain specific weaknesses in laws of war. First, legal provisions are subject to different interpretations. Second, written law does not adequately deal with all forms of warfare, and there are limitations in application and enforceability. Third, the technology of destructive forces has advanced so rapidly that the written laws cannot cover all the myriad possibilities (Roberts and Guelff, 1989, p. 15). In spite of these weaknesses, the alternative is less desirable. If the violence is to be stopped, permanent, international institutions have to be developed, empowered and operationalized.

## Genocide and Justice: Prevention and Punishment

If future massacres and genocides are to be prevented, individuals who wage aggressive war, or plan and execute genocide, must be apprehended and held accountable. While this is the first step, it is usually after the fact. Prevention is the key.

The first step toward prevention is knowledge or the ability to predict situations in which genocide might occur. Toward this end there have been a number of proposals to create different variations of what have been called "genocide early warning systems" (Charny, 1982; Kuper, 1985 and 1992; Littell, 1991). In order for these to be effective it is necessary to be able to identify the genocidal possibility in a society. For the most part observers believe that there are five general indicators[12] that might serve as portents of the potential for genocide.

First, instruments and mechanisms of *recruitment*. When a group or movement prints, uses or distributes anti-Semitic or racist or other dehumanizing material for recruitment of members this is a possible demonstration of genocidal possibility.

Second, the use of the media or other means to distribute anti-Semitic, racist, or other dehumanizing appeals.

Third, the mechanisms used to achieve political power involve the techniques identified above, which are attached to the use of violence and intimidation. The violent tactics encouraged or used against opponents include the creation of paramilitary training camps to teach the use of weapons, bombing, beating, assassination, and so on.

Fourth, the construction of an environment of unquestioning obedience to authority. The movement or state creates a "quasi-religious structure of authority and sanctions, with political hymns, shrines, martyrs, liturgies" all designed to establish a situation in which an individual loses any semblance of identity and believes that he owes his allegiance to the leader (Littell, 1991, p. 315).

Fifth, the use of secrecy and other methods to create an exclusionary organization that separates insiders from outsiders. These include secret binding rituals established to cement the follower's relationship to the organization. Among these are rituals of induction and separation as well as the use of deception or disinformation to confuse the public and maintain extreme secrecy. Tactics may include the use of infiltration and subversion of public and other institutions such as the police, schools and perhaps others.

In short, the usual indicators of genocide include widespread abuses of human rights, brutal political oppression, "inflammatory use of the media," accumulation of arms and organized killings. When these are present the institutions created to deter atrocity and genocide must be prepared to act to prevent the assertion of power of terrorist groups or to intervene to save lives.

After an early warning is triggered policies must follow if prevention is to occur. The question of what to do after an early warning has been issued was answered, at least partially, in a 1985 UN study on how to enforce the Genocide Convention.

The study argues that, basically, it is essential to link early warning with appropriate responses (George and Holl, 1997, p. 2). The first step, consequently, is to improve what they call "receptivity to warning" (p. 4). For the most part policymakers are not receptive and most policy response are after the fact. That is, policy making is usually reactive rather than proactive. As George and Holl note, "policy-makers generally prefer to put off hard choices as long as possible" (p. 5). Information is often, therefore, discounted or ignored since the issuing of a warning might entail confrontation with difficult or unpopular policy decisions (ibid.). These types of problems with information processing often lead to the fact that a warning is not taken seriously and preventive action is delayed until after the crisis is in full swing or over. This is referred to as "the warning-response gap," and six reasons are outlined to account for its' existence.

First, if the warning involves a situation perceived not to be a threat to the state's national interest, the state is likely to postpone action or not take any at all.

Second, events are sometimes not clear and information is murky, so uncertainty leads to the postponement of action.

Third, early warning requires interpretation and analysis, and in some cases there is a shortage of knowledge concerning the internal operation of the group or state involved. For example, the U.S. intelligence agencies, after the September 11, 2001, terrorist attacks, advertised for speakers and readers of Arabic because they had a shortage of people who could communicate in that language.

Fourth, policymakers may be slow to act because they do not wish to get into a situation from which they might not be able to extract themselves successfully.

Fifth, since there are so many possible crises, the "overload induces passivity" (ibid., p. 11).

Sixth, decision makers may be worried about the Vietnam-Somalia syndrome discussed earlier.

If a warning is given, however, there are specific steps that should be taken. These

> could include: the investigation of allegations; activating different organs of the United Nations and related organizations, both directly and through national delegations, and making representations to national Governments and to interregional organizations for active involvement; seeking support of the international press in providing information; enlisting the aid of other media to call public attention to the threat, or actuality, of genocidal massacre; asking relevant racial, communal and religious leaders, in appropriate cases, to intercede, and arranging the immediate involvement of suitable mediators and conciliators at the outset.
>
> Finally, there is the possibility of sanctions which could be applied with public support by means of economic boycotts, the refusal to handle goods to or from offending States, and selective exclusion form participation in international activities and events. Representations would also be made to Governments to enlist their support in the application of sanctions. (Lawson, 1991, p. 668)

The UN invoked its sanctions power only twice during the first forty-five years of its existence: Rhodesia, 1966, and South Africa, 1977. In the last decade, the UN invoked sanctions eleven times: Iraq, 1990; former Yugoslavia, 1991; Libya, 1992, 1993; Somalia, 1992; Liberia, 1992; Haiti, 1991; Union for the Total Independence of Angola, 1993; Rwanda, 1994; Khmer Rouge, 1995; Burundi, 1996 and Sierra Leone, 1997 (Lopez, 2000, p. 67). Generally speaking, the argument has been made that these do not stop genocide because very often the countries or groups committing genocide do not respond to the impact of sanctions since there are certain conditions absent within the country which are necessary to make them effective. These conditions include: "police and military institutions guided by civilian oversight and ... disciplined by the rule of law; a functioning constitution; and independent and functional judiciary system; and the existence of a degree of social peace characterized by the absence of large scale crime or political violence" (ibid., p. 69).

Since sanctions have most often had the effect of hurting the civilian population while leaving the elite relatively unscathed, the new proposal is for something called "smart sanctions." These include *"targeted financial measures*, including asset freezes, more comprehensive approaches to *arms embargoes*, and *restrictive international and participation bans"* (ibid., p. 78).

Essentially, the argument is that prevention is more likely to be successful and cost effective than intervention after a conflict has started. In fact, scholars calculated the costs of prevention as opposed to intervention to stop a conflict already ongoing. The list of costs, as outlined by Brown and Rosecrance (1999, p. 18), include refugee costs, including economic burdens, solving political and social problems and military complications; "Direct Economic Costs" and Economic Opportunity Costs" such as the loss of investments and imports, lost markets, disruptions to labor supplies and other regional instability; "Military Costs" that involve higher budgets for defense and associated military skirmishes; "Instability Costs" including all the problems involved in such instability and "Costs of International Peace Operations." Their analysis of Bosnia, Rwanda, Somalia, Haiti, the Persian Gulf, Macedonia, Slovakia, Cambodia and El Salvador leads them to conclude that, "In international conflict as well as many other realms of human activity, an ounce of prevention is worth a pound of cure" (ibid., p. 232). Specifically, they point out that preventive action is far superior. They also debunk the arguments against such action deployed by the United States and other countries opposed to such preventive action. First, the argument that the "interests of international powers are not engaged by such conflicts in far-off lands," the "so why should we care" attitude is challenged by the notion that "regional turmoil—even in far corners of the world—affects the interests of major powers" and "undermines the credibility of the United Nations, international law, and international norms of behavior, as well as the international reputations of the great powers" (ibid., p. 226).

Second, the argument that the international powers often do not know "what to do because they cannot predict where conflicts will break out" is shown to be defective by analyzing data from both Bosnia and Rwanda, where ample warning was given, and by the discussion of early warning systems above.

Third, the argument that the "international community lacks the capacity to engage in large numbers of conflict prevention efforts," the idea that the United Sates, for example, cannot become the world's policeman, is also "specious." They argue that, of course, action cannot be taken in every case, but the Persian Gulf War indicated the ability to project military power over long distance. Moreover, since the United States spends more on military than any other nation, "more, in fact, than the next ten countries combined," if it is not capable of such intervention, "then the competence of those in charge of the U.S. defense establishment has to be called into question" (ibid., p. 227).

Prevention also involves, they argue, more than military response, including as well, "long-term efforts to promote political and economic development in potential trouble spots before violence emerges" (ibid.). This means that a form of engagement is necessary as well as the means to overcome the main objections of many Western policymakers, in particular those in the United States.

Domestic political considerations influence intervention and prevention. We have already noted how most of these are not particularly telling and how many are bogus. For review, the five main objections identified by Brown and Rosecrance are:

1. The fear that "international actions will lack public support" (p. 227). We have already pointed out that pubic opinion is variable and susceptible to leadership. Brown and Rosecrance note that "The key, as always, is for the executive to make a strong and explicit case on interest or moral grounds for the United States to be involved" (ibid.).
2. The fear that prevention will cost too much economically. But they demonstrate that prevention is much less costly than violent intervention after a conflict is in motion, and we saw this clearly in the case of Rwanda.
3. The fear of casualties. Yet, as they note, "It is far riskier to send troops into war (as coalition leaders did in the Persian Gulf) or into situations where brutal conflicts have raged for years (as they did in Bosnia) than to use them in prevention efforts" (p. 228).

4. Policymakers claim they do not want open-ended commitments because of the "Vietnam syndrome," which was discussed earlier. Again, long-term commitments have been made and operations, such as those in the Middle East, are still ongoing with no resolution. If this type of commitment may be made, why not prevention?
5. Domestic political considerations including the existence of interest groups opposing intervention of any sort and the isolationist impulse among policymakers. Again, these prove to be questionable since preventive intervention is more likely to be successful and cost less than later military intervention.

In the long run, therefore, the analytic and political argument for the implementation of an early warning system leading to prevention is powerful. Of course, prevention does not always work. The mechanisms outlined above very often do not effectively dissuade those who wish to use genocide as a political weapon to achieve their desired goals. In these cases additional measures are often necessary.

## Humanitarian Intervention

The basic idea of a right of states to intervene in the affairs of another state to save lives is controversial. The NATO intervention in Kosovo and the Australian-led intervention in East Timor, as well as U.S. intervention in Afghanistan under the rubric of the "war on terrorism," function to bring the idea of humanitarian intervention back into the spotlight (Bayzler, 1987; Teson, 1988; Harff, 1991; and Kader, 1991).

Humanitarian intervention was first discussed by the Dutch writer Hugo Grotius, who argued that a state could use force to prevent another state from mistreating its own citizens. However, as Slomanson notes (1990), Grotius insisted that the state's oppression of its own citizens had to be "so ruthless and widespread that it would shock the sensibility of the international community" (p. 371). While it seems perfectly logical to assume that nation-states should have the right to intervene in cases of massive abuse of human rights, humanitarian intervention is suspect among the nations of the world because in the 1800s some states used humanitarian intervention as an excuse to pursue their own political and economic ends.

In early 1827, for example, England, France and Russia intervened militarily for the ostensible purpose of ending the atrocities in the Greco-Turkish War of 1827. After the invasion they announced a Treaty for the Pacification of Greece and proclaimed their primary motive as "putting an end to ... daily fresh impediments to the commerce of the European States" (ibid., p. 371). Other precedents for intervention have been cited, such as the 1849 intervention by the president of the United States with the sultan of Turkey on behalf of the Jews being persecuted in Damascus and Rhoads; French intervention in Lebanon in 1861; allied intervention to stop Nazi atrocities; the 20,000 U.S. troops sent by Lyndon Johnson to the Dominican Republic in 1965, and U.S. intervention in Panama, Nicaragua, Somalia and Afghanistan among others.[13] Generally speaking, there is no recognized or agreed upon right of humanitarian intervention outside the framework of the UN. Determination of the necessity for intervention is supposed to be made by the Security Council.

Beitz (1988, p. 182) and Bayzler (1987, pp. 598–607) suggest that intervention is justified if several overlapping criteria are met:

1. The existence of large-scale atrocities or gross violations of basic human rights in the offending society;
2. Humanitarian motives that take precedence over other motives such as territorial acquisition;
3. Other possible remedies are exhausted, and intervention will not cause significant harm elsewhere.

Even if these were accepted by the nations of the world as triggers to cue action, humanitarian intervention might remain a rare and endangered species of international activity. Nation-states are generally unconcerned about the plight of peoples unless there is some threat to their own interests. Thus, one must not forget that the most common occurrence in the face of violations of human rights and human dignity is for nothing to happen. Generally, states have been given the right to kill their populations because outside intervention would violate their sovereignty, and no state wants to set the precedent of intervention because it might find itself being accused of human rights violations. In fact, the recent interventions demonstrate that humanitarian intervention is likely to occur when the situation is perceived as not difficult, or does not involve high costs to the intervening powers. If there is an existing power with a relatively large army that is suspected of committing gross violations of human rights, such as Russia in Chechnya, it is unlikely that intervention will take place. The intervention in Somalia was an interesting case, since instead of a government, anarchy was perpetuated by small bands of relatively lightly armed gunmen. As a result the intervention was not seen as a violation of state sovereignty—technically, there was no state, or at least no central government, and the intervening troops were under the auspices of the UN. Thus, no precedent is set. In other cases of intervention the UN is usually invited in by the state to attempt to restore stability.[14] These problems and the recent examples of genocide increased attention on the subject of humanitarian intervention.

The Secretary General of the UN, Kofi Annan, recently urged international leaders to be more ready to intervene to protect civilians, providing the UN authorized the intervention. Annan also pointed out the dilemma facing the UN. Using Kosovo as an example, he noted that the NATO action was taken without UN authorization because Russia and China threatened to veto the use of force against Yugoslavia. Annan said that "A global era requires global engagement" (Winfield, 1999, p. 4). Again, however, principle ran afoul of the notion of sovereignty as the president of Algeria rejected outside interference in internal affairs. Annan replied by pointing out that if the UN could intervene this might serve as a deterrent, stating. "If states bent on criminal behavior know that frontiers are not the absolute defense; if they know that the Security Council will take action to halt crimes against humanity, then they will not embark on such course of action in expectation of sovereign impunity" (p. 5).

The question is whether the UN can adapt and, further, whether important members want it to adapt. The tragedies of Rwanda, Sierra Leone, Sudan, Kosovo and East Timor demonstrated the shortcomings and pointed out how the UN is powerless, since it does not have a standing force of its own.

Brian Urquhart (2000), the chief advocate for a UN force for humanitarian intervention, points out that the "so-called international community" is an "institutional arrangement, unpredictable and slow to act. It usually responds only when disaster has already struck and when its members, usually in the UN Security Council, can agree to take action. Even then, since the UN has no standing forces or substantial resources of its own, its action, if it can be agreed upon, is likely to be to little and too late" (p. 19).

He notes how the influence of national sovereignty remains the major impediment and quotes U.S. Senator Jesse Helms as telling the UN Security Council that "a United Nations that seeks to impose its presumed authority on the American people, without their consent, begs for confrontation and ... eventual American withdrawal" (ibid.).

Urquhart argues that sovereignty is in the process, he hopes, of being replaced by a new idea of "human security," which "has emerged as the result of a vaguely defined and fitful international conscience on the part of the liberal democracies, and it has been encouraged both by the prodigious growth of nongovernmental organizations and by the communications revolution. However, the rules and the means for protecting human security are still tentative and controversial, not least because virtually any situation threatening human security is likely to raise questions of national sovereignty. No government wants to set up a system which may, at some point in the future, be invoked against itself" (p. 19) (ibid.).

# Foreign Policy to Prevent Genocide

What is ultimately needed, he argues, is "A constitutional international system with a shared but consistent responsibility for both international and human security; an enforceable system of international law; an international rapid reaction force prepared to take the necessary risks; an adequately funded UN with the resources and the authority to carry out the tasks assigned to it—all of these now seem to be dreams with little chance of fulfillment. And yet we talk incessantly of "globalization"; we know all too well the capacity of human beings for reaching the depths of self-destruction as well as the heights of achievement; we have at last agreed that the rights of the human individual are paramount; and we know that, as a practical matter, we are all more than ever in the same boat" (p. 22).

Most interventions under UN auspices have been either peacekeeping or peace enforcement. They have both grown, but there are problems with the way they have been carried out. Peacekeeping involves "military or paramilitary operations that are undertaken with the consent of all major belligerent parties. These operations are designed to monitor and facilitate implementation of an existing truce agreement and support diplomatic efforts to reach a long term settlement" (p. 22).

Peace enforcement "is the application of military force or the threat of its use, normally pursuant to international authorization, to compel compliance with generally accepted [international] resolutions or sanctions. [Its] purpose ... is to maintain or restore peace and support diplomatic efforts to reach along-term political settlement" (Heidenrich, 2001, pp. 148, 150). Both have grown over the years. Prior to 1988 there were only thirteen UN peacekeeping operations and they have thirty-six since that time. The number of peacekeepers has likewise increased to around 80,000, costing more than $3 billion annually (DeVecchi and Helton, 1999, p. 2).

However, the main obstacle to a UN peacekeeping force remains the concept of sovereignty, since the acquisition of its own army by the UN means that it has acquired one of the attributes of being a nation-state (Kennedy and Russett, 1995, pp. 56–71), and while such a force has been proposed, as well as a European proposal to build a 60,000–person European Rapid Reaction Force composed of units from the different countries, it has not happened.

The veto in the Security Council and the gridlock imposed by the dynamics of a 185–member organization make changes, especially those that would expedite humanitarian intervention to save lives, difficult and slow. Therefore, while the Australians finally intervened in East Timor this occurred only after the Indonesian government agreed to allow an international force to restore order. Intervention came about because the Indonesians were threatened by the International Monetary Fund, the World Bank, the UN and Washington (Mufson and Lynch, 1999, p. 5).

The primary question appears to be whether the UN is able to meet the challenges of the post–Cold War period. These include stopping the violence and replacing it with something stable and longer lasting—in short, building new nations. Under these conditions when to intervene and in what circumstances becomes an all-encompassing and important foreign policy question. The likely unfolding series of humanitarian disasters awaiting us in the new century means that such questions will not disappear. Nor will the desire for self determination on the part of numerous groups slip back into the margins of history. As Richard Falk (1999) has noted, "The best we can hope for is some sort of compromise. Both Kosovo and East Timor suggest the form it might take: no support for claims of self-determination that would shatter an existing state unless a people is being victimized by genocidal behavior, by repeated crimes against humanity, and—in exceptional cases—by severe abuses of basic human rights that are targeted at a given ethnic community and sustained over a period of years" (p. 1). He also suggests that the needs of minorities might be protected by forming "strong regional communities" and granting substantial autonomy and self-administration to groups within existing states. This assumes, of course, the willingness of both participants. Humanitarian intervention, it would appear, must meet certain conditions if it is to be successful.

First, the intervening powers must have a "clear idea of the political objectives they hope to achieve. They should try to pursue one objective at a time; multiple objectives muddy the waters. The imposition of sanctions or the use of military force should also not be aimed at punishing troublemakers. Rather, these instruments should be used to change behavior or to bring those responsible to justice" (Oudraat, 2001, p. 29).

Second, intervening powers need to "correctly assess the economic, political, and military characteristics of the target, which will often be nonstate actors." This means that when sanctions will be successful they should be used and when military force is the only alternative it should be employed. To know this, however, means that one must have accurate intelligence concerning the targets. So, for example, "imposing economic sanctions in poor states (Burundi) or failed states (Somalia) is at best futile. Similarly, the effectiveness of the use of force depends on the characteristic of the target. Aiming the use of force at the 'conflict' instead of at the belligerent parties, as was done in the early 1990s in Bosnia and Somalia, led to dramatic political failures" (Oudratt, 2001, p. 29).

Third, the lead in intervention has to be taken by one country or by an international organization. This means that leadership is a key to success. "Leadership gives direction to interventions and is key to building strong coalitions" (ibid.). Without such leadership the policy to be followed may become confused and not successful. Generally, such interventions should be led by the UN Security Council, but, in fact, the most successful ones come from individual states. "A leader must chart an effective course of action and articulate its position to others. True leaders know how to translate national interests into regional and international interests and how to persuade other states to get on board" (ibid.).

Fourth, the leaders have to build strong international coalitions to support the action. This helps to provide legitimacy for the intervention.

Fifth, the intervening powers must provide sufficient resources to make the action successful. They must have "enough firepower and the right mix of forces—air power and ground troops—to get the job done" (ibid., p. 30).

Sixth, intervening powers have to adopt the "appropriate strategies." There is debate over what types of strategies to follow. One perspective is that force is most effective when applied "immediately and comprehensively. The second believes that coercive instruments can—and often should—be imposed gradually" (ibid.). Both might be accurate given the circumstances. If there is an immediate threat to human life and international peace, strong sanctions and military intervention must be immediate, while in less urgent situations the incremental approach may suffice.

Finally, any strategy should contain an "exit strategy. But exit strategies should not be confused with exit schedules. Exits must be based on local political and strategic conditions—not arbitrary and rigid timetables. They should also encompass a post intervention strategy designed to tackle long-term economic and political problems. Outside powers considering intervention should realize that interventions entail more than the imposition of economic sanctions or the use of military force. They should be prepared to make long-term—even open-ended—commitments" (ibid.).

While this all seems to be an application of good old-fashioned common sense, it is surprising how often these conditions are not met and how, therefore, the resulting intervention is viewed as a failure. It is almost as though they are being designed not to succeed so that there will be less pressure on, in this case, the United States to participate in or lead such interventions. Yet, outlined above are mechanisms that might help to create the conditions under which humanitarian intervention might successfully stop the short-term violence. It would be wonderful if the theoretical formulations outlined above were all that was necessary to guarantee the success of such interventions. In the real world of international politics, however, nation-states do not act primarily to guarantee human rights and there are always unanticipated complications. In the case of U.S. foreign policy we have to ask what it should look like in the new century faced with the same old threat of genocide?

# 8

# U.S. Foreign Policy in the New Century

At one time, prior to the rise of the nation-state, individual rights were not generally imagined, as people existed in small communities often at the whim of a ruler or local authority figure. Today they are face to face with the state and, as we have seen, the state has repeatedly killed large numbers while it continues to repress even larger numbers. The difficulty presented by the violence in Bosnia, Rwanda, Kosovo and elsewhere clearly demonstrates how intractable the modern world remains when faced with horrible crimes of war and genocide.

As we have seen, while the United States led NATO to intervene through aerial bombing to stop the massacres in Kosovo, it was unwilling to use ground troops to completely halt the carnage on the ground and, therefore, thousands of people were killed. And, while the United States finally undertook initiatives to bring the conflict in Bosnia to a conclusion, it was indecisive and wavered for years, while in Rwanda it took no action at all and East Timor breathed a sigh of relief when the Australians decided to take the initiative to stop the ongoing violence.

What role should the United States have played?

Specifically, the U.S. government should have taken a leadership role in encouraging, through the UN, a series of progressive steps aimed at, first, stopping the violence, as outlined in the previous chapter, and, second, at building and supporting a stable environment to support human rights and foster a move toward democratic governance. As outlined in the previous chapter, a range of alternatives is available. These could have included sanctions against the potentially offending government, threatening to supply their opposition with weapons or imposing "no fly" and "no artillery" zones. If these fail, the next step would be the use of air power against their positions to demonstrate the resolve to stop the murder and torture. Last would be the intervention under the auspices of an international organization such as the UN or a regional multilateral group such as NATO.

As long as nations and groups are willing to use force and pursue policies of genocide to achieve desired ends, the United States should actively encourage the development of internationally based means to demonstrate that this is not an acceptable activity and that the pursuit of that activity will be extremely costly to the perpetrator. As Levi (1991) notes, "the efficacy of any law forbidding the use of force must therefore continue to depend upon the unpredictable outcome of every state's profit and loss calculation, which weighs expected benefits from the use of force against expected costs" (p. 295). If the world continues to see that genocide pays, that the expected consequences of genocide are control of large amounts of territory and the creation of an independent, ethnically based state, the world will continue to see it pursued as a policy option.

From 1945 to a few short years ago, the United States pursued a policy of containing what it perceived as aggressive Communist expansion and now, in 2002, attempts to frame a similar policy to contain terrorism. It is now time to reformulate the policy of containment and extend the application to genocide. If we could devise a policy that "worked" in the seemingly unmanageable era of possible nuclear annihilation, why can we not design a policy to deal with the more common yet more pervasive dangers of ethnonational violence and genocide?

As the Cold War faded from memory it was replaced by a seemingly more intractable and difficult to understand situation. In place of the bipolar face-off between the United States and the Soviet Union the new reality witnessed the emergence of the United States as the strongest power in international politics and the former Communist states swirling in chaos and controversy. To deal with this changed reality, foreign policymakers had to come up with new formulations concerning how the United States would act in the international politics of the post–Cold War era. Policymakers and academics scrambling to reformulate policy devised new foreign policy prescriptions—call them prescriptions because academics and foreign policy professionals seem to be hooked on the Kennan model.[15] Write an article with a catchy new phrase, such as "containment," and the new foreign policy will magically appear. Like an antibiotic it will immunize the world from destruction for, historically, a relatively short period of time while we search for the next discovery to combat the newly mutated germs—except in this case the germs are old germs against which immunities have not been discovered. The disease of hatred, based on or motivated by ethnicity, religion or territorial

## U.S. Foreign Policy in the New Century

ambition, eventuating in violence and genocide, is allowed to grow and reappear because the first illness is never truly eradicated or controlled. So, what are the new prescriptions?

Since the end of the Cold War academics and policy professionals have been breaking out new slogans such as "cooperative engagement" or "cooperative security" fostered by "transparency" (Carnegie Corporation, 1994) or the "Recovery of Internationalism" (Hendrickson, 1994). Nations are supposed to cooperate to end war. This is simply a different way of talking about multilateral solutions to violent conflict, and it ignores that unfortunate fact that they have not worked, nor been applied, in places like Bosnia or Rwanda. "Cooperative security" is to accomplish the goal through "institutionalized consent rather that through threats of material or physical coercion" (Carnegie, p. 3). The relationships are supposed to be "collaborative" instead of confrontational and "defense of the home territory" is the "sole legitimate national military objective of states" (ibid., pp. 3–4). Somehow this magical formula is supposed to ensure that conflict will not start. Everything is to be open, or "transparent," so nothing is hidden. This system is also going to be "inclusive and nondiscriminatory." But, as the *Carnegie Quarterly* summary points out, the idea of cooperative security "is and probably will remain, an aspiration that will be only incompletely fulfilled" (ibid., p. 6). It will not solve all problems, "eliminate all weapons, prevent all forms of violence, resolve all conflicts, or harmonize all political values. It will not prevent the underlying causes of conflict, including those currently fueling civil disorder around the world. What it will do is provide the conceptual framework by which the international community could organize joint responses to conflict" (ibid.). If it will not accomplish any of these, what will it do, concretely? The obvious problem, in the short run, is to stop the violence, and in the long run to make sure that it does not continue to occur. In their prescriptions for both there is no new miracle drug. The UN and multilateral mechanisms of humanitarian intervention are available, as I argued above, and they must be applied with renewed vigor by a reformed and reinvigorated UN. But how do you convince the nation-states to accept the recommended dosage?

It is not at all clear that there exists any wish to do that. In fact, the notion of recovering internationalism as a basis for U.S. foreign policy appeared, before September 11, 2001, to be based on the wish to withdraw. After criticizing the disarray of the Clinton foreign policy as it was demonstrated in cases such as Bosnia, Somalia, Haiti, North Korea and China, Hendrickson (1994) argued that there are intrinsic difficulties in peacemaking and peacekeeping and that these were clearly shown in Somalia. There is also, he contends, a lack of public support for such activity and this resulted in the new U.S. policy of retreat from participation in UN peacekeeping operations.

In addition, few of the present cases of genocide involve U.S. interests and the basic Westphalian norm of nonintervention remains paramount. Hendrickson advocates a middle position

> between realpolitik and revolution—the former holding that there are no legal and moral rules binding together the society of states, and the latter seeking the abolition of the state system by denying legal or ethical standing to the principle of sovereignty. It is difficult to see how a stable international order could be achieved today if the internationalist norms forbidding intervention and preventive war were continually violated by the world's most powerful state. (Hendrickson, 1994, p. 41)

It depends, I suppose, on how one wishes to see the intervention carried out. If it is unilateral intervention that is one thing. If, on the other hand, one is talking about multilateral institutions, such as a UN force, that is quite another set of circumstances. As long, of course, as the Westphalian norms of sovereignty and nonintervention prevail, and as long as there is no leadership preparing the way for people to overcome their isolationist tendencies, we are, I fear, doomed to an ever increasing number of Bosnias and Rwandas and Kosovos. In essence, Hendrickson makes it very clear that he is proposing that the United States "abandon the illusion of a kind of leadership we are not really prepared to exercise on behalf of a vision of world order the price of which we have no intention of paying" (p. 43). But, national and international realities intrude, and I showed in chapter 2 that the American public is not completely opposed to U.S. participation in interventions to stop genocide and that a political movement may be built in the United States to increase support for such action.

All of the above discussion should signal a move to a more encompassing idea of national interest than the isolationist impulses that have traditionally dominated discussions of U.S. foreign policy. In the post–Cold War era where it is necessary to control the more egregious examples of ethnonational violence, it is necessary to view multilateral intervention as in the national interests of more powerful democratic states, especially if that intervention is aimed at supporting weaker democracies. If such support is not overt and forthcoming the lesson to small vulnerable countries may be that there is no international order and that their real friends lie elsewhere. This neglect or withdrawal into isolationism will also weaken the strong democracies by giving the "appearance of hypocritical self-interest that begins to gnaw at their moral (and thus their political) credibility" (Judt, 1995, p. 37).

In other words, we begin by redefining our national interest. It also means that the United States should reevaluate its role in peacekeeping and peace enforcement, or, if you will, the role the military should play in foreign policy.

While modern war appears to have changed, and while most wars are no longer fought between states, apparently humans go to war for the same reasons, to acquire territory and resources, defeat their enemies, convert the heathen and do away with evil, secure the release of captives or prevent violations of people's rights. War today has become the major source of identity and employment in deteriorating states. As Michael Ignatieff (1997) points out, "these states have been left to their own devices and bereft of outside support, they have broken up along ethnic and tribal lines. In these regions, low intensity conflict has become a way of life. War, like a virus, has worked its way into the very tissue of the Great Lakes regions parts of West Africa, the Southern Caucasus, and the Afghan region. It is the major employer, the chief economic activity. All power comes from the barrel of an AK-47" (p. 12).

After the Kosovo bombing observers began to reevaluate the way modern wars are fought with a view towards attempting to ascertain whether or not the use of ground troops was becoming a rare and rarely used instrument in order to minimize western, in particular United States, casualties. In evaluating the result of the Kosovo intervention many questions were raised concerning precedents and whether the operation was successful in achieving the articulated humanitarian goals. The debate continues, though with less attention on it, since the Kosovar Albanians are now attempting to gain their independence and a guerilla war remains a real possibility. While Kosovo remains a messy situation, the question of how to intervene to preserve human rights is a continuing source of debate.

Some argue that NATO did the "right thing in the wrong way" (Ash, 2000b, p. 60). This of course ignores the question of whether or not politically they could have done anything else. The moral question is if this is how it is to be done, should it be done at all since there are so many unpredictable aspects including civilian casualties? Ash sums up the dilemma by noting that it has usually been the case that peace has been maintained by preparing for war. In the Cold War era we had, he notes, "the moral and political conundrum of nuclear deterrence. Deterring Soviet aggression depended on our seriously threatening to do something which, if we ever had to do it, would have been immoral" (ibid.). Now, he believes, we have the "conundrum of non-nuclear compliance." To prevent genocide or preserve human rights, to force a dictator such as Milosovic to "treat their own citizens with minimal decency, we have to generate a credible military threat. This involves seriously preparing to do horrible things—both endangering innocent civilians in the guilty state and risking our own soldiers' lives in ground action" (ibid.). And, the "more awful the threat, the less likely it is we will have to do what we say we will do" (ibid.). Whether we are interested in generating such a threat in the face of genocide remains a realistic question. We appear, Ash notes, "structurally incapable of generating such a threat. The Western liberal societies that care most about stopping gross violations of human rights in other countries also have the most difficulty in willing the means best suited to achieve that end. This is our post-Kosovo dilemma" (ibid.).

Yet, after the terrorist attacks on the United States, a threat was generated as the United States took the lead in using military force to overthrow the Taliban government in Afghanistan and to attempt to capture the individuals responsible for the attacks. Here too, however, ground forces were used sparingly as the main initiative was pursued through the use of air power and was accompanied by extensive media coverage all designed to demonstrate that this is, in fact, the new and safer way to conduct war.

In a review of several books on the manner in which the United States has fought recent wars, Michael Ignatieff (2000) noted that "relying exclusively on air power has limits: planes are effective against fixed strategic targets, like petroleum storage, bridges and command bunkers; but even then air power rarely succeeds, by itself, in destroying a regime's ability to command and control its forces" (p. 43). More important, he points out that "Air power alone cannot protect civilians at risk" (ibid.). In the post–Vietnam era he concludes, the "American way of war" is to attempt to make it "risk-free and casualty averse war waged in the expectation of impunity" (ibid.). Ignatieff calls this "virtual war."

It is war on the model of a video game with explosions and media hype concerning the success of the bombing, but it is war that is without significant, as in final victory, results. Even more important is the question of whether this type of war can be successful in humanitarian intervention to protect human rights. The answer is probably that this type of action alone cannot successfully protect human rights and thus raises the further question of whether the United States will "only take part in such situations if risk to its own combatants is minimal." In other words, will the United States support and participate in interventions only if they involve air power? (ibid.) As summarized by Ignatieff: "In the new American way of war, the Air Force has the leading role as the high altitude precision specialist; the Navy follows as a platform from which to launch planes and missiles; and the Marines can be used to secure beachheads and evacuate Americans at risk" (ibid.). This position, Ignatieff argues, I think correctly, is the same as a "refusal to admit the presence of tragedy in warfare—the inevitability of mistakes, unintended consequences, and terrible accidents—which undermines the credibility of . . . [a] belief in technology" (ibid.). Mistakes happen and no human action, whether war or any other, is entirely predictable. As he notes, "where violence is used, what can go wrong usually does" (p. 46). He concludes that the means developed by the military and the U.S. policymakers cannot achieve the rhetorical end they advocate. It will, he argues, be difficult for Americans to recognize that "American power is deeply vulnerable because of the contradiction between high moral goals—commitment to human rights and humanitarianism—and military means that are concerned, above all, to avoid risk" (ibid.).

American policymakers, however, have been less than forthright in their view of what action the United States should take to prevent genocide. For the most part they are busy justifying past and present policy and actively pointing out the great success of air power in achieving stated goals. For example, Harold Hongju Koh, former assistant secretary of state for Democracy, Human Rights, and Labor, when interviewed concerning his perception of what needed to be done to prevent genocide, argued that the United States has "established an intelligence network within the U.S. government and among several countries which participated" in a conference on atrocity prevention convened October 1999. He said it was not possible to get an agreement because the countries wanted any principles to be part of an endorsement of the International Criminal Court that the United States refused to sign. But it was signed by Clinton on December 31, 2000. Koh outlined some disappointments, such as the failure to arrest Radovan Karadzic and General Mladic, and noted that Rwanda was a disaster that showed the need for early intervention. Consistent with other evaluations by United States officials, he apparently neglected to point out the U.S. role in delaying both the arrest of Karadzic and Mladic and intervening in Rwanda. He maintained that the U.S. State Department made notable achievements. In short, even former officials are reluctant to condemn U.S. inaction although a forthright examination of U.S. policy is a necessary place to begin analysis of what now must be done (Fein, 2001, pp. 11–12).

U.S. participation in multilateral institutions has become questionable, and as early as 1998 Urquhart urged that the "United States must decide what interests and problems are of real importance and might realistically be advanced by American intervention." Unilateralism is "neither wise nor sustainable" in view of both the domestic situation in which the United States is reluctant to act entirely alone and of an international situation in which America's ability to have its own way will diminish (1998a, p. 51). The United States uses an ineffective UN as a scapegoat. Always noting how the UN did not or will not act to prevent genocide, the real politics of intervention is subverted as attention is diverted from the fact that the UN is the creation and creature of the nations of the world and without their allocating to it money and man power it is effectively powerless.

Other then rhetoric and debate, action is virtually impossible. The UN does, however, act as the main forum for the expression and support of human rights in the world and the United States needs to become a more active participant in that endeavor.

David Rieff (1999) argues that the movement for human rights is one of the major ideas of the twentieth century, but "it has yet to become an integral part of the fabric of American democracy. So far, what power the human rights movement has obtained derives not from an evolution of popular sentiment—as occurred, for example, with regard to civil rights or the environment—but from the press and the political elite" (p. 10). People will accept American participation in humanitarian intervention, especially if it involves the possibility of American casualties, only if the "human rights movement shows more willingness to engage in straightforward political activism, to get its hands dirty. It must lobby people in churches and shopping malls in the Midwest as assiduously as it lobbies Capitol Hill or the Ford Foundation. It must take its case to the public, not just rely on its influence and its certainty that it does an enormous amount of good in the world" (p. 11).

Of course, it is often the case that nothing works, that the lessons of the past are not learned and that the interventions in Kosovo, however controversial, and East Timor, however successful, do not necessarily become precedents. While the United States supported military intervention to counter communism during the Cold War, it has been less likely to support intervention for humanitarian purposes. Whatever the barriers to humanitarian intervention, and they are many, the method of intervention most likely to be successful is no secret and was outlined in the previous chapter. What is most necessary at this point is both a movement among citizens of the United States to support human rights and to intervene to stop the violations of those rights, and the development of an ethic that would be incorporated into the American socialization process whereby citizens would understand why these rights are of paramount importance.

This, of course, is unlikely in the short run. Therefore, what I want to show in the following chapters is how a long-run alteration in the process of political socialization might lead to such change, and then to conclude by reexamining how a movement to prevent genocide might be built within the United States.

# 9

# Reflections on "Ethics," "Morality" and "Responsibility": Thinking about a New Political Consciousness for a New Century

In chapter 3 I defined politics as involving two elements: choice and decision. We have now arrived at a point where it is imperative to ascertain what those choices mean.

In a marvelous film, *Breaker Morrant*, the lead character, Harry Morrant, on trial for following orders to execute Boer prisoners during the Boer War in South Africa (1899–1902), notes as he is on his way to the firing squad, "These days it is so very easy to be on the wrong side." Harry phrased, concisely and eloquently, a central moral question of our time: How does one choose, or even know, the "right" side when so many choices appear morally repugnant? When confronted with seemingly ambiguous alternatives, all clamoring for allegiance, deciding which choices are the moral ones may appear eminently difficult in an era when any action appears to threaten the innocent. Choices that in hindsight might seem very clear, are, in the heat of the moment, not always so easily discernable.

For example, the NATO bombing of Yugoslavia was viewed by some as an inhumane and disproportionate response to the Serbian attempt to ethnically cleanse the Kosovar Albanians. Others argued that it was a much too limited response that should have included the use of ground forces to fully stop the atrocities. The choice may have appeared ambiguous, but in this confusing modern era, most choices will remain ambiguous, and one must often choose the lesser of two evils. In the real world the ideal choice rarely presents itself.

Looking back on the Holocaust in particular and genocide in general, from this perspective, it might seem as though it would be easy to pick the right side. In the case of the Holocaust hindsight makes that choice appear self-evident.

Since the Holocaust was the first public genocide, the first genocide about which large numbers of people had any knowledge, it has become the paradigmatic genocide, the one we all use to talk about crimes against humanity—it is our ruler, our measuring rod, our basis of comparison. It also marks the symbolic and real decline of the somewhat naive view of the enlightenment that the thin veneer of Western civilization could control the baser impulses of humans to kill each other in large numbers. With this perceptual chasm bridged, the defeat of Nazi Germany signaled to the victors that they should try to put the genie back into the bottle. Thus, they hoped, perhaps optimistically and naively, to establish moral and ethical guidelines that they devoutly wished would keep such events from being repeated. To accomplish this, as noted previously, it was decided that it was necessary to punish those who committed the most egregious crimes and demonstrate to the world that certain actions would not be tolerated by what ultimately turned out to be an illusory "international community of nations." Hence, the defeat of Nazi Germany and Japan led to war crimes trials and the incorporation into international law of the Nuremberg Principles.

The victorious coalition put on trial the high-ranking German and Japanese officials thought to be responsible for laying waste to a large portion of the planet. The result of the trials made individual responsibility a part of international law and set precedents that have, in spite of their incorporation into international law, not been followed in subsequent instances of genocide. In the post-Holocaust period perpetrators have, for the most part, gotten away with genocide, and when trials have occurred, they focused on apprehending lower level officials instead of those most responsible. While this trend appears to be changing, the legacy of this view of responsibility created a situation in which notions of morality and responsibility were redefined so that the lessons of the Holocaust, if not lost, were applied in a different fashion.

The implication, of course, was that any definition of morality which could be used to hold perpetrators responsible for their behavior became murky. How could one talk about ethics, morality and responsibility within this context? In order to attempt to structure such a discussion it is necessary to begin by attempting to define that about which we are speaking. What do these terms mean in the new century?

## Ethics and Morality after the Holocaust

There are numerous ways to define the key concepts in the terminology of moral discourse. I want to begin this discussion by narrowing the boundaries and proposing to accept some stipulative definitions. First, it is necessary to draw a distinction between law and morality.

The use of international law as a mechanism to punish the perpetrators raises important issues of meaning. Hence, it is essential to note that morals are not laws. Even though moral judgements often use words similar to those used in courts of law, they are different. Law, as Philip Hallie (1979) notes, "moves and lives in public institutions; life-and-death [morality] (which is the area ... closest to criminal law) moves and lives in individuals" (p. 270). Laws are made and enforced by public institutions, moral judgments are personal and there are no mechanisms of enforcement. There are times when law and morality may be in harmony, but usually, the needs of the state are placed before those of the moral conscience of the individual.

This is an important distinction, and it was for Harry Morrant. Given orders to execute Boer prisoners, he did as he was told by the representatives of the authority of the British army. When it became inconvenient for Britain to admit the practice, when they needed scapegoats to appease the German government in their attempt to get out of the war, Harry and his fellow Australian troopers, who were by the definition of the times "good soldiers," became victims of the perceived needs of the state. Or, as stated in the film, they became "scapegoats for the empire."

So that is the very dilemma faced by all who wish to see moral principles as part of state law. In fact, if Harry and his fellows had not followed orders they would have been court-martialed or shot, which they eventually were anyway. So, what does one do when confronted with this dilemma? The easy solution is to council those in such a situation to follow their own consciences. But this is the luxury of academics in warm offices writing about the real world. In that world of ambiguity it is not often as clear as it appears in hindsight. So the issue phrased by Harry goes to the heart of the distinction between law and morality.

In order to address this distinction, morals must be situated in public spaces; they are not, and cannot be, only private. They have to be communal and based on some concept of community (Hallie, 1979, p. 271). Morality and law, when applied in a nation with moral principles, of which there are very few if any, would, theoretically, have the same common goal—to restrain the destructive power of humans.

Law and morality, in this case, would both rest on fundamental principles—beliefs that are accepted by a society or group. A principle such as "innocent until proven guilty," is, for example, a presumption of U.S.

criminal law, while the "presumption at the foundation of life-and-death morality is that all human life is precious" (ibid., p. 273).

Law and morals also have codes which make demands upon individuals to learn to control certain "passions." The difference is that while law threatens punishment from without, by the state, morality "is inwardly experienced self control. When the moral law within you rules your passions, you are good. When your inward government is in chaos, in anarchy, you are bad" (ibid.). In short, morals are a matter of human character and are based in a community. They cannot be divorced from history or from action since they must concern themselves with how human beings behave, but, generally, when we talk about moral principles we mean some internal restraint on behavior resulting from standards or norms that have arisen within a community—however defined. As we shall see, a community might mean a small contiguous group or a larger international setting in which there may or may not be general agreement upon these ideas.

Missing from this type of discussion, however, is an important dimension of critical reflection. Given the ambiguity of reality, questions of right and wrong, of ethics and of morality must, as all others, be the subject of critical evaluation. So, even though the terms "ethics" and "morality" are often used interchangeably, a distinction is helpful. "Morality" may be defined, following McCollough (1991), as referring to "commonly accepted rules of conduct, patterns of behavior approved by a social group, values and standards shared by the group. It consists of beliefs about what is good and right held by a community with a shared history" (pp. 6–7).

"Ethics," on the other hand, is the critical analysis of morality. "It is a reflection on morality with the purpose of analysis, criticism, interpretation and justification of the rules, roles, and relations of a society." In this sense, ethics "is concerned with the meaning of moral terms, the conditions in which moral decision making takes place, and the justification of the principles brought to bear in resolving conflicts of values and of moral rules." In other words, ethics involves a reflection and critical analysis of "what we say, what we do, and what we are" (ibid., p. 7).

Those of us who examine the Holocaust and genocide and how to prevent these from reoccurring are, therefore, engaged in ethical reflection on morality, and what we are trying to do is to incorporate these into laws that will impose some sense of responsibility and ultimately be used to punish those who commit genocide. The key to understanding the ethical implications of the moral principles derived from examining the genocide, therefore, may very well be centered in the idea of responsibility.

## Responsibility after the Holocaust

If attempts to regulate the worst aspects of human behavior are to have any major impact there must be some way to assign responsibility—to assure that individuals are held accountable for the acts they commit. This becomes difficult in an era that has witnessed a perversion of language unmatched in any period of history. While politicians and self-proclaimed moralists propound and preach about the lack of responsibility, the meaning of the term remains ambiguous. There is no reason for this confusion since Stanley Milgram clarified the idea of responsibility many years ago (Milgram, 1974).

While Milgram's work has been controversial, it remains the foundation for all later examinations of obedience and responsibility. In fact, in spite of repeated attempts to elaborate Milgram's essential interpretations (Blumenthal, 1999; Kelman and Hamilton, 1989), his remains the clearest conceptualization of the perversion of the idea of responsibility in the modern era.

For Milgram, "responsibility" no longer meant what it had in a previous time. In the modern era, he argued, responsibility now referred to the single-minded pursuit of selfishness—to get what you can for yourself and the hell with everyone else—especially if they get in your way or you perceive them as standing in your way. In short, any notion of responsibility is thought to be divorced from any idea of the public good or community. In the contemporary era it is tied to what Milgram referred to as the "agentic state." If there is any responsibility it is to authority, to obey orders, to be the agent of others and to do what you are told. Accordingly, an individual is not to cause trouble, and least of all, to be responsible for the consequences of his or her actions because if an unethical or immoral act is committed, it is not the individual's fault as he or she acted in the name of obedience. Hence, you are able to convince yourself that your actions are actually the responsible thing to do; you obeyed and did not cause trouble. It is, after all, the troublemakers, the questioners, who are irresponsible. This, it turns out, is a very "Nazi"-like notion of "responsibility."

It is also a new notion of responsibility. It is responsibility without compassion, without caring, without concern for others. Since there is no notion of the public good, of community, because responsibility is defined individualistically, we are unable to hold others responsible and we find it difficult to decide, as Harry Morrant noted, which is the wrong side. In fact, one has to wonder if there is any clear way to decide which side is "right" and which is "wrong"? There certainly does not seem to be any consensus among nations or groups as they appear reluctant to accept a moral-ethical code that defines responsibility? There are, of course, at least two excellent reasons to raise these issues.

First, there are numerous impediments to a general acceptance of any moral ideas that cut across cultural and national boundaries. Second, the prescriptions offered by scholars are, most generally, based upon suppositions that ignore some of the unpleasant realities of the real world of politics and human behavior.

## Impediments to Choosing the "Right Side"

### Culture and Nationalism

All observers do not agree that there are universal humanitarian standards. Some argue that even the idea of codes such as individual human rights are culture bound and tied to Western ideology. Proponents of cultural relativism, and those who hesitate to apply human rights principles to their own situation because of their use of power to abuse individual rights, do not accept human rights standards as universal. In fact, some argue that "indigenous-aboriginal peoples, have achieved both dignity and, equally important, a harmony with nature without the conception of rights" (Forsythe, 1991, p. 3). There are nation-states that go even farther and argue that rights such as freedom of religion and freedom from sexual discrimination violate their cultural traditions and are not appropriate for a multicultural world. In short, it is their right to engage in activities such as cutting off a person's hand for stealing or stoning a woman to death for committing adultery without outside interference in their affairs. Ideas of human justice and equality are, according to these perspectives, culture bound and tied to imperialistic notions of the West. These ideas are tied not only to culture, but also to the nation-state that claims, according to the doctrine of sovereignty, the right to be free from outside interference in its treatment of its citizens. In fact, of course, the rise of the nation-state left the individual without intervening institutions, and the state repeatedly killed and dominated ever larger numbers of people in the last century. Culture and nationalism, therefore, remain major impediments to a more generally acceptable morality.

### Scholarly Wishful Thinking and the Appeal of Violence

Among the many recent attempts to face these impediments and outline a more universal morality, two, in my view, stand out. Lifton and Markusen's (1990) effort to develop what they call a "species mentality," and Kelman and Hamilton's (1989) concern with ways to break the habit of obedience and create a "global perspective."

Lifton and Markusen (1990) argue that what they call the species mentality is an alternative that is life enhancing rather than life destroying. They define this as

> full consciousness of ourselves as members of the human species....
> Species consciousness contributes to a sense of self that identifies with the entire human species. But the self cannot live, so to speak, on the human species alone. Its traditional forms of immediate identification—other people, family, work, play, religion, ethnic groups and nation—give substance to the species identification and are necessary to it. (P. 258)

This is, of course, nothing other than the old notion of the importance of community. Since it is really a reexpression of some of the oldest traditions it is not a startling insight. Nor is their prescription concerning how to achieve this goal.

To achieve the species mentality, they argue, the human self has to realign elements of the self so that concern and caring are now extended from the immediate self and family to the species as a whole. While they do not specifically discuss the politics involved in transforming the present mentality into the species mentality, they do identify several traditions of species consciousness. Here Lifton and Markusen point out that "Species consciousness has been advocated over the centuries by spiritual traditions of moral and intellectual power" (p. 263). Their list of advocates includes Gandhi; Martin Luther King Jr.; religious traditions including Hindu, Muslim and Jewish; Marx; and the reaction of the world to Nazi atrocities after World War II, among others. In the long run, their concern, like that of most students of genocide, is to stop the murder. To accomplish this they call for all people to "join in a vast project—political, ethical, psychological—on behalf of perpetuating and nurturing our humanity.... We become healers, not killers, of our species" (p. 279).

Kelman and Hamilton (1989) are likewise interested in psychological mechanisms to deter obedience and in the creation of a general purpose morality. Their view, I surmise, is that if the habit of obedience is broken, the next step will be to move to the creation of the species mentality, except that in their case they call it a "global perspective." Kelman and Hamilton offer a more detailed analysis of the concrete problem of obedience. Specifically, they explore how the habit of obedience might be broken by changing social structures, increasing political participation, changing the socialization process and creating "collective support systems that are needed to develop a more responsible citizenry—a citizenry prepared to apply human values and moral principles in evaluating the political authorities' policies and demands" (p. 308).

According to Kelman and Hamilton, individuals are bound to authority systems, in a manner originally identified by Milgram, by role definitions, chain of command, and the general bureaucratic hierarchy. Potential victims are dehumanized or neutralized and individuals respond differently to authority situations according to their conceptions of responsibility and their political orientations. The important thing is to promote personal responsibility, and Kelman and Hamilton recommend two means to reduce what they call rule- and role-oriented behavior and induce or encourage value-oriented behavior.

First, by reducing the impact of forces that bind the individual to an authority system, the individual citizen "will be more familiar with it and feel more capable of judging its demands" (ibid., p. 322). It is also necessary, they argue, to change the social structure, the education experiences, and the group support structure so that individual citizens will be empowered and begin to feel a renewed sense of personal efficacy. According to their formulation: "Empowerment means having the opportunity and the right to make decisions about one's own life and to participate in decision making on public issues. Efficacy means possessing the skills, the knowledge, the material resources, and the social supports that enhance people's ability to determine their own fate and to influence public policy" (p. 323). They are related, and the way to enhance them is to disperse authority by increasing decentralization of political and economic institutions. Decentralizing authority is a key idea in Kelman and Hamilton's theory, and they believe that it will have a "liberating effect" because those who experience having some authority are less likely to abuse that authority and less likely to obey other authority figures.

But this neglects a sad and repetitious reality. It is not necessarily the case that dispersing authority makes it more humane. Lt. Calley, one of Kelman and Hamilton's primary examples, was clearly in a position of authority, as were Himmler and Eichmann and Milosovic. The simple fact of dispersing authority will make little difference if there are more fundamental problems facing the creation of a more humanitarian ethic.

Kelman and Hamilton then argue that education promotes empowerment and enhances efficacy (p. 325). Education may enhance empowerment and efficacy, but empowerment and efficacy do not necessarily enhance morality. Einsatzgruppen were composed of highly educated individuals who were willing to obey and kill. Education, even at the highest levels, does not necessarily mean that people will not obey. Heidegger went along with and, at first, celebrated the Nazi rise to power (Farias, 1989), as did numerous professors, lawyers, physicians and other highly educated citizens of the Third Reich. To offset this potential criticism Kelman and Hamilton reason that exposing people to different perspectives and changing the structure of decision-making groups by breaking down the boundaries and emphasizing dissent as an obligation of citizenship are also necessary. The ideal of citizenship, they argue, should promote dissent, and the citizen should have allegiance to multiple authorities (Kelman and Hamilton, 1989, p. 330).

Generally, they sum up their analysis of authority by noting that individuals have to reacquire a sense of personal responsibility—perceive themselves as personally causing harmful outcomes. Their proposed corrective involves education directed toward individualizing potential victims so that they no longer would be seen as "anonymous members of stereotyped categories" (ibid., p. 337). While this is similar to Lifton and Markusen's idea of a species mentality, neither examines the political and psychological reality of a world that does not always operate in the fashion they would like.

## Reflections

Of course it is difficult to find fault with any resolve to stop the epidemic of mass death. Indeed, my quarrel is not with that resolve, but with what is missing. Suppose we begin our quest with the opposite assumptions. That is, suppose humans really do not wish to get along with each other? Suppose, instead, there is something in all of us that moves us toward the very darkest part of our nature. Suppose we, in some deep recess of our psyche, like, or perhaps learn, how to perpetrate violence and are willing to use it against our fellow humans and view this as a legitimate means to achieve our own goals. This means that the creation of the species mentality or a global perspective, or any other alternative morality, will be much more difficult than simply stating it on a piece of paper. In fact, of course, the history of the species appears to substantiate the power of violence to draw us in ways we do not like to admit.

Without acknowledging the power and appeal of violence, without acknowledging that there may be something within all of us that appeals to our darker nature, without acknowledging that we too may be capable of the most horrendous acts, it is unlikely that the genocidal mentality will undergo the miraculous change so desired by so many observers. As with most attempts to suggest alternative world views, they neglect to discuss, in convincing fashion, how to get from where we are to where they would like to see us go.

While these ideas about what a more humane perspective would resemble are important and necessary, they are not sufficient since they neglect certain sad ironies and realities. Both Anthony Storr (1991) and Stanley Milgram (1974) point out that some of the very themes of moral behavior that scholars wish to incorporate into their new moralities may, in fact, cause violence. As I pointed out above, there is no general agreement on the desired morality that is to guide behavior. According to different cultural and national circumstances individuals may very well believe that your "right side" is their "wrong side." Consequently, we are back to Harry's observation.

What is defined in one religion, culture or nation as conscientious behavior, might very well be immoral in another. In fact, Rainer Baum (1988, p. 56) notes that "conscientiousness can take the place of conscience very easily." A person may be very conscientious about his behavior and perform with complete moral indifference. Baum argues that moral indifference is the opposite of moral responsibility, which involves concern about the consequences of our actions. But this is not true either. Moral indifference in one culture or one nation may not be the same in another. All cultures and states have constructed elaborate justifications, guidelines for how they wish their subjects to behave. The reason it is easy to carry out what might be considered immoral acts even under the guidelines of Lifton and Markusen and Kelman and Hamilton is because they are justified in terms of a higher good. The great irony is that in the name of good, evil is committed, and as Kren (1988) argues, "the primary source of violence is found in the willingness of individuals to be self sacrificing for an ideal, ideology, or cause. When individuals speak of a willingness to die for a cause, they also mean a willingness to kill. 'Give me liberty or give me death' is soon followed by 'give me liberty or I will give you death' " (p. 255).

The human desire to change the world to bring about their own particular vision of a "better" society, to change the world from what it is to what it should be, may also be a source of destructive behavior. Just as Christianity led to the Crusades and the Inquisition, visions of an ideal democracy and the city on the hill and manifest destiny led Anglo-Americans to exterminate and steal the land of Native Americans.

The conditions created within a group or society as a means to move toward some particular vision create the environment within which certain kinds of behavior are rewarded and others discouraged. What happens is that force and violence win out and become the consensual tools to achieve success. In international politics genocide becomes a tool of success as leaders choose to follow that path while the world watches and does nothing. Power triumphs. What is most important are the sets of behaviors receiving the institutionalized rewards of a society, national or global, and the kinds of models that are created. If one recognizes rewards for violence, for war and aggression, that is the form of behavior most likely to be displayed. If, on the other hand, one sees violence and aggression punished and peaceful negotiation rewarded, that will be the form of desired behavior. One does not need to be a very perceptive observer to note what is now rewarded and celebrated.

So, now we return to Harry's dilemma. In a world that rewards an ethic of violence, counterviolence is necessary to protect people from the aggression. As Storr (1991) points out, while we would all like to "rid

# "Ethics," "Morality" and "Responsibility"

ourselves of our proclivities for violence," if we did we "might find that we could no longer stand up for ourselves or assert our separate identities. Aggression seems closely linked with self-preservation, self-assertion, and self-affirmation. An aggressive attack upon another individual involving the use of physical force is a crude, extreme example of self-assertion at the expense of the other" (p. 7). The paradox is that if one is not willing to die for a cause and use violence to stop, in the case of our discussion, genocidal violence, then it will continue. The matter, therefore, of replacing one morality with another, or of imposing one set of community standards as opposed to another, is only the starting point for a solution to the problem of genocidal violence.

## Summing Up

The longer I study violence and human behavior the more suspicious, and perhaps cynical, I become about academic prescriptions to halt the violence or to replace one morality with another. No religion has been free of murder, no nation-state has failed to kill to achieve the goals leaders wish to pursue. To be able to make Harry's judgment, to be able to ascertain which is the "wrong side," is more complicated than simply putting forth some definitions.

Our contemporary world is not homogenous and there are major disagreements over what once might have appeared to be fundamental, agreed-upon ideas of how humans were to behave toward each other—although they clearly never did act in that fashion. The old rules of the major ethical and religious traditions have given way to justifications for virtually any form of behavior humans may wish to pursue. While there are movements afoot to return to the older ethical traditions, these meet with controversy, and there is little agreement over what tradition would best serve as the guideline for behavior.

So perhaps the optimal solution is unlikely and there are always unforeseen consequences for any action. The difficulty of proposing to solve moral dilemmas in a morally ambiguous world, in a world where morality and responsibility are secondary to ambition and power, remain. While we must, therefore, tell Harry we are sorry that it is still so very easy to find oneself on the wrong side, at least we are able to become aware of alternatives. If it were possible to inculcate a vision of morality and institutionalize ideas of responsibility it would follow that a movement to prevent genocide would emerge. This is a long-term step toward prevention, the first being the previously outlined means to stop the violence. In short, it is possible to make the "right" side more amenable to international human rights and to recognize which is "right" if one has experienced a socialization process in which such an ethic is inculcated.

# 10

# Inculcating an Ethic to Prevent Genocide

## Introduction

People are not born with political ideas.[16] As far as is discerned, everything we know about politics, and this includes genocide and/or human rights, ethics or morality, is learned or taught to us either formally, as, for example, through the process of education, or informally, through the process of cultural transmission. The process operates something like the following: Born into a particular political culture, the agents of socialization (generally speaking these include family, educational systems, media, peers, and other influences such as religion) transmit the norms of that culture to young people. These norms are taught to every person in order to try to convince individuals to accept them as "natural" and to exhibit "approved of" or "desirable" forms of behavior. By extension, if this process is successful, it operates to control what is regarded as "deviant" ideas or behavior.

This is important because the most efficient means of insuring conformity and obedience is to transmit, through political socialization, norms of behavior that are congruent with the dominant ideology in a society. If people can be convinced that these norms are "legitimate," that this is the way they *should* behave, then it will not be necessary for those in power to resort to force to put down dissidents—those who do not conform to the norms. Obviously, if all citizens, or even a majority, internalize and/or accept the desired definitions of normality, if they conform and obey the leaders, then there will be no "deviants." To accomplish this all states and all organizations socialize new members in an attempt to reproduce their desired vision of reality (Hirsch, 1971; Matthews, 1960; Wheeler, 1966). One of the most important aspects of this process is to create an agreed to, or collective, memory so that all or most individuals in a nation or society will value positively the same set of symbols and will share a view of what is and is not legitimate. This is how cultures and societies define deviance. Behavior in the political realm that is defined as not legitimate, invokes sanctions and the populations are, consequently, controlled. If most people, for example, regard military service as a positive virtue and as necessary for anyone running for high office, such as the president of the United States, then not serving or avoiding service in a war with which he disagrees may not help the candidate's approval. If, in addition, all or most believe that all or most of the wars in which a nation fought were "just," or that the nation never started the wars but was provoked and was acting to defend values that are believed to be positive, such as defending democracy or the free world, then it becomes very difficult to question that memory, and people who do might be subjected to derision or, even worse, to a range of retribution that might include a black list to prevent them from securing certain jobs, and, in cases such as the antiwar protesters in the 1960s, violence by the state.

All societies, all cultures, all states perpetuate themselves, or try to, by inculcating new members into the ongoing set of living arrangements. The most pervasive mechanism to accomplish this has been for the modern state to set up state-sanctioned systems of public education.

Schools in all societies function to train people for the roles they are to play in those societies. Generally, education serves the dominant political and economic forces in a state. The idea that education serves political ends goes back a long way in history—some take it back to Plato, some to Rousseau. However far back one wishes to travel, it is clear that at one time education was designed to serve the ends of the dominant religious forces—to inculcate "the faith" and ensure its continuation.

As the nation-state replaced religion as the major power in the world this function was inevitably secularized and transferred to the state. Education became the inseparable adjunct of the state. Its function was to serve the state in the same way it served religion—to perpetuate it and inculcate a particular ethic that teaches citizens to revere certain their particular state and view others with, if not outright hostility, at least some semblance of suspicion.

Throughout history, with increasing ferocity and deadliness in the twentieth century, genocide has been perpetrated by the modern nation-state, which, until recently, has made few if any moves to prevent or punish that crime. This chapter examines the relationship between how individuals learn to view the state and techniques that might help to temper nationalism and contribute to internationalizing world views so that individuals begin to see themselves as experiencing the same problems, frustrations and desires as their fellow beings. If this basic sense of likeness, of empathic identification, can be communicated and internalized, then basic changes might begin to occur.

Since nationalism is the psychological foundation upon which international perceptions are currently constructed, it must be modified by instituting a process of political resocialization from one that emphasizes nationalism to one that emphasizes internationalism and human rights as an overarching ethic. The mechanism suggested to accomplish this goal is to focus on the socialization of what has been referred to as "covenanted internationalism," which, in turn, emphasizes the first universal ideology—international human rights.

## Learning to Live Together

Whether future generations will live together peacefully or continue the outrage of mass murder depends to a very large extent upon how future generations learn to perceive not only the state, but each other, and how educators and political decision makers act with regard to increasing people's awareness of human interdependence. Interestingly, this view of international perceptions is not a new proposition. In 1926 George Bradford Neumann wrote: "international relations are of far greater importance now than ever before in peace times and there does not appear any indication that this importance will decrease, but it rather appears that it will continue to increase" (p. 5). Neumann enumerated selected indicators of the growing importance of international relations and noted that social scientists and educators were focusing ever greater attention on international concerns. In a surprisingly contemporary phrase, he pointed out that "modern technology is causing the world's physical distances to shrink ... [but this] does not necessarily mean that world brotherhood will result" (p. 7). In fact, he argued, only "the development of more friendly attitudes in the nations and people concerned" can lessen hostility (ibid.).

Finally, Neumann noted that new perceptions of the international state system were needed, but were not being developed: "new attitudes toward humanity in general and other nations in particular must take the place of those which have obtained—a new loyalty, an internationalistic loyalty, not simply a nationalistic loyalty" (p. 6). If all this sounds vaguely familiar it is not surprising. Contemporary scholars have once again discovered, or rediscovered, the importance of international perceptions and knowledge (Ravitch and Finn, 1987; Grosvenor, 1989; Delli Carpini and Keeter, 1996), and are asking questions first phrased over fifty years ago by Neumann: "Are the people of the nations being prepared for these new conditions...? Or are the youth of today being attitudinally prepared to live in a social order which is rapidly ceasing to exist...?" (pp. 6–7).

Political attitudes and views of the world do not appear in a vacuum but are learned through the process of political socialization, which occurs within a definite cultural context. This includes the national culture, which bends international perceptions in certain nationalistic directions. Children are taught the politically constructed boundaries of the international nation-state system. Indeed, it would not be an exaggeration to say that national identity is learned early in life along with some of the more basic socialization experiences.[17] An individual's identity becomes intertwined with the nation-state and we use leaders and patriotic figures and patriotic rituals as guidelines to place ourselves within the international political community. What this means is that when children internalize nationalistic identifications and orientations they formulate a world view based upon the reconstructed account of their nation's history and its affiliation with or hostility to other nations. Unlike the indoctrination to the nation-state, which fosters total loyalty and identification, attachment to the international domain is more selective and, therefore, more disconnected.

It is, consequently, disingenuous for observers to decry the lack of international knowledge or identification when there are few or no agents from which to acquire these perceptions. It is unlikely that any nation-state will include, as part of the process of socialization, information that presents a positive view of international attempts to override the power of the individual state. This is supported by the findings from research studies, which continuously indicate the strength of nationalist sentiments.

In 1926 Neumann surveyed 110 high school students and found "a strong tendency toward nationalism" (p. 89). When Lambert and Klineberg (1967) asked American children what nationality they would "most like to be if they were not American," most chose British, Italian and Canadian (pp. 32–33). The people most often considered similar to them were also the British, Canadians, French, Italians and Germans. Those most often thought of as different are from Africa, or are Chinese, Japanese, or Russian. In addition, a study conducted by the Educational Testing Service found what the authors called a "we-they" view with the United States set far apart from all the other countries (Pike and Barrows, 1976). The United States was seen as the most desirable, richest, strongest, and largest country by their fourth grade respondents (p. 108). In other words, these different studies yield remarkably similar results. One common thread, also found by Lambert and Klineberg (1967), are the very definite stereotypes, based on nationalism, which are attached to these perceptions (p. 102). As far back as 1926 Neumann, noted that nationalism was a pervasive and important ideology. Noting its complexity, he nevertheless defined it as a "reverence bordering in sacredness for the political institutions. Often symbols such as the flag or Constitution are regarded as sacred and any criticism is seen as unpatriotic" (Neumann, 1926, pp. 17, 18). Similar perceptions remain today. One study (Hirsch and Hirsch, 1990) disclosed that students interviewed categorized the United States as a "free country," as opposed to Communist countries, which were seen as "not free" and "bad." Communism was also viewed as a form of social organization that does not reward or encourage individuality or competition; it makes everyone "the same as everyone else." Conversely, the United States was seen as a free nation where people can choose to be different. The United States was also seen as not as warlike as other nations. Thus, Americans are "good, wealthy and free," as are the Canadians, French, and Germans. These perceptions are, quite clearly, not based on information or knowledge, but on vague, and sometimes incorrect, perceptions of reality.

Perceptions of reality are created linguistically and individuals derive meaning from the cultural, social and political context. In the social construction of reality, language carries the cultural imperatives and transmits the dominant themes of a culture into the minds, feelings and habits of the people. Language is the carrier and formative agent of the ideologies and myths that form the basis of perceptions.

All cultures and every nation-state construct political myths that usually involve glorification and romanticization of the nation-state. Whether in war or peace, the state is correct and the enemies of the state, any other state, are wrong. Moreover, as Mosse (1990) notes and Fussell 1989) documents, "God" and righteousness are always on the side of your state. Nationalism and Christianity created myths to justify violent action by one state against another, and the myth was further extended to justify the death of an individual in service to the state as a worthy, sometimes Christlike, sacrifice (Mosse, 1990, p. 35). Nationalism became the new religion as love of the Fatherland or Motherland replaced love of God as the new mythology with which people could identify. These myths are phrased metaphorically and "suppress the recognition of reality" (Edelman, 1971, p. 74). They eventually become self-perpetuating and serve as mechanisms used by individuals to organize their views of the world, which are based on nationalism.

Overall it seems quite remarkable that, given this evidence of the deep-seated nationalism, hope for a peaceful future remains a constant finding of research—even in the face of absolute tragedy.

In his remarkable book, *Children of War*, Roger Rosenblatt (1984) found a similarly hopeful phenomenon. When children he interviewed had been exposed to some of the most unspeakable inhumanity and cruelty, many expressed kindness and hope instead of a desire for revenge. This suggests that, even though the world is now locked into a system of international politics that operates on the imperatives of nationalism and the nation-state system, there are young people who would like the future to be different. In turn, this might imply that the power of memory to lock people into stereotypic responses and to perpetuate hate and hostility might be mitigated by some, slim to be sure, hope for the future. Is it possible, if people believe that they must share their fate on this small planet, that the seemingly continuous cycle of violence might somehow be broken? My argument is that transforming national loyalties into international and human loyalties is one hesitant step toward a more peaceful planet. Ascertaining how to transform these international perceptions based on nationalism into truly international perceptions is the task remaining.

## Political Socialization and International Perceptions

Having just noted the historical importance of the nation-state and the overwhelming presence of nationalistic themes, it is now necessary to examine how these themes can be transformed into perceptions more compatible with international harmony. How, in other words, can the process of political socialization be recast from one in which international perceptions are actually based on nationalism, to one in which they are truly international?

For the most part, studies have focused on national identity and have ignored or paid little attention to international concerns. While the international political system has undergone remarkable and swift transformation since the end of the World War II, our perceptions of it appear to remain mired in the morass of nationalism. If international perceptions remain tied so closely to national identity, and if the process of political socialization does not begin to focus on the formation of international identity instead of national identity, it is unlikely that narrow nationalism will be lessened. Fortunately, it is not difficult to see how this process of change might occur.

Political socialization studies generally find that knowledge and attitudes are transmitted to young people via a series of socialization agents. These include the family, the peer group and other significant groups, and the media—in particular television, and education. In the case of international perceptions, all of these could have a potential impact, but education would appear to be the most logical agent of transformation.

There are, however, formidable obstacles. Political decision makers view educational institutions as extensions of the state. For them, schools should function to train people for the role they will play in society. Historically, education fulfilled this function as it served the dominant political and economic forces in a nation-state and taught citizens to identify with the nation.

Nations, in the persona of the political decision makers, consequently, think of education as a means to achieve national aspirations. As a result, the focus remains centered on national sovereignty and is not conducive to truly international identity. In fact,

> As long as the framework for international education is based on the notion that education, like military power, is but a means to achieve national ambitions, progress in building better cross-cultural and global relations among people and nations is likely to be incidental and haphazard. Education viewed solely as a matter of getting ahead is divisive at local, national and international levels. The need is to devise a system that educates all comers, rich and poor, foreign and domestic, to full humanity. (Becker, 1973, p. 106)

One way to accomplish this is to try to change the socialized content from competitive nationalism to cooperative internationalism. The single best mechanism to inculcate cooperative internationalism is by focusing on the "world's first universal ideology"—international human rights (Weissbrodt, 1988, p. 1).

## Human Rights and Political Socialization

As noted above, all observers do not agree that ideologies supportive of human rights are universal. Yet, without the protection offered by safeguarding human rights there is nothing to restrain the modern state.

Where most political, religious, philosophical, or economic ideologies have been tied to a particular tribe, group, nation or group of nations, human rights represents a more universal idea that offers one method to protect the individual from the all-pervasive power of the state. Despite this growing importance, political education, which is one aspect of political socialization, seldom portrays identity or rights as international. Students are taught about national identity. The nationalistic orientation of almost all history and civics courses means that human identity and human rights are not seen as international—rarely are the international documents studied to the same extent as the national documents.

For example, it is far more common to learn the Declaration of Independence or the Preamble to the Constitution than the Universal Declaration of Human Rights. In other words, schools prepare students to fit into the particular national context and to venerate the nation-state. Studies find over and over again that this type of "nationalistic education incorporates instruction designed to portray the most positive views of the nation-state and the most negative views of ideas, symbols, and people considered to be contranational" (Nelson, 1980, p. 270). These national identifications, as I have repeatedly argued, are not completely compatible with true international identity. What is needed is a new way of looking at the relationship between the individual and the international community.

## Covenanted Internationalism

Young people, as Schaar argues (1981), "need a clear and intelligent comprehension of life to guide their earnestness, their seeking, ... and their indignation ... If the larger community does not provide out of its own resources of ideas and experiences the material for the fabrication of such identity-forming ideologies, young people will find their material elsewhere" (pp. 278–79). Some may "escape into a private utopia," while others might submerge their nascent identity into the consumer fads of America, and still others, "especially those on the economic, ethnic and cultural margins—will develop negative and hostile ideologies" (p. 279). Young people need points of positive identification, and since there is little positive attention focused on international identity, young people may find their identity in virulent forms of patriotism and nationalism. Perhaps a new definition of patriotism or nationalism is called for.

A model of patriotism that is in fact compatible with humanism and internationalism does exist. Schaar (1981) argues that "covenanted patriotism" is the only "conception of patriotic devotion that fits a nation as large and heterogeneous as our own" (p. 293). Covenanted patriotism, he argues,

> sets a mission and provides a standard of judgement. It tells us when we are acting justly and it does not confuse martial fervor with a dedication to country ... the covenant is not a static legacy, a gift outright, but a burden and a promise. The nation exists only in repeated acts of remembrance and renewal of the covenant through changing circumstances. Patriotism here is more than a frame of mind. It is also activity guided by and directed toward the mission established in the founding covenant. This conception of political membership also decisively transcends the parochial and primitive fraternities of blood and race, for it calls kin all who accept the authority of the covenant.... This patriotism is compatible with the most generous humanism. (Ibid.)

Covenanted patriotism is an alternative to the blind adherence to patriotic ritual devoid of critical and moral reasoning which has traditionally characterized nationalism.[18] Covenanted patriotism, on the other hand, is based on knowledge of, for example, the Bill of Rights. There is

# Inculcating an Ethic to Prevent Genocide

no apparent reason that covenanted patriotism could not be socialized in a manner similar to that in which patriotism is inculcated today. In addition, there is no apparent reason for not extending the notion to include what I call "covenanted internationalism." This means that international identity, like covenanted patriotism, would be guided by and directed toward the international mission established in international human rights covenants. Specifically, the numerous eloquent human rights documents found in the UN (Davies, 1988).[19] In addition to all the UN documents, covenanted internationalism would also be based on teaching the common human history of human rights. Thus, the historical basis of human rights as espoused in documents such as the Declaration of Independence, the U.S. Constitution and the Declaration of the Rights of Man (France, 1791) would all be included as the foundation from which people in general, and children in particular, would begin to form their international identity. Socialization would be built upon an invocation of these documents as the common frame of human identity and as the common hope for a better life for all people. For as Smith (1992a) so eloquently argues:

> Recognition and remembrance involve more than regard for truth: they express compassion for those who have suffered, respect for their dignity as persons, and revolt against the injustice done to them. In the deepest sense, recognition and remembrance are related not only to what happened, but to questions of who *we* are, what *society* is, and how life and community can be protected against visions that would destroy both. To remember those who have come before us is an expression of ourselves—our care, our capacity to join in a community, our respect for other human beings. And through our capacities for memory and foresight, a community comes to include those who are living, those who have died, and those yet to be born. (P. 14)

This vision must be based on a profound change in the way we now socialize our young people to identify with nationalism and obedience. A process based on covenanted internationalism and stressing human rights may be a viable alternative. By itself, however, it is necessary, but not sufficient. Covenanted internationalism must be part of a larger ethic, an ethic aimed at the preservation rather than the destruction of human life.

But the key question remains: If a life preserving ethic, based on covenanted internationalism and a new sense of community is to be implemented, how does that process occur in a real world dominated by nation-states and ruled by the incentives of power and violence—how, in short, do we learn to live together?

There are, of course, several obvious problems. First, nationalism still predominates and human rights are still abused by many nations. This contemporary reality will remain until a life-preserving ethic based on covenanted internationalism replaces the virulent form of old-fashioned patriotism. Without international identity there can be no international authority that supersedes the nation-state and enforces the eloquent claims to human rights.

Second, and related, is the fact that the topic of international human rights occupies a very minor place in the overall socialization patterns in most nation-states. Even formal educational courses such as history, civics and even political science at the collegiate level remain nation-centered with a focus on country and national identity. Moreover, Carol Hahn (1987) notes that "Most curriculum guides, syllabuses, textbooks, and examinations still emphasize descriptions of national governmental and political institutions and elite political actors (mostly male)," and teachers are generally unfamiliar with international human rights documents. If education is to become truly international or global "political education about, for, and in the spirit of human rights can and should begin early and continue throughout the school years" (p. 184).

Political socialization research could provide insight into how the process might work. One way to conceptualize the process of political socialization is to see it as involving two steps: first, political awareness and personalization, and, second, institutionalization (Niemi, 1973, p. 121). As the first step, political awareness and personalization involves the young person learning that there are authorities above and beyond the family and school, and viewing those authority figures as helping them personally. At this stage children have little awareness of the actual operation of politics or of political institutions. The second step, which occurs as the child grows older, is institutionalization, or learning that there are political institutions. This stage involves the young person becoming aware of political institutions and how the political process works.

Socializing a life-preserving ethic could very well follow a similar sequence by beginning to teach about people as individuals and moving away from the emphasis on leaders and wars. Examining the similar problems experienced by all human beings and personifying them with specific examples representing experiences of everyday life provides a point of identification for young children. In addition, these examples would provide a balance between showing history the way it was lived as well as how it was made by selected leaders. Following this, attention should be devoted to the international political institutions and, in particular, to the human rights documents. The emphasis would be on pointing out how we are all entitled to protection offered by these documents and must all work together to establish these protections throughout the world community. These common protections and the

## Inculcating an Ethic to Prevent Genocide

identification of common problems may then provide the basis for building a sense of community based on covenanted internationalism. The community sense becomes the base for the spreading of the life-preserving ethic.

As Suzanne Shafer (1987) points out, education aimed at fostering international identity must incorporate all the other forms of education that have received individual labels. These include multicultural education, peace education, education that focuses on transnational concerns such as the environment and energy resources. However, the fact that these are viewed as separate, as indicated by their discrete labels, demonstrates that there is presently no integrated approach to change the perspective. Implementation of these changes is not a simple matter. There are few enough who are interested in and believe that this is the direction humanity must move in order to forestall the repeated cycles of destruction, and there are even fewer qualified to teach and communicate the knowledge base.

For example, a noteworthy instance occurred in the State of California, which recently mandated a very fine curriculum on the teaching of human rights and genocide. One of the primary authors of that curriculum reported that there are few if any teachers qualified to implement the necessary courses (Kuper, 1989). Despite such problems, attempts to move in this direction remain ongoing and appear to be in the process of being more widely diffused throughout the world. In pursuing the desired results there are at least two central questions to be answered:

1. "Does the existing political education produce obedient and compliant or alienated citizens who let an elite rule and do not themselves exercise their rights to participate in public policy decision making?
2. Does the existing approach produce citizens who repeat the rhetoric of 'rights for all' but who are not supportive of these rights in concrete situations? Or will young people grow up respecting international human rights both at home and abroad and possessing knowledge, skills, and attitudes that will lead them into active citizen participation?" (Hahn, 1987, p. 185)

When these questions can be answered honestly to indicate that obedience is not the overwhelming product of the socialization process and that a choice to support human rights replaces the choice to support the policy of the nation-state, perhaps then young people will grow up respecting human rights at home and abroad instead of displaying outdated nationalism that results in hatred and hostility.

To achieve this admittedly idealistic goal requires a system of education transmitting international identity based on covenanted internationalism and moving toward an effective world community of legal, political, economic and educational institutions carrying the message of common humanity and signifying a transformation of the nation-state system. If and when the socialization process is so transformed it will signal that a new historical era has dawned. The age of the preeminent state, "intent upon sacrificing private interests and personal life at the alter of global competition" (Beres, 1985, p. 397) will be replaced by an age of "understanding, tolerance and friendship among all" (Universal Declaration of Human Rights, 1948).

While this note of optimism is necessary to reinforce the hope that humanity has the capability to move to a more just, humane and peaceful future, a dose of realism must be added. The obstacles are many and in the real world it may not even be so easy to identify which ethic is aimed at the preservation of life. Yet, if a movement to prevent genocide is to germinate in the United States, at a minimum, the above two steps, an education process inculcating support for international human rights and action to support those rights, and a government willing to participate in that action, are necessary conditions. So, we are brought full circle to the beginning of our exploration.

# Conclusion: A Politics to Prevent Genocide

I want to conclude with great words of wisdom, but I cannot summon them from the depths of my consciousness. Instead, allow me to point out that we have heard it all before. Nothing in the previous nine chapters is entirely original or startling. Nothing is surprising. Common sense alone would tell us that if genocide is ever to be prevented the elements outlined above are both necessary and sufficient, and without them humans will continue to kill each other in large numbers. Having stated the obvious I could now review all the formulations in this book and note how genocide will be prevented when they are implemented. In reality, however, I am profoundly suspicious of such discussions—even my own. I do believe that genocide could be prevented and that humans could create a better, more just and humane environment for themselves if, as all the clichés note, the will and leadership were present to travel that path. After all, I begin by noting that people make their own history and that politics involves making decisions and choices, so if we made the ethical and moral choices we could bring to pass a better life for all on the planet. In addition, I argued that a political movement could be built in the United States to support the ethic of human rights and a foreign policy to prevent genocide and that American public opinion would be very likely to support such action but not likely to participate in it in large numbers. So what is left?

Instead of reviewing in detail all that has been written—after all, stating it once should be sufficient—let me summarize some of what we know about international violence and genocide and U.S. responses to that violence. First, we know that there was an exponential increase in international violence associated with failed states and ethnonational hatred and aspirations. We know, further, that the United States responded to that violence in a sporadic and haphazard fashion. When U.S. interests were perceived to be threatened, such as in the Iraqi invasion of Kuwait which threatened the supply and price of oil, American intervention was immediate and the United States led a coalition to turn back the invasion. On September 11, 2001, when terrorists flew airliners into the World Trade Center and the Pentagon and America was seen as under attack, the response was likewise immediate and swift as a coalition to fight terrorism was initiated and proceeded to overthrow the Taliban government in Afghanistan and to attempt to capture or kill the leaders of the terrorist effort. In other cases, less was done.

There was more rhetoric than action. Intervention took place in the case of Bosnia only after several years of dithering and hesitation and outright lies concerning what was going on in that sad area. The response was several years late and after 250,000 people were killed. We know that the Clinton administration was fully aware of what was taking place and we know that they manipulated the situation, claiming that public opinion was opposed to U.S. humanitarian intervention to stop that violence. We know that this was not the case, that public opinion wanted the violence halted and that the Clinton administration failed to exercise leadership to bring the humanitarian crisis to a halt. We know that the Clinton administration failed to take any action in Rwanda, actually prohibiting the use of the term "genocide" so that they would not have any obligation under the UN Convention on the Prevention and Punishment of the Crime of Genocide to intervene to stop the violence. We know that the United States led NATO to bomb the former Yugoslavia to stop the ethnic cleansing in Kosovo but refused to consider the use of ground troops, and we know that the United States breathed a sigh of relief when Australia took the lead in halting the massacres in East Timor. Moreover, we know that in other genocidal situations, such as Sierra Leone and the Sudan, little or no action was taken, and we know that when other large powerful states such as Russia abused human rights little or nothing was said about it by the U.S. government. In short, we know that the United States hesitated to take a leadership role in the prevention of genocide, and we also know that only when the United States is ready to undertake such a leadership role to implement the policies outlined in this book will the scourge of modern genocide be halted. Furthermore, we know what these policies should be; at least we know what the possible options are, and we know that a movement has to be built within the United States so that citizens will support such action and will take an active role in pressuring their government to take the lead in initiating and carrying out the policies necessary to

## Conclusion: A Politics to Prevent Genocide

prevent genocide—to, in the short run, stop the violence and, in the long run, fashion an ethic of prevention.

While we also know that this is highly unlikely there are positive signs indicating that there may be hesitant movement toward prevention. These include:

1. The proposed creation of a UN rapid reaction force or police force and a proposal to create a 60,000-person European force ready to take action to prevent atrocity. These would be potential forces that might go into action upon the initiation of an early warning.
2. The creation under UN auspices of the International Criminal Tribunal for the Former Yugoslavia. In particular the extradition and trial of Milosovic the former leader of the Serbs, and the similar creation and operation of The International Criminal Tribunal for Rwanda.
3. The creation of the International Criminal Court and discussions and debates concerning jurisdiction.
4. The indictment of Augusto Pinochet, former military dictator in Chile.
5. Proposed Cambodian trials of the leaders of the Khmer Rouge for genocide.
6. The conviction in February 2001 of three former members of the Bosnian Serb armed forces who were found guilty of rape and sexual enslavement of Muslim girls and women in Foca in 1992. They were found guilty of crimes against humanity and violations of the laws and customs of war. This is path breaking. It is the first time that sexual enslavement has been punished as a crime against humanity
7. Globalization of finance, trade, communication, which may erode national sovereignty but which is also questioned by some as not supportive of human rights as global corporations support the violation of human rights and environmental protections.

There are, obviously, always complexities to these types of formulations. In some cases they may be viewed as positive signs leading toward prevention while in others some may believe they have the opposite impact.

For example, Robert Kaplan (2001) asserts that the nation-state itself is in danger. As he argued in 1994 and repeated in 2001, he foresees the "weakening, dilution, and perhaps even crackup of larger, more complex, modern societies in the next 10 or 15 years in places such as Nigeria, Ivory Coast, and Pakistan" (p. 54). He views this as part of a destabilization process fueled by economic growth that supports political upheavals as people yearn for their own piece of the state. Further, this is all made more threatening by the demography as the number of young males ages 15–29 fuels the violence. They are unemployed and frustrated and being part of a violent movement provides identity and a sense of mission and purpose. Finally, ironically, he believes that "serious institutional crises," is sparked by democracy as "Everyone wants to be democratic, no use denying it. But democracy tends to emerge best when it emerges last. It should be the capstone to all other types of development, when you already have middle classes that pay income taxes, when you already have institutions run by literate bureaucrats, when the major issues of a society (such as territorial borders) are all resolved and you already have a functioning polity. . . . Right now, we're seeing democracy evolve in many places around the earth accompanied by unemployment and inflation rates every bit as dire as Germany in the 1930s, when Hitler emerged under democratic conditions, and in Italy when Mussolini came to power in the early 1920s" (p. 56). These he views as destabilizing, while others see the decline of the nation-state and the quest for democracy as positive.

In fact, R.J. Rummel (1994) argued that one focus of U.S. foreign policy and an important mechanism for preventing genocide is to foster democracy. Rummel's thesis is that the more power a government has the more it can, as he believes, "act arbitrarily according to the whims of the elite, and the more it will make war on others and murder its foreign or domestic subjects. The more constrained the power of governments, the more power is diffused, checked and balanced, the less it will aggress on others and commit democide [he uses this concept in place of genocide]." This contention leads him to conclude that totalitarian governments, in particular the former communist governments, slaughtered their people by the "tens of millions," while some democratic governments can barely execute those who commit homicide. He concludes, "The way to end war and virtually eliminate democide appears to be through restricting and checking power, i.e., through fostering democratic freedom" (pp. 1–2).

Rummel bases his case for democracy as a means to prevent genocide on what he refers to as "three facts and one practical necessity" (p. 2). First, "democracies by far have had the least domestic democide, and now with their extensive liberalization have virtually none. Therefore, democratization (not just electoral democracies, but liberal democratization in terms of civil and political rights and liberties) provides the long run hope for the elimination of democide" (ibid.).

His second "fact" is that democracies do not make war on each other, and the third is that "a fundamental national interest of democracy is peace, the avoidance of war and international trade and prosperity" (ibid.). His so-called "practical necessity" is that the UN is inadequate to

## Conclusion: A Politics to Prevent Genocide

the task of humanitarian intervention and that a parallel international organization of democracies, called by him "Alliance of Democracies," should be the main force when the UN is paralyzed.

There is no doubt that democracy should be encouraged, but Rummel's proposal contains numerous problems not the least of which is that it is very undemocratic. The democratic states, or at least those labeled by themselves and others as such, pick and choose who is to be a member and who is to participate in the interventions to stop atrocity. Left out are states not admitted to the club, which would raise important questions about the legitimacy of such actions. In addition, there are other problems that may be illustrated by referring to U.S. actions cited above. Rummel clearly stacks the deck by ignoring key information. Democracies have committed violations of human rights, if not genocide.

The United States, for example, committed genocide against the indigenous peoples of this continent and supported regimes and groups, such as the contras, who violated human rights without hesitation. The fact that the United States has done so does not mean it is not a relatively more benign place to live. There is an unfortunate tendency to get very defensive in this type of discussion and to be willing to accuse others of atrocity but not admit doing so yourself. The idea that somehow we alone are virtuous is a denial of the basic principles that still guide the nation-state in international politics. Like it or not, sovereignty and self-interest still reign supreme and the fact remains that the United States, under both Republican and Democratic administrations, has been reluctant to participate in the creation of an ethic or a movement leading toward prevention.

In addition, Rummel's argument that the key to controlling genocidal violence is political power is only partially accurate. Controlling power is the most important short-run consideration, but changing perspectives, changing the socialization process and world views as well as transforming the conditions that give rise to genocide and other forms of violence, are essential aspects of a more comprehensive policy for the long-run control of such violence.

Indeed, while there are signs that democracy is growing, Rummel's assertions are too simplistic. The fact is that a very sound argument may be made for what some now refer to as "national security liberalism," with caveats included. Simply stated, the proposition claims that the United States has both the ability and the interest to promote democracy abroad and that this will lead to what used to be called "democratic peacemaking." The idea dates to Woodrow Wilson and included the idea that promoting liberal democracy abroad at the nation-state level, along with open world markets and international institutions, to regulate conflict would bring about a more peaceful world (Smith, 2002, p. 263). This was all part of what is now known as "America's liberal grand strategy"

(Ikenberry, 2002, p. 274) which "sees the character of the domestic regimes of other states as hugely important for the attainment of American security and material interests. Put simply, the United States is better able to pursue its interest, reduce security threats to its environment, and foster a stable political order when other states particularly the major great powers are democracies rather than non-democracies" (ibid., p. 275). This rests not only on the view that democracies do not fight each other, but also on a wide range of "related claims." The "overall idea is that "democracies are more capable of developing peaceful, continuous, rule-based institutionalized, and legitimate relationships among each other than is possible with or between non-democracies" (ibid., p. 282). Related to this is economic growth and trade, since when states feel a stake in a stable international order, they are less likely to create conditions to violate that. Finally, it involves the building of international institutions that constrain and socialize nation-states. Rule and roles are created to channel states in particular directions (ibid., p. 287). All of this, the hope is, will create a common identity among states that will promote "the establishment of a peaceful and durable order" and ultimately overcome the restrictions of sovereignty (ibid., p. 288).

There remain, however, strong disagreements over the final demise of sovereignty. Stephen Krasner (2001) summed these up, noting an onslaught of forces, including monetary unions, CNN, the Internet, and nongovernmental organizations that appear to be threats to the sovereign state, but the nation-state historically has adapted to new challenges and most likely will survive these as well. So, while Kaplan's challenges appear to be real, and some states will most likely break apart, the most established will adapt and survive. Sovereignty is defined as the idea that "states are autonomous and independent from each other. Within their own boundaries, the members of the polity are free to choose their own form of government. A necessary corollary of this claim is the principle of non-intervention. One state does not have the right to intervene in the internal affairs of another" (p. 21).

The notion that the campaign for human rights is an unprecedented challenge to sovereignty is, according to Krasner, just not correct. He points out, "Over the centuries the emphasis has shifted from religious toleration, to minority rights (often focusing on specific ethnic groups in specific countries), to human rights (emphasizing rights enjoyed by all or broad classes of individuals). Human rights became the main focus after World War II when the United Nations Charter endorsed both human rights and "the classic sovereignty principle of nonintervention" (ibid., 22). In the last half century, around twenty or so human rights accords have been signed that "cover a wide range of issues including genocide, torture, slavery, refugees, stateless persons, women's rights, racial discrimination, children's rights, and forced labor. These U.N. doc-

## Conclusion: A Politics to Prevent Genocide

uments, however, have few enforcement mechanisms, and even their provisions for reporting violations are often ineffective" (ibid.). Given the trends, he argues that the new initiatives will "coexist with, not displace, the sovereign-state model" (p. 29). The positions are not incompatible, and a new U.S. foreign policy must take cognizance of both trends.

Yet, the continuing enigma of human violence troubles and perplexes me. The terrorist attacks of September 11, 2001, along with the continued presence of using and creating hatred to motivate cadres to kill others to achieve political objectives for aspiring leaders, creates an environment in which the prevention of genocide, in fact the prevention of political violence at whatever level, is a remote hope. What hope there is abides in the precarious consciousness of human actors to seize the initiative, to think about replacing the previous age of genocide with an age of peace and justice. Of course, these are clichés that must be replaced by policy. Perhaps a final word concerning the relationship between terrorism, genocide and policies designed to alleviate these threats will move us toward a conclusion that might translate into active attempts to prevent both.

### Terrorism and Genocide in the New Century

Since September 11, there have been discussions concerning the relationship between genocide and terrorism, or more specifically the Holocaust and the acts of September 11. However horrible the terrorist attacks are, they do not compare in magnitude to the death and destruction resulting from the genocides of the last century. The purpose of terrorism is to frighten or terrorize members of a group. The threat of action is designed to result in compliance with the terrorists' demands. The purpose of genocide is to kill all members of a racial or ethnic group as cited in the UN definition. Therefore, no matter how disgusting the acts of September 11 or other acts of terror, genocide remains a much more dangerous proposition for larger numbers of people.

Terrorism, however, as a result of the attacks and the sustained effort to hunt down those responsible for those attacks, is and has been at the center of public consciousness for the last five or six months. Genocide, even during the height of the killing in Bosnia and Rwanda, never occupied such a central point of saliency in the public mind. In addition, there has never been a time when political leadership in the Western developed nations undertook a sustained effort to wage a "war on genocide." In fact, quite the opposite was the case as they took little or no action to stop the killing and to hunt down the perpetrators of genocide.

In spite, therefore, of the fact that both are political acts in the sense that they are designed to achieve political goals, there remain important differences. Terrorism is designed to bring about political change that the terrorists believe cannot be accomplished any other way. Genocide is usually also designed to achieve a political goal, an ethnically cleansed area that will become a pure state purged of other groups, but it may also be an end in itself—the extermination of the European Jews as an example. The killing of the Jews may have served political ends, but it was also an end in itself. Is genocide, then, an act of terrorism, or is the use of terror a tactic that might be employed in the pursuit of a genocidal policy?

Both terrorism and genocide violate laws and are criminal offences. Genocide is illegal under the UN Convention, and terrorism is illegal under the laws of most nations and under international law as well. Both might be crimes of war and crimes against humanity. Terrorism might be part of a strategy of genocide in the sense that states might practice terrorism in the pursuit of genocidal policies such as the terror against the Armenians by the Ottoman Empire or the terror used by Hitler against the Jews. States, therefore, may commit both terrorism and genocide, and they might use terrorism as a means to achieve genocidal goals.

Mechanisms to deal with both terrorism and genocide also have similarities. Most observers believe that there are "two ways to cope with terrorism" (Snow, 2002, p. 14). One is antiterrorism, and the other is counterterrorism. Antiterrorism involves "defensive measures used to reduce the vulnerability of potential targets to attack and to lessen the effects of attacks that do occur" (ibid.). The focus here is to make it difficult for the terrorist to complete their acts successfully. A main example is increased security at, for example, airports. Similarly with genocide, "anti-genocide" might involve the creation of the early warning system that has been discussed so widely.

Counterterrorism involves "offensive and military measures taken by the military and other agencies against terrorist or their sponsoring states to prevent, or deter, or respond to terrorist acts" (ibid., p. 15). Here the focus is to eliminate the ability of the terrorists to carry out their acts and generally to take an offensive position in attacking the terrorists at the base of their operations. In this case there has been little in the way of countergenocide in the sense that there has been no worldwide coalition formed to pursue those responsible for acts of genocide, and there has been no overall mobilization of, in particular, U.S. forces to combat genocide in a fashion similar to that mobilized to fight terrorism.

What, then, is the relationship between terrorism and war? Is the "War Against Terrorism" the new form of war in the twenty-first century? The rhetoric of war has been the foremost characterization in the aftermath of the September 11 attacks. The attacks were said to be an act of war against the United States, and the United States is said to be carrying on a war against terrorism. If the United States is at war against terrorists

## Conclusion: A Politics to Prevent Genocide

it is, as one observer has noted, "a very different kind of war than any previously fought" (ibid., p. 17). There are no sustained military actions in which units of one side face off against the other, there are few if any pitched battles, and the taking of territory in a sustained campaign is not part of the action. The term that has garnered some acceptance in describing this new form of warfare is "fourth generation warfare" (ibid.). The first generation was war as it was fought up until the Napoleonic Wars, that is, war fought primarily by private armies in the employ of a noble or some organization who paid for and equipped the troops. The Napoleonic era ushered in the time of mass war, as large armies were recruited and faced each other such as in the American Civil War, and generation three is the lightning blitzkrieg campaigns of the Germans in World War II (ibid.). The new, fourth generation of war is said to be different in that there is no distinction between military and civilian targets, and success is not defined as controlling territory but in terms of the damage done to the morale of the population (p. 18). Yet, this is not entirely new. In fact, terrorism has been around for a long time and wars have been fought using tactics designed to demoralize an enemy, for example, the guerilla war waged by the Vietcong and North Vietnamese against U.S. forces in Vietnam. Overall, therefore, the question of designing policies to combat both terrorism and genocide are similar.

As Snow points out, antiterrorist policy is "largely reactive," in the sense that it is after the fact (p. 33). Airport security is strengthened after the attacks of September 11. Anti-genocide policy has been reactive, but there is now a movement to attempt to make it proactive with the previously mentioned early warning system. Yet, both face the same long-term problems, namely, that military reactions, or even early warning implementations, most likely would eliminate some terrorists or perpetrators of genocide but would leave intact the root causes of the problems that gave rise to both in the first place. Snow believes that "without basic reforms, it will be like killing a few mosquitos and leaving the swamp" (p. 33).

There appears to be some general agreement on the policies to be followed to implement such basic reforms. First, the approach cannot follow the simplistic formula of a "war on terrorism" or genocide. While any program must include a military component, peacekeeping, peace enforcement and state building must also be involved. These have been met with skepticism and a negative reaction by the Bush administration but, if neglected, will allow the basic problems that gave rise to the terror or massacres to continue and to cause more. State building means that the conditions that resulted in the poverty and hopelessness that are the root causes of both must be replaced by economic, political and social stability, which creates an environment of peace and hope for the people. To be sure, it is a difficult task, but one must ask how often we will allow ourselves to be doomed to repeat the seemingly endless cycles of violence before we begin to address the factors that precipitate that violence.

However, the world that emerged after September 11, 2001, was not the world envisioned by human rights advocates and those of us who wanted to prevent genocide. Summarized very concisely by Michael Ignatieff (2002) as the integration of American power "into a transnational legal and economic order, organized around the UN, the WTO, the International Criminal Court, and international human rights organizations" (p. 4). Instead, he argues, the new order that is emerging is one "crafted to suit American imperial objectives" where the United States uses the "pieces of the transnational legal order that suit its purposes (the WTO, for example), while ignoring or even sabotaging those parts (the International Criminal Court, the Kyoto Protocol, the ABM Treaty) that do not" (p. 4). In addition, the new war on terrorism justifies what Ignatieff refers to as "complicitious silence about the human rights violations of major partners" and justifies unilateral action and nonparticipation in the very actions that should be supported, including the building of democratic foundations and nation building (p. 5). Ignatieff points out that there have been successes in Poland, the Czech Republic, the Baltic states, South Africa (p. 6) and East Timor as well ("Lessons for Nation Builders," 2002, p. 1). In fact, East Timor is a lesson worthy of attention. For over twenty-four years, East Timor was a place where Indonesian troops and their allies, the local militias, destroyed a fifth of the population and much of the infrastructure of the island. The carnage was stopped, as noted earlier, only when Australia led a coalition of UN troops into East Timor. Today the island has, as reported by the *New York Times* (ibid.), "The institutions of democracy and will hold presidential elections before it becomes an independent nation on May 20" (ibid.). East Timor is an advertisement for nation building following the policies outlined in previous chapters—that is, the deployment of a "strong peace keeping force with robust rules of engagement. The UN forces were able to stop militia raids into East Timor from West Timor, which is part of Indonesia, by getting permission for their peacekeepers and police to aggressively protect themselves and the Timorese people. They can shoot first if threatened" (ibid). Obviously, the UN learned lessons from the previous failures and these were applied to East Timor and should be applied to future situations including Afghanistan. Instead of thwarting such efforts and demanding that its lead be followed as it pursues a unilateral policy, the United States should join actively in participating in such actions and take the lead in moving the world in that direction. There is no secret as to how to accomplish the goals I have advocated. In fact, sources as diverse as Klaus Schwab, president of the World Economic Forum, and Kofi Annan, Secretary General of

## Conclusion: A Politics to Prevent Genocide

the UN, essentially agree on the task before those who wish to prevent both genocide and terrorism. As Schwab (2002) so eloquently noted,

> Borrowing from the hard-earned lessons of World War II, and enriching those insights with what we have learned since, it seems clear that we cannot continue to live in a world where the voices of the poor go unheeded, where economic development benefits only the rich and where conflict is allowed to germinate and grow in a culture of misunderstanding. It is in the enlightened self-interest of the privileged and the advantaged to ensure that this does not happen. More important, it is the moral obligation of us all. (P. 28)

These are, of course, ideals, words, and they do not necessarily translate into policy. What all who advocate a policy to prevent genocide ardently wish is that the more times they are repeated, and in particular by those in positions of social, economic and political responsibility, the words will translate into action and will in turn be transmitted into the consciousness of large and ever larger numbers of people who will in the short run support the policies necessary to prevent genocide and to build a movement to support that activity, and, in the long run transform the socialization process and the policy process so that they too will give rise to thoughts and actions to liberate us from the repetitive destruction of genocidal violence.

# Notes

1. In 1993 Zbigniew Brzezinski claimed that "167,000,000 to 175,000,000 lives have been deliberately extinguished through politically motivated carnage" (p. 17). Some of the genocides usually included are:

1915–1923: 1,500,000 Armenians
1932: 10,000,000 Ukranians
1933–1945: 6,000,000 Jews
1939–1945: 500,000 Gypsies
1939–1945: 50,000 Homosexuals
1959: 65,000 Tibetan Buddhists
1965–1973: 160,000 Hutu peasants
1966: 15,000 Ibos
1975–1979: 1,500,000 Khmer (Cambodians)
1981–1989: 15,000 Bahai
1988: 75,000 Hutu
1992–1994: 250,000 Bosnian Muslims
1994: 1,500,000 Tutsi

2. In May 1984 the International Court of Justice rendered a preliminary decision against the United States, and the United States refused to accept its jurisdiction.

3. Reservations: First, that "before any dispute to which the United States is a party may be submitted to the jurisdiction of the International Court of Justice under this article, the specific consent of the United States is required in each case."

Second, "That nothing in the Convention requires or authorizes legislation or other action by the United States of America prohibited by the Constitution of the United States as interpreted by the United States."

Understandings:

1. "That the term 'intent to destroy, in whole or in part, a national, ethnical, racial, or religious groups as such' appearing in Article II means the specific intent to destroy, in

whole or in substantial part, a national, ethnical, racial or religious group as such by the acts specified in Article II."
2. "that the term 'mental harm' in Article II(b) means permanent impairment of mental faculties through drugs, torture or similar techniques."
3. That the pledge to grant extradition in accordance with a state's laws and treaties in force found in Article VII extends only to acts which are criminal under the laws of both the requesting and the requested state and nothing in Article VI affects the right of any state to bring to trial before its own tribunals any of its nationals for acts committed outside a state." (Under this the Nuremberg Trials may not have taken place because the idea of "conspiracy" does not exist in European law.)
4. "that acts in the course of armed conflicts committed without the specific intent required by Article II are not sufficient to constitute genocide as defined by this convention."
5. "That with regard to the reference to international penal tribunal in Article VI of the Convention, the United States declares that it reserves the right to effect its participation in any such tribunal only by a treaty entered into specifically for that purpose with the advice and consent of the Senate." (Again the Nuremberg or Tokyo trials could not have been held unless approved by the United States Senate).

4. The relationship between racial myths, culture and oppression is explored in Poliakov (1971) and Mosse (1978). The connection between culture and genocide or oppression is examined in Harris (1973), Henry (1965) and Becker (1975).

5. I am indebted to Professor Scott Keeter of George Mason University, who introduced me to this source of data and downloaded some of it for me.

6. Two colleagues read an earlier version of this chapter and made me aware of these questions: Professor Roger Smith of the College of William and Mary and Dr. Judyth Twigg from Virginia Commonwealth University. I am indebted to them for their insightful comments.

7. Since the end of the conflict numerous books and articles have been written about what happened, why it happened, and how international and U.S. policy failed to prevent it from happening. Rather than detail these sources in the text they are found in the references.

8. This section is derived from the last two chapters of my previously published book: *Genocide and the Politics of Memory: Studying Death to Preserve Life*. Chapel Hill, N.C.: University of North Carolina Press, 1995. Since I still maintain that the basic approach outlined there is the best way to prevent genocide, I have taken most of what I wrote at that time and brought it up to date for this volume.

9. These principles are found in Falk, Kolko, and Lifton, 1971, pp. 106–7.

The Nuremberg Principles of 1946
1. Principles of International Law Recognized in the Charter of the Nuremberg Tribunal and in the Judgment of the Tribunal as formulated by the International Law Commission, June–July 1950.

Principle I
Any person who commits an act which constitutes a crime under international law is responsible therefor and liable to punishment.

Principle II
The fact that internal law does not impose a penalty for an act which constitutes a crime under international law does not relive a person who committed the act from responsibility under international law.

Principle III
The fact that a person who committed an act which constitutes a crime under interna-

tional law acted as Head of State or responsible government official does not relieve him from responsibility under international law.

Principle IV

The fact that a person acted pursuant to order of his Government or of a superior does not relieve him from responsibility under international law, provided a moral choice was in fact possible to him.

Principle V

Any person charged with a crime under international law has the right to a fair trial on the facts and law.

Principle VI

The crimes hereinafter set out are punishable as crimes under international law:
a. Crimes against peace:
  (i) Planning, preparation, initiation or waging of a war of aggression or a war in violation of international treaties, agreements or assurances.
  (ii) Participation in a common plan or conspiracy for the accomplishment of any of the acts mentioned under (i).
b. War crimes:
Violations of the laws or customs of war which include, but are not limited to, murder, ill-treatment or deportation to slave-labour or for any other purpose of civilian populations of or in occupied territory, murder or ill-treatment of prisoners of war or persons on the seas, killing of hostages, plunder of public or private property, wanton destruction of cities, towns, or villages, or devastation not justified by military necessity.
c. Crimes against humanity:
Murder, extermination, enslavement, deportation and other inhuman acts done against any civilian population, or persecutions on political, racial or religious grounds, when such acts are done or such persecutions are carried on in execution of or in connexion with any crime against peace or any war crime.

Principle VII

Complicity in the commission of a crime against peace, a war crime, or a crime against humanity as set forth in Principle VI is a crime under international law.

10. Australia, Canada, China, France, India, the Netherlands, New Zealand, the Philippines, the Soviet Union, the United Kingdom, and the United States.

11. For the most part, the primary precedents include the Hague Convention on Land Warfare of 1907 which set the so-called "laws and customs of war on land." According to this convention poison or poisoned weapons were forbidden and prisoners must be treated fairly and not tortured or mistreated. In addition, according to Article 2J "the attack or bombardment by whatever means, of towns, villages, dwellings, or buildings which are undefended is prohibited."

A second precedent was the Versailles Treaty of 1918, by which Kaiser Wilhelm was to be tried as a war criminal. A special tribunal of five judges from the United States, Great Britain, France, Italy and Japan was to be convened. Germany was forced to recognize the right of the Allies to set up these trials and was supposed to hand over any person accused of war crimes. Also, they were to "furnish all documents and information of every kind, the production of which may be considered necessary to ensure the full knowledge of the incriminating acts, the discovery of the offenders and the just appreciation of responsibility" (Falk, Kolko, and Lifton, 1971, p. 42).

Additional precedents included the Geneva Protocol on Poison Gas and Bacteriological Warfare of 1925, the Pact of Paris (Kellogg-Briand Pact) of 1928, and the Geneva Conventions on the Law of War of 1949, which was updated in the 1977 Geneva Protocols.

12. Littell (1991, pp. 314–315) identifies fifteen.

13. Since 1990 the United States has intervened militarily in Third World countries around twenty-five times. The list includes: 1898–1902, Cuba; 1903–1914, Panama; 1906–1909, Cuba; 1912–1925, Nicaragua; 1914–1919, Mexico; 1915–1934, Haiti; 1916–1924, Dominican Republic; 1917–1922, Cuba; 1918–1920, Panama; 1926–1933, Nicaragua; 1950–1953, Korea; 1958, Lebanon; 1961, Cuba; 1962–1963, Congo; 1964–1973, Vietnam; 1965, Dominican Republic; 1975, Cambodia; 1980, Iran; 1981–1991, Nicaragua; 1983–1984, Lebanon; 1983, Grenada; 1986, Libya; 1989–1990, Panama; 1990–1991, The Gulf War—Iraq; 1990, Liberia; 1992, Somalia (Cingranelli, 1993, pp. 236–237).

14. In March 1993, the UN was involved in twelve different operations. These include: UN Truce Supervision of Israel's borders with Lebanon, Syria and Egypt; UN Disengagement Observer Force in the Golan Heights between Israel and Syria; UN Interim Force in Lebanon near the border with Israel; UN Military Observer Group in India and Pakistan to supervise the cease-fire in Kashmir; UN Peacekeeping Force in Cyprus overseeing the Turkish-Greek cease-fire; UN Iraq-Kuwait Observation Mission in the demilitarized zone between the two nations; UN Angola Verification Mission II to observe the attempt to restore peace to Angola; UN Observer Mission in El Salvador to supervise the end of the civil war in that country; UN Mission for the Referendum in Western Sahara to watch over disputed territory and try to resolve the issue; UN Protection Force in Croatia, Bosnia-rate which is having little effect in stopping the Serbs from taking over large amounts of territory; UN Transitional Authority in Cambodia attempting to reconcile the factions but is getting little cooperation from the Khmer Rouge, who previously committed genocide against their own people; UN Operation in Somalia to supervise transport of food to starving people (*Richmond Times-Dispatch*, Sunday, December 6, 1992, p. A18).

15. In July 1947, George F. Kennan published an article in *Foreign Affairs* under the pseudonym "X" that was part of an ongoing debate over what the Soviet Union was planning to do in world politics. Kennan argued that the Soviet Union was primarily motivated by communist ideology, which led to a drive for world power. This could only be "contained" by applying counterforce whenever necessary at various political and geographic locations. It was as a result of this article that the policy of "containment" emerged.

16. This is derived from chapter 13 in Herbert Hirsch, *Genocide and the Politics of Memory* (Chapel Hill: University of North Carolina Press, 1995), pp. 161–180.

17. Many of the studies of political socialization tend to confirm that children's early experiences provide them with their basic view of the world. The first six years of a young person's life influence the way in which he will define "reality." Children learn their socially defined roles, but they also begin to acquire a political identification. In particular, among the first political perceptions learned are views of authority—that is perceptions of political leaders—and orientations toward relating to authority. While it has not been adequately tested, scholars hypothesize that national identity—identification with the nation state—is also learned early and reinforced by the later agents such as the school and the media (Hirsch, 1971).

18. Nationalism became ascendant in the modern era. Schaar (1981, p. 299) identifies four factors involved in the rise of nationalism:
1. "The decline of religious faith as the basic bond among people and as the primary source of cultural life."
2. "the breakdown of cultural isolation consequent upon the development of improved means of transportation and communication."
3. "consolidation and growth of centralized state power."
4. "the dissolution of the monarchical and dynastic principle of political legitimacy."

19. These documents include the following: UN Charter (1945); Universal Declaration of Human Rights (1948); Convention on the Prevention and Punishment of the Crime of Genocide (1948); Convention Relating to Status of Refugees (1951); Convention Relating to the Status of Stateless Persons (1954); Declaration of the Rights of the Child (1959); Convention Against Discrimination in Education (1960); Protocol Instituting a Conciliation and Good Offices Commission to be Responsible for Seeking a Settlement of any Disputes Which May Arise Between States Parties to the Convention Against Discrimination in Education (1962); United Nations Declaration on the Elimination of all Forms of Racial Discrimination (1963); International Convention on the Elimination of all Forms of Racial Discrimination (1965); Declaration on the Promotion Among Youth of the Ideals of Peace, Mutual Respect and Understanding Between Peoples (1965); Protocol Relating to the Status of Refugees (1967); International Covenant on Economic, Social and Cultural Rights (1966); International Covenant on Civil and Political Rights (1966); Declaration on the Elimination of Discrimination Against Women (1967); Declaration on the Rights of Mentally Retarded Persons (1971); International Convention on the Suspension and Punishment of the Crime of Apartheid (1973); Declaration on the Rights of Disabled Persons (1975); Declaration of the World Conference to Combat Racism and Racial Discrimination (1978); Declaration on the Elimination of all Forms of Intolerance and of Discrimination Based on Religion or Belief (1981); Convention on the Elimination of All Forms of Discrimination Against Women (1981).

# References

Alinsky, Saul. 1971. *Rules for Radicals*. New York: Random House.
Alvarez, Alex. 2001. *Governments, Citizens, and Genocide: A Comparative and Interdisciplinary Approach*. Bloomington: Indiana University Press.
Anderson, Terry. 1995. *The Movement and the Sixties: Protest in America from Greensboro to Wounded Knee*. New York: Oxford University Press.
Ash, Timothy Garton. 2000a. "Anarchy and Madness." *The New York Review of Books* (February 10): 48–53.
———. 2000b. "Kosovo: Was It Worth It?" *The New York Review of Books* (September 21): 50–60.
Associated Press Release. 1998a. *Little Cause to Celebrate at Human Rights Declaration Birthday*. December 6.
———. 1998b. *Human Rights Declaration Feted in Paris Ceremonies*. December 10.
Baum, Rainer. 1988. "Holocaust: Moral Indifference as the Form of Modern Evil." In Alan Rosenberg and Gerald E. Myers, eds., *Echoes from the Holocaust* (pp. 53–90). Philadelphia: Temple University Press.
Bayzler, Michael. 1987. "Re-Examining the Doctrine of Humanitarian Intervention in the Light of Atrocities in Kampuchea and Ethiopia." *Stanford Journal of International Law* (summer): 588–607.
Becker, Elizabeth, and Philip Shenon. 1999. "U.S. Priority is to Maintain Good Ties with Indonesia, Officials Indicate." *New York Times*, September 9, pp. 1–7.
Becker, Ernest. 1975. *Escape from Evil*. New York: The Free Press.
Becker, James M. 1973. "International and Cross-Cultural Experiences." In George Henderson, ed., *Education for Peace: Focus on Mankind* (pp. 103–24). Washington, D.C.: Association for Supervision and Curriculum Development.
Beitz, Charles R. 1988. "The Reagan Doctrine in Nicaragua." In Steven Luper-

Foy, ed., *Problems of International Justice* (pp. 182–95). Boulder, Colo.: Westview Press.

Bennett, W. Lance. 1989. "Marginalizing the Majority: Conditioning Public Opinion to Accept Managerial Democracy." In M. Margolis and G. Mauser, eds., *Manipulating Public Opinion* (pp. 321–61). New York: Dorsey.

Bennett, W. Lance, and David L. Peletz. 1994. *Taken by Storm: The Media, Public Opinion and U.S. Foreign Policiy in the Gulf War*. Chicago: University of Chicago Press.

Beres, L.R. 1985. "Genocide." *Policy Studies Review* 4, no. 2: 397–406.

Berger, Peter L., and Richard John Neuhaus. 1977. *To Empower People*. Washington, D.C.: American Enterprise Institute for Public Policy Research.

Bilton, Michael, and Kevin Sim. 1992. *Four Hours in My Lai*. New York: Viking Penguin.

Blinken, Antony J. 2001. "The False Crisis Over the Atlantic." *Foreign Affairs* 80, no. 3 (May/June): 35–48.

Blumenthal, David R. 1999. *The Banality of Good and Evil: Moral Lessons from the Shoah and Jewish Tradition*. Washington, D.C.: Georgetown University Press.

Boot, Max. 2000. "Paving the Road to Hell: The Failure of U.N. Peacekeeping." *Foreign Affairs* 79, no. 4 (March/April): 143–48.

Brogan, D.W. 1952. "The Illusion of American Omnipotence." *Harper's*. December.

Brown, Michael E., and Richard N. Rosecrance, eds. 1999. *The Costs of Conflict: Prevention and Cure in the Global Arena*. New York: Rowman & Littlefield.

Brugger, Seth. 2001. "Don't Reject the Germ Protocol." *Washington Post*, July 22, pp. B7–8.

Brzezinski, Zbigniew. 1993. *Out of Control*. New York: Charles Scribner's Sons.

*Bulletin of the International Tribunal for the Former Yugoslavia*. 1996. May 14.

Burner, David. 1996. *Making Peace with the 60s*. Princeton, N.J.: Princeton University Press.

Burns, James MacGregor, and Georgia Sorenson. 2000. *Dead Center. Clinton-Gore Leadership and the Perils of Moderation*. New York: Scribner.

Burns, John F. 1992. "Confessed Executioner Remembers Little Girl." *Richmond Times-Dispatch*, November 22, pp. Al, A12, A13.

Calley, William L. 1972. "Lieutenant Calley: His Own Story." In Jay W. Baird, ed., *From Nuremberg to My Lai* (pp. 213–34). Lexington, Mass.: D.C. Heath.

Carnegie Commision on Preventing Deadly Conflict. 1997. *Preventing Deadly Conflict: Final Report*. New York: Carnegie Corporation of New York.

Carnegie Corporation of New York. 1994. "Cooperative Engagement." *Carnegie Quarterly* 32, no. 3 (summer).

Carroll, James. 1997. "Shoah in the News: Patterns and Meanings of News Coverage of the Holocaust." Discussion Paper D-27, The Joan Shorenstein Center on the Press, Politics and Public Policy. John F. Kennedy School of Government, Harvard University. Pp. 1–17.

Chalk, F., and K. Johassotin. 1990. *The History and Sociology of Genocide: Analyses and Case Studies*. New Haven: Yale University Press.

Charny, Israel W. 1982. *How Can We Commit the Unthinkable?* Boulder, Colo.: Westview Press.

# References

Chomsky, Noam. 1999. *The New Military Humanism: Lessons from Kosovo*. Monroe, Maine: Common Courage Books.

Cingranelli, David L. 1993. *Ethics, American Foreign Policy, and The Third World*. New York: St. Martin's Press.

"Clinton Defends Bypassing U.N. to Intervene in Kosovo." 1999. *Richmond Times-Dispatch*, September 22, p. A4.

CNN. 1999. "Serb Parliament Meets on Kosovo Peace Talks." Retrieved February 4. <CNN.com>.

Cobb, Roger W., and Marc Howard Ross, eds. 1997. *Cultural Strategies of Agenda Denial: Avoidance, Attack, and Redefinition*. Lawrence: University Press of Kansas.

Cohen, Ben. 1993. "Why Europe Failed to Halt the Genocide in Bosnia." *The Washington Report on Middle East Affairs* (April/May): 39–40.

Committee on Conscience. 2000. *Genocide Warning: Sudan*. Washington, D.C.: United States Holocaust Memorial Museum. November 15.

Craig, Stephen C., and Stephen Earl Bennett, eds. 1997. *After the Boom: The Politics of Generation X*. Lanham, Md.: Rowman & Littlefield.

Crocker, David A. 2000. "Truth Commission and Transitional Justice." *Report from the Institute for Philosophy and Public Policy* (fall): 23–31.

———. 2000. "Retribution and Reconciliation." *Report from the Institute for Philosophy and Public Policy* (winter/spring): 1–6.

Cumings, Bruce. 2002. "The American Century and the Third World." In G. John Ikenberry, ed., *American Foreign Policy: Theoretical Essays* (pp. 187–201). New York: Addison-Wesley.

Curtiss, Richard H. 1993. "Bosnia 1993: Showdown for U.S., U.N., and Shape of the New World Order." *The Washington Report on Middle East Affairs* (March): 7–8, 70, 95.

———. 1995. "Bosnia Talks Show What a Superpower Can Do When Lobbies Are Absent." *The Washington Report on Middle East Affairs* (December): 15, 102–3.

Daalder, Ivo H., and Michael E. O'Hanlon. *Winning Ugly: NATO's War to Save Kosovo*. Washington, D.C.: Brookings.

Danner, Mark. 1997a. "The US and the Yugoslav Catastrophe." *The New York Review of Books*. (November 20).

———. 1997b. "America and the Bosnian Genocide." *The New York Review of Books* (December 4): 55–65.

———. 1997c. "Clinton, the UN, and the Bosnian Disaster." *The New York Review of Books* (December 18).

Davies, Peter, ed. 1988. *Human Rights*. New York: Routledge.

Delli Carpini, Michael X., and Scott Keeter. 1996. *What Americans Know About Politics and Why It Matters*. New Haven, Conn.: Yale University Press.

Des Forges, Alison. 1999. *"Leave None to Tell the Story." Genocide in Rwanda*. New York: Human Rights Watch.

DeVecchi, Robert P., and Arthur C. Helton. 1999. "Mission Implausible: Are We Asking too Much of the U.N.?" *Washington Post*, September 19, pp. B1–B4.

Edelman, Murray. 1971. *Politics as Symbolic Action*. New York: Academic Press.

Epstein, Jason. 1999. "Always Time to Kill." *The New York Review of Books* (November 4): 57–64.

Falk, Richard. 1999. "Mission Implausible: Caught Between National Interests and Nationalism." *Washington Post*, September 19, p. B1.

Falk, Richard A., Gabriel Kolko, and Robert Jay Lifton, eds. 1971. *Crimes of War*. New York: Random House.

Farber, David. 1994. *The Age of Great Dreams: America in the 1960s*. New York: Hill and Wang.

Farias, Victor. 1989. *Heidegger and Nazism*. Philadelphia: Temple University Press.

Feher, Michael. 2000. *Powerless by Design: The Age of International Community*. Durham, N.C.: Duke University Press.

Feil, Scott R. 1998. *Preventing Genocide: How the Early Use of Force Might Have Succeeded in Rwanda*. New York: Carnegie Corporation of New York. April.

Fein, Helen. 1979. *Accounting for Genocide*. New York: The Free Press.

———. 2000. "Three P's of Genocide Prevention: With Application to a Genocide Foretold—Rwanda." In Neil Riemer, ed., *Protection Against Genocide: Mission Impossible?* (pp. 41–66). Westport, Conn.: Praeger.

———. 2001. "U.S. Government Moves Toward Prevention, Koh Says: Commentary." *The ISG Newsletter* (spring): 10–12.

Fischer, Tim. 2000. *Seven Days in East Timor*. St. Leonards NSW, Australia: Allen & Unwin.

Fishkin, James S. 1996. *The Voice of the People: Public Opinion and Democracy*. New Haven, Conn.: Yale University Press.

Forsythe, David P. 1991. *The Internationalization of Human Rights*. Boston: Lexington Books.

Foyle, Douglas C. 1999. *Counting the Public In: Presidents, Public Opinion and Foreign Policy*. New York: Columbia University Press.

The FP Interview. 2001. "True Believer." *Foreign Policy* (March/April): 26–41.

Freeman, Michael. 1991. "The Theory and Prevention of Genocide." *Holocaust and Genocide Studies* 6, no. 2: 185–99.

Fussell, Paul. 1989. *Wartime: Understanding and Behavior in the Second World War*. New York: Oxford University Press.

Gaddis, John Lewis. 1999. "Living in Candlestick Park." *Atlantic Monthly* (April): 65–74.

The Gallup Organization. 1999a. *Gallup Social and Economic Indicators, Kosovo in Crisis: U.S. Role and Clinton Approval, May 27, 1999*. Retrieved June 7. <www.gallup.com/poll/indicators/Indkosovo.asp>.

———. 1999b. "East Timor Has Yet to Register Strongly on Americans Consciousness." *Poll Releases*, October 4.

*Gallup Tuesday Briefing*. 2002. "Tuesday Briefing." Retrieved January 2. <tuesday briefing@gallup.com>.

George, Alexander L., and Jane E. Holl. 1997. *The Warning—Response Problem and Missed Opportunities in Preventive Diplomacy*. New York: Carnegie Corporation of New York. May.

Gitlin, Todd. 1993. *Sixties: Years of Hope, Days of Rage*. New York: Bantam Books.

Glenny, Misha. 1996. *The Fall of Yugoslavia: The Third Balkan War*. New York: Penguin Books.

Graham, Bradley. 1991. "Joint Chiefs Doubted Air Strategy." *Washington Post*, April 5, pp. A1–3.

# References

Grosvenor, Gilbert M. 1989. "The Case for Geography Education." *Educational Leadership* 47: 29–32.
Gurr, Ted Robert. 2000. "Ethnic Warfare on the Wane." *Foreign Affairs* 79, no. 3 (May/June): 52–64.
Gutman, Roy. 1993. *A Witness to Genocide*. New York: Macmillan.
Gutman, Roy, and David Reiff. 1999. *Crimes of War: What the Public Should Know*. New York: W.W. Norton and Co.
Haas, Richard N. 2000. "The Squandered Presidency: Demanding More from the Commander-in-Chief." *Foreign Affairs* 79, no. 3 (May/June): 136–40.
Hahn, Carol. 1987. "The Right to a Political Education." In Norma Bernstein Tarrow, ed., *Human Rights and Education* (pp. 173–87). Elmsford, N.Y.: Pergamon Press.
Hall, Brian. 1994. *The Impossible Country: A Journey Through the Last Days of Yugoslavia*. New York: Penguin Books.
Hallie, Philip. 1979. *Lest Innocent Blood Be Shed*. New York: Harper and Row.
———. 1997. *Tales of Good and Evil, Help and Harm*. New York: Harper's.
Halsell, Grace. 1993. "Women's Bodies a Battlefield in War for 'Greater Serbia.'" *The Washington Report on Middle East Affairs* (April/May): 8–9.
Harff, Barbara. 1991. "Humanitarian Intervention in Genocidal Situations." In Israel Charny, ed., *Genocide: A Critical Bibliographic Review*, vol. 2 (pp. 146–72). London: Mansell.
Harris, Marvin. 1973. *Cows, Pigs, Wars, and Witches: The Riddles of Culture*. New York: Vintage Books.
Hawk, David. 1986. "Some Recommendations of the Whitaker Report are Achieveable." *Internet on the Holocaust and Genocide* 5 (January): 3.
Heidenrich, John G. 2001. *How to Prevent Genocide: A Guide for Policymakers Scholars, and the Connected Citizen*. Westport, Conn.: Praeger.
Hendrickson, David C. 1994. "The Recovery of Internationalism." *Foreign Affairs* 73 (September/October): 26–43.
Henry, Jules. 1965. *Culture Against Man*. New York: Vintage Books.
Hirsch, Herbert. 1971. *Poverty and Politicization: Political Socialization in an American Subculture*. New York: Free Press.
———. 1995. *Genocide and the Politics of Memory: Studying Death to Preserve Life*. Chapel Hill: University of North Carolina Press.
———. 1999. "Preventing Genocide in the Post–Cold War World." In Roger W. Smith, ed., *Genocide: Essays toward Understanding, Early-Warning, and Prevention* (pp. 223–388). Williamsburg, Va.: Association of Genocide Scholars.
Hirsch, Herbert, and Gail M. Hirsch. 1990. "Learning to Live Together: Political Socialization and the Formation of International Identity." *International Journey of Group Tensions* 20, no. 4 (winter): 369–90.
Hitchens, Christopher. 2002. *The Trial of Henry Kissinger*. New York: Verso Books.
Hoffman, Eva. 2000. "The Uses of Hell." *The New York Review of Books* (March 9): 23.
Holsti, Ole R. 1996. *Public Opinion and American Foreign Policy*. Ann Arbor: University of Michigan Press.

Honig, Jan Willem, and Norbert Both. 1996. *Srebrenica: Record of a War Crime*. New York: Penguin Books.

Horowitz, Donald L. 1994. "Ethnic and Nationalist Conflict." In Michael T. Klare and Daniel C. Thomas, eds., *World Security: Challenges for a New Century* (pp. 175–87). New York: St. Martin's Press.

Huntington, Samuel P. 2002. "American Ideals versus American Institutions." In G. John Ikenberry, ed., *American Foreign Policy: Theoretical Essays* (pp. 204–37). New York: Addison-Wesley.

Hyland, William G. 1999. *Clinton's World: Remodeling American Foreign Policy*. New York: Praeger.

Ignatieff, Michael. 1997. "The Gods of War." *The New York Review of Books* (October 9): 10–13.

———. 2000. "The New American Way of War." *The New York Review of Books* (July 20): 42–46.

———. 2002. "Barbarians at the Gate." *The New York Review of Books* (February 28): 4–6.

Ikenberry, G. John. 2002. "America's Liberal Grand Strategy: Democracy and National Security in the Post-War Era." In G. John Ikenberry, ed., *American Foreign Policy: Theoretical Essays* (pp. 274–96). New York: Addison-Wesley.

Institute for War and Peace Reporting. 1999. "The Kosovo Numbers Game." Retrieved August 9. <www.iwpr.net/in>.

Ives, Stephen B. 2001. "Vengeance Did Not Deliver Justice." *Washington Post*, December 30, p. B2.

Jentleson, Bruce W. 2000. *American Foreign Policy: The Dynamics of Choice in the 21st Century*. New York: W.W. Norton and Co.

Johnson, Robert H. 1997. *Improbable Dangers: U.S. Conceptions of Threat in the Cold War and After*. New York: St. Martin's Press.

Jones, David H. 1999. *Moral Responsibility in the Holocaust: A Study in the Ethics of Character*. Lanham, Md.: Rowman & Littlefield.

Judah, Tim. 2000. *Kosovo: War and Revenge*. New Haven, Conn.: Yale University Press.

Judt, Tony. 1995. "What Are American Interests?" *The New York Review of Books* (October 5): 37–38.

Kader, David. 1991. "Progress and Limitations in Basic Genocidal Law." In Israel Charny, ed., *Genocide: A Critical Bibliographic Review*, vol. 2 (pp. 141–45). London: Mansell.

Kaplan, Robert D. 1993. *Balkan Ghosts*. New York: Vintage.

———. 1994. "The Coming Anarchy," *Atlantic Monthly* (February): 44–76.

———. 2001. "Hope for the Best, Expect the Worst." *Foreign Policy* (May/June): 53–56+.

Kelman, Herbert C., and V. Lee Hamilton. 1989. *Crimes of Obedience: Toward a Social Psychology of Authority and Responsibility*. New Haven, Conn.: Yale University Press.

Kennan, George F. 1947. "Sources of Soviet Conduct." *Foreign Affairs* (July): 566–82.

Kennedy, Paul, and Bruce Russett. 1995. "Reforming the United Nations." *Foreign Affairs* 74, no. 5 (September/October): 50–71.

KFOR Online—The Kosovo Protection Corps. 1999. <www.kforonline.com>.

# References

Kiernan, Ben. 2000. "Bringing the Khmer Rouge to Justice." *Human Rights Review* (April/June): 92–108.

Kissinger, Henry A. 2001. "The Pitfalls of Universal Jurisdiction." *Foreign Affairs* (July/August): 86–96.

Krane, Jim. 2002. "Anan Gov'ts Must Fight Poverty." Associated Press. February 4. <http://daily news: Yahoo.com>. Retrieved February 9.

Krasner, Stephen D. 2001. "Sovereignty." *Foreign Policy* (January/February): 20–29.

Kren, George M. 1988. "The Holocaust: Moral Theory and Immoral Act." In *Echoes from the Holocaust*, ed. Alan Rosenberg and Gerald E. Myers (pp. 245–61). Philadelphia: Temple University Press.

Kull, Stephen D. 1995. "Americans on Bosnia: A Study of U.S. Public Attitudes." Program on International Policy Attitudes, University of Maryland.

Kuper, Leo. 1985. *The Prevention of Genocide*. New Haven, Conn.: Yale University Press.

———. 1989. "Reflections on Education against Genocide." Special supplement to the *Internet on the Holocaust and Genocide* 19. September.

———. 1992. "Reflections on The Prevention of Genocide." In *Genocide Watch*, ed. Helen Rein (pp. 135–61). New Haven: Yale University Press.

Kuperman, Alan F. 2000. "Rwanda in Retrospect." *Foreign Affairs* 79, no. 1 (January/February): 94–118.

Lambert, Wallace E., and Otto Klineberg. 1967. *Children's Views of Foreign Peoples*. New York: Appleton-Century-Crofts.

Laurence, Edward J. 1998. *Light Weapons and Intrastate Conflict*. New York: Carnegie Corporation of New York. July.

Lawson, Edward, ed. 1991. *Encyclopedia of Human Rights*. New York: Taylor & Francis.

Le Carre, John. 1995. *Our Game*. New York: Ballantine Books.

Leber, Jeri. 1993. "Bosnia: Questions About Rape." *The New York Review of Books* (March 25): 3–6.

Legro, Jeffrey W., and Andrew Moravcsik. 2001. "Faux Realism." *Foreign Policy* (July/August): 80–82.

Leitenberg, Milton. 1994a. *The Prevention of Genocide: Rwanda and Yugoslavia Reconsidered*. Working Paper. New York: Institute for the Study of Genocide.

———. 1994b. "Rwanda, 1994: International Incompetence Produces Genocide." *Peacekeeping and International Relations* 23 (November): 6–10.

Lemkin, Raphael. 1944. *Axis Rule in Europe*. Washington, D.C.: Carnegie Endowment for World Peace.

Leopold, Evelyn. 2001a. "Praise, Criticism Greet U.S. Signing of Court Treaty." Retrieved January 1. <http://dailynews.yahoo.com>.

———. 2001b. "U.S., Israel Sign Landmark Criminal Court Treaty." Retrieved January 1. <http://dailynews.yahoo.com>.

———. 2001c. "U.S. Changes Tone of UN Small Arms Conference." *Reuters* (July 10): 1–3.

"Lessons for Nation Builders." 2002. *New York Times*, February 7.

Levi, Werner. 1991. *Contemporary International Law*. Boulder, Colo.: Westview Press.

Lifton, Robert Jay, and Erik Markusen. 1990. *The Genocidal Mentality: Nazi-Holocaust and Nuclear Threat*. New York: Basic Books.

Littell, Franklin H. 1991. "Early Warning: Detecting Potentially Genocidal Movements." In Peter Hayes, ed., *Lessons and Legacies: The Meaning of the Holocaust in a Changing World* (pp. 305–15). Evanston, Ill.: Northwestern University Press.

Lopez, George A. 2000. "Economic Sanctions and Genocide: Too Little, Too Late, and Sometimes Too Much." In Neil Riemer, ed., *Protection Against Genocide: Mission Impossible?* (pp. 67–84). Westport, Conn.: Praeger.

Luper-Foy, Steven, ed. 1988. *Problems of International Justice.* Boulder, Colo.: Westview Press.

Lute, Douglas E. 1998. *Improving National Capacity to Respond to Complex Emergencies: The U.S. Experience.* New York: Carnegie Corporation of New York. April.

Maas, Peter. 1996. *Love Thy Neighbor: A Story of War.* New York: Vintage Books.

Machedo, Stephen, ed. 1997. *Reassessing the Sixties: Debating the Political and Cultural Legacy.* New York: W.W. Norton and Co.

Marcuse, Herbert. 1972. *Counter-Revolution and Revolt.* Boston: Beacon Press, 1972.

Margolis, Eric. 1999. "NATO Stalls, and Killing Continues." *Foreign Correspondent.* Retrieved January 25. <foreign@foreigncorrespondent.com>.

Mastanduno, Michael. 2002. "The United States Political System and International Leadership: A 'Deadly Inferior' Form of Government?" In G. John Ikenberry, ed., *American Foreign Policy: Theoretical Essays* (pp. 238–57). New York: Addison-Wesley.

Matthews, Donald R. 1960. *U.S. Senators and Their World.* New York: Vintage Books.

McCollough, Thomas E. 1991. *The Moral Imagination and Public Life: Raising the Ethical Question.* Chatham, N.J.: Chatham House Publishers, Inc.

McNamara, Robert S. 1995. *In Retrospect: The Tragedy and Lessons of Vietnam.* New York: Times Books.

Mendelson, Edward, ed. 1995. *As I Walked out One Evening: Songs, Ballads, Lullabies, Limericks, and other Light Verse by W.H. Auden.* New York: Vintage International.

Mendlovitz, Saul, and John Fousek. 2000. "A UN Constabulary to Enforce the Law on Genocide and Crimes Against Humanity." In Neil Riemer, ed., *Protection Against Genocide: Mission Impossible?* (pp. 105–22). Westport, Conn.: Praeger.

Meyer, Karl E. 1993. "The Roots of Bosnia's Anguish." *The Washington Report on Middle East Affairs* (April/May): 61.

Milgram, Stanley. 1974. *Obedience to Authority.* New York: Harper and Row.

———. 1977. *The Individual in a Social World.* Reading, Mass.: Addison-Wesley.

Minear, Richard H. 1971. *Victor's Justice: The Tokyo War Crimes Trials.* Princeton, N.J.: Princeton University Press.

Mirsky, Jonathon. 2000. "The Never-ending War." *The New York Review of Books* (May 25): 54–64.

Moore, Barrington, Jr. 1970. *Reflections on the Causes of the Human Misery and Upon Proposals to Eliminate Them.* Boston: Beacon Press.

Morgan, Edward P. 1991. *The 60s Experience: Hard Lessons about Modern America.* Philadelphia: Temple University Press.

# References

Morganthau, Tom, and John Barry. 1995. "On the March." *Newsweek*, December 11, pp. 28–32.
Mosse, George L. 1978. *Toward the Final Solution*. New York: Harper and Row.
———. 1990. *Fallen Soldiers*. New York: Oxford University Press.
Mufson, Steven. 2000. "An Uneasy Union of Morality and Pragmatism." *Washington Post*, February 6, p. B1.
Mufson, Steven, and Colum Lynch. 1999. "E. Timor Puts U.N. on Spot." *Washington Post*, September 26, pp. 1–6.
Nacos, Brigitte L., Robert Y. Shapiro, and Pierangelo Isernia. 2000. *Public Opinion and the International Use of Force*. New York: Routledge.
Neier, Aryeh. 2001. "The Quest for Justice." *The New York Review of Books* (March 8): 31–35.
Nelson, Jack L. 1980. "The Uncomfortable Relationship between Moral Education and Citizenship Instruction." In Richard Wilson and Gordon Schochet, eds., *Moral Development and Politics* (pp. 256–85). New York: Praeger.
Nelson, Lars-Erik. 2000. "Clinton and His Enemies." *The New York Review of Books* (January 26): 18–22.
Neumann, George Bradford. 1926. *A Study of International Attitudes of High School Students*. New York: Teachers College Press.
Niemi, Richard. 1973. "Political Socialization." In Jeanne N. Knutson, ed., *Handbook of Political Psychology* (pp. 117–38). San Francisco: Jossey-Bass.
Nolan Janne E., ed. 1994. *Global Engagement: Cooperation and Security in the 21st Century*. Washington, D.C.: Brookings Institution.
Novick, Peter. 1999. *The Holocaust in American Life*. Boston: Houghton Mifflin.
Olson, James S., and Randy Roberts. 1999. *Where the Domino Fell: America and Vietnam, 1945–1995*. St. James, N.Y.: Brandywine Press.
Organization of African Unity. 2000. *Rwanda: The Preventable Genocide*. <www.oau-ous.org/Document/ipep/ipep.htm>.
Oudraat, Chantal De Jonge. 2001. "Humanitarian Intervention: The Lessons Learned." *Current History Magazine* (December): 419–29. Reprinted in Helen E. Purkitt, ed., *World Politics 01/02* (pp. 23–31). Guilford, Conn.: McGraw Hill/Dushkin.
Pace, David. 1999. "Congressional Negotiators Restore School of the Americas Funding." *Cable News Network*, September 23, 1999, pp. 1–2.
Page, Benjamin I., and Robert Y. Shapiro. 1992. *The Rational Public: Fifty Years of Trends in Americans' Policy Preferences*. Chicago: University of Chicago Press.
The Pew Research Center for the People and the Press. 1999a. Kosovo Release, 12 pages. April.
———. 1999b. *Continued Public Support for Kosovo, But Worries Grow*. April.
———. 2002. *Worries Over New Attacks Decline: Terrorism Transforms News Interest*. <www.people-press.org/122001rpt.htm>.
Pike, Lewis, and Thomas Barrows. 1976. *Other Nations, Other Peoples: A Survey of Student Interests and Knowledge, Attitudes and Perceptions*. Washington, D.C.: U.S. Department of Health, Education, and Welfare.
Poliakov, Leon. 1971. *The Aryan Myth*. New York: New American Library.
Power, Samantha. 2002. *The Problem from Hell: America and the Age of Genocide*. New York: Basic Books.

Program on International Policy Attitudes. 1994. College Park: University of Maryland. April.
———. 1995. College Park: University of Maryland. April.
———. 1996. College Park: University of Maryland. June.
Ravitch, Diane, and Chester Finn. 1987. *What Do Our Seventeen-Year-Olds Know?* New York: Harper and Row.
Reisman, W. Michael. 2002. "The United States and International Institutions." In G. John Ikenberry, ed., *American Foreign Policy: Theoretical Essays* (pp. 40–58). New York: Addison-Wesley.
Rice, Condoleeza. 2000. "Promoting the National Interest." *Foreign Affairs* 79, no. 1 (January/February): 45–62.
Rieff, David. 1999. "The Precarious Triumph of Human Rights." *New York Times Magazine*, August 8, pp. 1–12.
Riemer, Neil, ed. 2000. *Protection Against Genocide: Mission Impossible?* Westport, Conn.: Praeger.
Roberts, Adam, and Richard Guelff, eds. 1989. *Documents on the Laws of War.* New York: Clarendon.
Rosenblatt, Roger. 1984. *Children of War.* New York: Anchor Press.
Ronayne, Peter. 1998. "An Unconventional Debate: The United States, NGOs, and the Genocide Convention." *The Miller Center Journal* 5 (spring): 77–89.
Roth, Kenneth. 2001. "The Case for Universal Jurisdiction." *Foreign Affairs* (September/October): 150–54.
Rummel, R.J. 1994. *Death by Government.* New Brunswick, N.J.: Transaction Publishers.
Schabas, William A. 2000. *Genocide in International Law.* Cambridge: Cambridge University Press.
Schaar, John. 1981. *Legitimacy in the Modern State.* New Brunswick, N.J.: Transaction Books.
Scharf, Michael P. 1997. *Balkan Justice: The Story Behind the First International War Crimes Trial Since Nuremberg.* Durham, N.C.: Carolina Academic Press.
Schwab, Klaus. 2002. "Building the Future." *Newsweek*; December 17, p. 28.
Seybolt, Taylor B. 2000. "Making Humanitarian Intervention Effective: An Analysis of Interventions in Somalia and Rwanda." *Draft Pugwash Occasional Paper First Written for the Venice Workshop* (May): 1–24.
Shafer, Suzanne M. 1987. "Human Rights Education in Schools." In Norma Bernstein Tarrow, ed., *Human Rights and Education* (pp. 191–205). Elmsford, N.Y.: Pergamon Press.
Shaw, Randy. 2001. *The Activist's Handbook: A Primer.* Berkeley: University of California Press.
Shively, W. Phillips. 1999. *Power and Choice: An Introduction to Political Science.* New York: McGraw-Hill.
Silber, Laura, and Allan Little. 1997. *Yugoslavia: Death of a Nation.* New York: Penguin Books.
Simon, Douglas W. 2000. "The Evolution of the International System and Its Impact on Protection Against Genocide." In Neil Riemer, ed., *Protection Against Genocide: Mission Impossible?* (pp. 17–40). Westport, Conn.: Praeger.
Singer, David. 1994. "Knowledge of Holocaust." *Society* (March/April): 31.

# References

Slomanson, William R. 1990. *Fundamental Perspectives on International Law.* St. Paul, Minn.: West Publishing Company.

Smith, Michael Joseph. 2000. "On Humanitarian Intervention." In Neil Riemer, ed., *Protection Against Genocide: Mission Impossible?* (pp. 123–40). Westport, Conn.: Praeger.

Smith, Roger. 1992a. "The Armenian Genocide: Memory, Politics, and the Future." In Richard G. Hovannisian, ed., *The Armenian Genocide: History, Politics, Ethics* (pp. 1–20). New York: St. Martin's Press.

———. 1992b. "Exploring the United States' Thirty-Five-Year Reluctance to Ratify the Genocide Convention." *Harvard Human Rights Journal* 5 (spring): 227–33.

Smith, Roger W., ed. 1999. *Genocide: Essays Toward Understanding, Early-Warning, and Prevention.* Williamsburg, Va.: Association of Genocide Scholars.

Smith, Tony. 2002. "National Security Liberalism and American Foreign Policy." In G. John Ikenberry, ed., *American Foreign Policy: Theoretical Essays* (pp. 258–73). New York: Addison-Wesley.

Snow, Donald. 2002. *September 11, 2001: The New Face of War?* New York: Longman.

Snow, Donald M., and Eugene Brown. 1997. *Beyond the Water's Edge: An Introduction to U.S. Foreign Policy.* New York: St. Martin's Press.

Sobel, Richard. 1998. "Portraying American Public Opinion toward the Bosnia Crisis." *Harvard International Journal of Press/Politics* 2: 16–33.

———. 2001. *The Impact of Public Opinion on U.S. Foreign Policy Since Vietnam.* New York: Oxford University Press.

Steel, Ronald. 1999. "East Timor Isn't Kosovo." *New York Times*, September 12, pp. 1–3.

Stimson, James A. 1991. *Public Opinion in America: Moods, Cycles, and Swings.* Boulder, Colo.: Westview Press, 1991.

Storr, Anthony. 1991. *Human Destructiveness.* New York: Ballantine.

Sudetic, Chuck. 1998. *Blood and Vengeance: One Family's Story of the War in Bosnia.* New York: Penguin Books.

Szechi, Daniel. 2000. "Apologizing for History." *History News Service.* Retrieved (March 20). <www.h-net.msu.edu.>

Taudevin, Lansell, and Jefferson Lee, eds. 2000. *East Timor: Making Amends? Analyzing Australia's Role in Reconstructing East Timor.* Darlilnghurst, NSW, Australia: Oxford Press.

Teson, Fernando R. 1988. *Humanitarian Intervention: An Inquiry into Law and Morality.* New York: Transnational Publishers.

Traub, James. 2000. "Sierre Leone: The Worst Place on Earth." *The New York Review of Books* (June 29): 61–65.

Truehart, Charles. 1999. "Mission Implausible: Putting Doctrine to the Test." *Washington Post*, September 19, pp. B4–B6.

Tutorow, Norman E., ed. 1986. *War Crimes, War Criminals, and War Crimes Trials: An Annotated Bibliography and Source Book.* New York: Greenwood Press.

UN Doc. E/CN.4/Sub.2/1985/6, by Whitaker.

Unger, Irwin, and Debi Unger. 1988. *America in the 1960s.* St. James, N.Y.: Brandywine Press.

United Nations Department of Public Information. 2000. *OAU Report*. Retrieved July 7. <www.un.org/News>.

Universal Declaration of Human Rights, 1948.

Urquhart, Brian. 1998a. "Looking for the Sheriff." *The New York Review of Books* (July 16): 48–53.

———. 1998b. "The Making of a Scapegoat." *The New York Review of Books* (August 12): 32–35.

———. 1999. "Mission Impossible." *The New York Review of Books* (November 18): 26–29.

———. 2000. "In the Name of Humanity." *The New York Review of Books* (April 27): 19–22.

U.S. Department of State. 1999. *Erasing History: Ethnic Cleansing in Kosovo*. Washington, D.C.: Report released by the U.S. Department of State. <www.state.gov/www/religions/eur/rpt-9905-ethnic-kosovo-2/html>.

U.S. Department of State Dispatches. November 2, 1992 (vol. 3, no. 44), November 16, 1992 (vol. 3, no. 46), December 28, 1992 (vol. 3, no. 52), February 8, 1993 (vol. 4, no. 6), April 9, 1993 (vol. 4, no. 8), and July 26, 1993 (vol. 4, no. 30).

U.S. Senate Committee on Foreign Relations. 1985. Hearing on the Prevention and Punishment of the Crime of Genocide. 99th Cong., 1st sess., March 5.

van Creveld, Martin. 1991a. *Technology and War: From 2000 B.C. to the Present*. New York: The Free Press.

———. 1991b. *The Transformation of War*. New York: The Free Press.

———. 1993. *Nuclear Proliferation and the Future of Conflict*. New York: The Free Press.

Walt, Stephen M. 2000. "Two Cheers for Clinton's Foreign Policy." *Foreign Affairs* 79, no. 4 (March/April): 45–62.

Wasserstrom, Jeffrey N., Lynn Hunt, and Marilyn B. Young. 2000. *Human Rights and Revolutions*. Lanham, Md.: Rowman & Littlefield.

Weiss, Thomas G., and Cindy Collins. 2000. *Humanitarian Challenges and Intervention*. 2nd ed. Boulder, Colo.: Westview Press.

Weissbrodt, David. 1988. "Human Rights: An Historical Perspective." In Peter Davies, ed., *Human Rights* (pp. 1–20). New York: Routledge.

Wheeler, Stanton. 1966. "The Structure of Formerly Organized Socialization Settings." In Orville Brim and Stanton Wheeler, eds., *Socialization after Childhood* (pp. 51–116). New York: John Wiley.

Whitaker, B. 1985. *Revised and Updated Report on the Question of the Prevention and Punishment of the Crime of Genocide*. Document E/CN. 4/5SUB/1985/6, July 2.

White, N.D. 1997. *Keeping the Peace*. Manchester: Manchester University Press.

Winfield, Nicole. 1999. "Annan Urges Humanitarian Intervention." *Salon* (September 21): 1–7.

Winters, Paul A., ed. 1995. *Interventionism*. San Diego: Greenhaven Press.

Wippman, David. 2000. "Can an International Criminal Court Prevent and Punish Genocide?" In Neil Riemer, ed., *Protection Against Genocide: Mission Impossible?* (pp. 85–104). Westport, Conn.: Praeger.

Wittkopf, Eugene R. 1986. "On the Foreign Policy Beliefs of the American People:

A Critique and Some Evidence." *International Studies Quarterly* 30 (December): 425–55.

Zimmerman, Warren. 1995. "The Choice in the Balkans." *The New York Review of Books* (September 21): 4–7.

———. 1998. "Bad Blood." *The New York Review of Books* (May 28): 39–42.

———. 1999. *Origins of a Catastrophe: Yugoslavia and Its Destroyers*. New York: Times Books.

# Index

Action, political, 31, 34
Afghanistan, 136, 176
Africa: conflicts in, 91; Great Lakes region of, 90-91, 147; low priority of, 89, 94; violations of human rights in, 105. *See also* Rwanda; Somalia; Sudan; Zaire
African Americans, 4, 13
Agenda conflicts, 59
Agentic state, 155
Albanians, slaughter of, 72, 96
Albright, Madeline, 100
Algeria, 40
Alinsky, Saul, 34, 38, 60
America's liberal grand strategy, 179-80
Amnesty International, 36
Annan, Kofi, 138, 184-85
Anti-genocide, 33, 182
Anti-Vietnam War movement, 21, 25-28, 33, 59. *See also* Vietnam War
Apologies, political, 70-71, 96
Appeasement, 87
Arkan (Zeljiko Raznatovic), 102-3
Armenian Genocide, 119-20
Arms trade: Bosnian embargo, 82-83, 85-86; and genocide in Rwanda, 91; illegal, 111, 113; profitability of, 12-13; and sanctions, 143-44
Arrogance of power, 71-72
Ash, Timothy Garton, 104-5
Australia, 92-93, 106, 113, 136, 139, 176, 184
Awareness, political, 28-29, 171-73
*Axis Rule in Europe* (Lemkin), 2-3

Bacon, Ken, 102
Batangas Province, genocide in, 128
Battle of Kosovo (1389), 75
Baum, Rainer, 160
Berger, Samuel, 100-102, 106-7
Biological weapons, convention on, 113
Bogomils, 75
Bosnia, 73-87; background of conflict, 74-77; classed as civil war, 78; genocide in, 2, 16, 45, 109; indifference to, 176; public interest in, 40-41, 46-47; state department reports on, 82-83; and Vietnam syndrome, 71-72
Boutros-Ghali, Boutros, 92
*Breaker Morrant* (film), 151, 153, 155, 159-61
*Brown v. Board of Education*, 22

Burundi, 89-90
Bush, George, 79, 83
Bush, George W.: foreign policy of, 109-10, 110-11; and multilateral agreements, 111-14; opposition to preventing genocide, 68, 110-14; unilateralism of, 113

Califano, Joseph, 23-24
California, education in, 173
Calley, William, 14, 15, 158
Cambodia, 9, 27, 42
Cambodian Genocide Program, 36
Campaign to End Genocide, 36
Change, political, 29-33, 37
Chechnya, 109, 137
Chemical Weapons Convention, 109
Cheney, Dick, 113
*Children of War* (Rosenblatt), 167-68
Citizenship, 158-59
Civilians: killing of, 114, 129; need to protect, 138; treatment of, 3
Civilization, standards of, 130
Civil Rights Act, 22-23
Civil rights movement: and the American political system, 25-26, 33, 59, 62; events of, 22, 24; reaction to, 21, 28
Clark, Wesley K., 101
Clinton, Bill: apologies of, 70-71; foreign policy of, 40, 47-48, 68, 91-92, 108-9; and genocide, 83; inaction of, 70, 87, 104, 176; and intervention, 84-85, 106-10; speeches of, 105, 107-8
CNN, 42, 180. *See also* Television
CNN effect, 58
Cohen, William, 100
Commerce, foreign, 63
Committee on Genocide, 9
Communism: American view of, 167; collapse of in Europe, 60, 77; containment of, 144
Community: importance of, 156-57; international, 124
Concentration camps: in Bosnia, 78, 80, 97-98; during World War II, 76, 119, 125-26

Congress, 62-63, 66-67
Cooperative security, 145
Counterviolence, 146-48, 160-61
Crimes against humanity: prosecution of, 129; punishment for, 114-15, 120, 131, 152
Croatia, 75
Cultural identity, 12, 156
Cultural transmission, 163

Dallaire, Romeo, 94
Definitional problematic, 7
Democracy, 60-62, 177-80
Demonstrations, political, 27-28, 65
Denationalization, 6
Denazification of Germany, 125
Development: economic, 24, 135, 180, 185; political, 135
Deviant behavior, 62, 163-64
Distant places, perceived unimportance of, 33-34, 39, 42-43, 51, 68
Domino theory, 100
Drive-by shootings, 13

Early warning systems, 120, 123-24, 131-33, 135, 177, 182
East Timor: attention paid to, 51; genocide in, 2, 95, 106, 119; intervention in, 50, 113, 136, 139; lessons of, 150, 184; U.S. inaction in, 176
Education: multicultural, 173; nationalism in, 166-67, 168-69, 171-72; political, 169-70; role in transmission of culture, 158, 163, 164, 165-66
Eichmann, Adolf, 117, 158
Einsatzgruppen, 127, 158
Eisenhower, Dwight, 4
Empowerment of people, 33, 158
Ethics, 154
Ethnic cleansing: and air strikes, 100, 101-2; in Bosnia, 50, 82, 85; in Kosovo, 96-98; in the twentieth century, 45, 76-78
Ethnic hatred, 90-91, 95-96. *See also* Racism

# Index

European Rapid Reaction Force, 139
Exit strategies, 133, 141
Ex Parte Quirin, 126

Falk, Richard, 140
Famine, as weapon of war, 73, 109
Freedom Summer, 22
Fulbright, J. William, 71

Genealogy, importance of, 15-16
Geneva Conventions, 82
Genocide: avoidance of term, 92, 108, 176; consequences of, 144; cost of prevention, 134, 135; defined, 2-4, 6-7, 8-9, 59; ideology of, 7-8; inaction on, 37, 69-70; individual choice in, 152; media coverage of, 42; and pluralism, 6-7; as a political tool, 10, 78, 136, 181-82; and politics, 11; prevention of, 115, 117, 120, 123, 144, 147-48; and public opinion, 33-34, 35-38, 40-44, 45; punishment for, 123-24, 182
Genocide Research Project, 36
Giap, Vo Nguyen, General, 71
Gitlin, Todd, 26-27
Globalization, 139, 177
Global perspective, 156-57, 159
Great Society, 21, 23-24
Grotius, Hugo, 136
Gulf of Tonkin Resolution, 62-63

Hallie, Philip, 153
Halo Effect, 54
Helms, Jesse, 5, 138
Hitler, Adolf, 30, 44, 45, 75-76, 178
Holbrooke, Richard, 99, 104
Holocaust, 44-45, 120, 152-54. *See also* Ethnic cleansing; Genocide
Homicide, 13
Humanitarian assistance, cost of, 93
Humanitarian impulses, manipulation of, 54
Human rights: campaign for, 150, 180, 184; and nationalism, 169, 171-72; respect for, 173-74
Human Rights Watch, 36, 91
Hutus, 89-90. *See also* Rwanda

Identity, international, 171, 173-74
Identity cleansing, 98
Ignatieff, Michael, 147, 148, 184
Individuals: choices of, 11, 17, 71, 151, 153; responsibility of, 152, 155
Indonesia, U.S. relations with, 106-7
Intelligence: failures of, 104-5, 133, 135; need for accuracy, 140; use of, 149
International Alert and Aegis Trust, 36
International Convention on the Prevention and Punishment of the Crime of Genocide: adoption of, 2-4; and Bosnia, 96; effectiveness of, 9-11, 119, 120, 124; and the United States, 4-6, 81-82
International Court of Human Rights, 9
International Court of Justice, 4-5
International Criminal Court, 32-33, 71, 114-17, 149, 177, 184
International Criminal Tribunal for Rwanda, 177
International Criminal Tribunal for the Former Yugoslavia, 102-4, 177
Internationalism, 120-21, 145, 165, 170, 171-72, 173-74
International Monetary Fund, 139
Intervention: American, 150; arguments against, 107; conditions for, 140-41, 149; cost of, 134; humanitarian, 58, 78-79, 136-41, 145, 176; justification for, 72, 137; multilateral, 46, 86, 146; as political tool, 136-37; public support of, 43, 44-45
Isolationism, 53-54, 146. *See also* United States, isolationism of
Izetbegovic, Alija, 83

Johnson, Lyndon Baines: foreign policy of, 4; political agenda of, 21-22, 23, 24; and the Vietnam War, 27, 62-63, 64, 65
Justice, 36, 128

Kaplan, Robert, 177-78
Karadzic, Radovan, 85, 149
Kennedy, John F., 4, 21-22, 25, 65
Kennedy, Robert, 27
KFOR (Kosovo Protection Corps), 103
King, Martin Luther, 22
Kissinger, Henry, 90, 116-17
Koh, Harold Hongju, 149
Kosovo: ethnic cleansing in, 2, 104; ground troops in, 99, 100-101, 102, 104, 108; ineffectiveness of air strikes in, 101-2, 105-6; public interest in, 40-41, 50, 51; UN intervention in, 136
Kosovo Liberation Army, 96
Kurds, 13

Law, international, 124; enforceable system of, 139; and individual responsibility, 126-27, 129-30, 131; of war, 120; and war crimes, 125, 130-31
Law and morality, fundamental principles of, 153-54
Leaders, national: isolation from public opinion, 67-68; pressure on, 32
Leadership: importance of, 54-55, 175; international, 120, 140-41; mobilizing public opinion, 24-25, 53-54, 135; need for moral, 114
Le Carre, John, 73
Lemkin, Raphael, 2-3, 9, 81
Lewis, Stephen, 94
Liberalism, 23-24
Lockhart, Joe, 100
*Love Thy Neighbor* (Maas), 86-87

Maas, Peter, 86-87
Mantle, Mickey, 14
Marcuse, Herbert, 37
Marginalization of the majority, 46-47, 51-52
Massacres, 11
McCarthy, Eugene, 27, 65
McNamara, Robert, 70
Medical neutrality, violations of, 98
Milgram, Stanley, 155

Milosovic, Slobodan: cease-fire agreements of, 83, 85, 99; defeat of, 103-4; and genocide, 95, 102-3, 115, 158; negotiations with, 104, 105; trial of, 177; use of news media, 77
Mladic, Ratco, 85, 102-3, 149
Morality: modern, 153-54, 159-60, 161; practicality of, 35-36, 121, 123
Muslims: Bosnian, 6, 16, 74-75; killing of, 45; and rape as political tool, 74, 177
My Lai massacre, 11-12, 14-15, 26-27. *See also* Vietnam War
Myths: cultural, 8, 15-17, 160, 164; founding, 61-62, 166; political, 167

Naming, blaming and claiming, 58-59
National interest, need to redefine, 100, 124, 132-33
Nationalism: and culture, 15-17, 156; education's role in, 164-65, 166-68; ingredient of genocide, 8; in modern Europe, 77; need to move away from, 120, 170, 171, 173
National Rifle Association, 111
Native Americans, 4, 14-15, 78, 160
NATO: air strikes in Kosovo, 50, 97, 98, 143, 151-52, 176; Chinese embassy bombing, 104-5; effectiveness of, 103-4, 105-6; and the European community, 101-2; inaction of, 74, 78; intervention in Kosovo, 86, 96-99, 147; relevance of, 84, 107
Nazis: liability of, 126-27; methods of, 77-78, 119
Ndadaye, Melchior, 90
Neumann, George Bradford, 165-67
News media: control of, 102, 148; importance of, 34, 52, 54-55, 58, 68; representation of public opinion, 46-47; use of, 77, 132
News stories: about the Holocaust, 44-45; misrepresentations in, 46-47; public interest in, 40-43, 45, 50-51
Nixon, Richard, 4, 24, 27, 28, 90
"No fly" zones, 143-44

Nongovernmental organizations, 3, 36, 115-16, 180
North American Free Trade Agreement (NAFTA), 109
Nuclear weapons, 109, 113
Nuremberg Principles, 125-27, 152
Nuremberg Trials, 71, 125-26, 127, 128

Obedience to authority, 132, 155, 157, 163, 170-71, 173
Oil, 78, 176
Order, international, 13, 83
Organization of African Unity, 91
Organizing, political, 33-35
*Our Game* (Le Carre), 73

Patriotism, 170-71. *See also* Nationalism
Pavelic, Ante, 76
Peacekeeping: international, 51, 139; in Kosovo, 102; U.S. public opinion on, 45; U.S. resistance to, 93, 112-13, 145, 183
Peace talks, 83
Pell, Claiborne, 5
Perry, William, 93
Persian Gulf War, 53
Physicians for Human Rights, 36
Political systems, fragility of, 1-2
Politics: access points in, 60, 63-64, 67; and genocide, 10, 29; humanization of, 37; money in, 67; moral, 26; role of third parties in, 64
Port Huron Statement, 26
Potsdam Declaration, 128
Powell, Colin, 81, 83, 113
Power, 16-17, 59, 132
Prevent Genocide International, 36
Pristina, 98-99
Property, destruction of, 96-97
Public good, 155
Public opinion, 150; grievances into issues, 58; influence of, 46-47, 64; uninformed, 52; world, 131

Racism, 8, 22-23, 132; and African tragedies, 91, 95-96; in foreign policy, 94

Rape, 73, 96, 98
Rape camps, 74, 78, 177
Raznatovic, Zeljiko (Arkan), 102-3
Reactions when threatened, 2
Reagan, Ronald, 4, 47
Red Cross, 3
Refugees: cost of, 134; helping, 48, 50-51; from Kosovo, 73-74, 97
Religion, role of in foreign policy, 94
Resources, use of, 57-58
Responsibility: defined, 155; denial of, 71; personal, 152, 155, 159
Rice, Condoleeza, 112-13
Rieff, David, 150
Risk, avoidance of, 149
Rosenblatt, Roger, 167-68
Rummel, R.J., 178
Rumsfeld, Donald, 113
Rwanda: and the arms trade, 91; cholera epidemic in, 92-93; cost of intervention, 94; genocide in, 9, 45, 89-94; and the international community, 91, 93; public interest in, 40, 42, 47-51
Rwandan Patriotic Front (RPF), 89-90

Safe havens, 47, 74, 78. *See also* Refugees
Sanctions, 133-34, 140, 143-44
Sarajevo, 2, 78
Schabas, William, 124
September 11, 2001: and failures of intelligence, 133; and the importance of the U.S., 11; in international politics, 13, 54, 109-10, 145, 176, 181; and public interest in the news, 42
Serbia, 6, 75
Sides, right and wrong, 151, 155, 159-60, 161
Sierra Leone, 34
Simpson, O.J., 14, 40
Simpson, Varnado, 11, 15
Slavery, 6. *See also* Rape camps
Smith, Roger, 124
Socialization, political, 61-62, 163-64, 166, 168-69
Social order, 1-2, 13

Somalia, 79, 86, 137
Sovereignty: and education, 168-69; effect of globalization on, 177; and human rights, 137, 179; role in international anarchy, 13, 116-17, 124, 146, 156; and the UN, 4-5, 139
Species mentality, 156-57, 159
Srebrenica, 84
Sri Lanka, 34
Stability, 73
Starvation, 73, 109
Steel, Ronald, 107
Strategic interests, 94, 110
Students for a Democratic Society, 26
Styer, General, 128
Sudan, 34, 109
Supreme Court, 63
Symbols, sacredness of, 166-67

Technology, 39
Television, 83; effect on public policy, 58, 79, 80; information from, 9-10, 42; as a propaganda tool, 77; and socialization, 168; as a threat to sovereignty, 180. *See also* News media; News stories
Tenet, George J., 101
Terrorism: causes of, 183-84; as feature of politics, 13; new focus on, 11; prevention of, 117, 182; purpose of, 6, 181-82. *See also* September 11, 2001
Third Reich, 2. *See also* Nazis
Tito, Josip Broz, 76
Tojo Hideki, 129
Tokyo War Crimes Trials, 127-28
Torture, 6, 73, 130
Tribal hatred, 95-96
Truman, Harry, 4, 127
Truth commissions, 114-15
Tudjman, Franjo, 83
Tutsis, 89-90, 109. *See also* Rwanda

Uganda, 89-90
United Nations, 2-4; Charter of, 180-81; credibility of, 134-35, 149; and genocide, 92; inaction of, 78; interventions of, 47, 79; peacekeeping, 84, 139; relationship with the United States, 84; Resolution 95 (1), 126; Resolution 771, 82-83; sanctions of, 133-34; Security Council, 91-92, 102, 103, 116-17, 138, 139; War Crimes Commission, 125
United States: credibility of, 79-80; criminal law of, 5-6, 153-54; culture of, 33, 60-62, 164; education in, 166-67, 173-74; European bias of, 50, 51; fear of casualties, 52-53, 85, 101-2, 105, 135, 143, 147-48; foreign policy of, 62-63, 78-79, 141, 143, 178, 179-80, 184; genocide committed by, 179; illusion of omnipotence, 71-72; importance of, 10-11, 69, 86, 119; inaction of, 39, 69-70, 78, 80-83, 89, 179; indifference of, 92, 99, 100; interests of, 51, 66, 106; and international treaties, 3-6, 32, 62-63, 111-14; and interventions, 44-45, 141, 175-76; isolationism of, 83-84, 86, 104, 111-12, 119, 136, 138; lack of leadership in, 109, 146, 176; lack of long-term vision, 100; peacekeeping role of, 146-47; political movements in, 21-28, 34, 111, 175; president of, 63-66, 66; and Rwanda, 47-51, 89-94; and safe havens, 74; sovereignty of, 117; suppport of arms trade, 111; unilateralism of, 149; use of armed forces, 93, 135; as viewed by the world, 86-87, 112, 113; violence of, 12-13, 14; as the world's policeman, 107-8, 110, 135
Universal jurisdiction, 115-16, 117
Urquhart, Brian, 138
U.S. Department of State reports on genocide, 96-99
USTASHA, 76-77, 77

Vance-Owen Plan, 78
Versailles Treaty, 126
Victims, dehumanization of, 8, 157-58
Vietnam-Somalia syndrome, 79-83, 92, 133

# Index

Vietnam syndrome, 71-72, 73, 78-81, 83, 101, 136
Vietnam War: apologies for, 70-71; horrors of, 11, 14; opponents of, 64; politics of, 24, 62-63, 65-66; and public opinion, 46, 51
Violence: acclimation to, 14; attraction of, 11-12, 14-15, 156-59; rewards for, 160; and self-preservation, 160-61; training in, 132

War: horror of, 11; international laws of, 120; modern, 147, 183; perceptions of, 53, 148-49
War crimes: by individuals, 126; prosecution of, 6, 125-26, 127-30; standards of justice for, 130
War criminals, 125, 127
Warning-response gap, 132-33
"War on terrorism," 109-10, 124, 136, 182-83
Watergate, 28

Watts riot, 24
Weathermen, 27
Whitaker Report, 9
William II of Hohenzollern, 126
Wilson, Woodrow, 179
World Bank, 139
World Court, 9. *See also* International Court of Justice
World Trade Organization, 109, 184
World War II, 53-54
Wright-Patterson Air Force Base, peace talks at, 83

Yamashita, General, trial of, 127-29
Yugoslavia: atrocities in, 74; dissolution of, 8, 40; formation of, 75; genocide in, 73-74, 76-77; German invasion of, 75-76

Zaire, 40, 42
Zimmerman, Warren, 80-81, 83
Zone of acquiescence, 51-52

**About the Author**

HERBERT HIRSCH is Professor of Political Science at Virginia Commonwealth University, Richmond.